MATRONS AND MAIDS

Matrons and Maids

Regulating Indian Domestic Service in Tucson, 1914–1934

Victoria K. Haskins

The University of Arizona Press
Tucson

The University of Arizona Press
www.uapress.arizona.edu

First paperback edition 2017

Printed in the United States of America
22 21 20 19 18 17 7 6 5 4 3 2

ISBN-13: 978-0-8165-2960-5 (cloth)
ISBN-13: 978-0-8165-3655-9 (paper)

Cover design by Lori Lieber Graphic Design, Inc.
Cover photo: "Papago Indian with unidentified woman" from the Arizona Historical Society.

Publication of this book is made possible in part by the proceeds of a permanent endowment created with the assistance of a Challenge Grant from the National Endowment for the Humanities, a federal agency.

Library of Congress Cataloging-in-Publication Data
Haskins, Victoria K. (Victoria Katharine), 1967–
Matrons and maids : regulating Indian domestic service in Tucson, 1914–1934 / Victoria K. Haskins.
p. cm.
Includes bibliographical references and index.
ISBN 978-0-8165-2960-5 (cloth : alk. paper)
1. Indians of North America—Employment—Arizona—Tucson—History—20th century. 2. Household employees—Arizona—Tucson—History—20th century. 3. Tucson (Ariz.)—Social conditions—20th century. 4. Tucson (Ariz.)—Economic conditions—20th century. I. Title.
E78.A7H24 2012
979.1′776—dc23
2012001807

∞ This paper meets the requirements of ANSI/NISO Z39.48-1992 (Permanence of Paper).

Contents

MATRONS AND MAIDS

1

Introduction

The Outing Matrons of Tucson

ONE LATE SPRING DAY in Tucson, Arizona, in 1933, when outing matron Gracie Taylor finally made herself sit down and write the report that the Office of Indian Affairs at Washington, DC, had demanded, she found herself utterly unable to do so. She hardly knew how to explain the situation, and all the resentments and anxieties she had been accumulating over the past months came spilling out instead. "I suppose that Mrs. Bronson wrote you what I said to her," she began desperately. "I have been almost sorry I asked her to say anything."

> I have just felt that I could not stay here by myself and Mrs. Bronson said she wouldn't stay in such a place. I have one white neighbor two blocks from me and there are no other white people closer than four blocks. I am not one to be too easily frightened as I have staid alone many times in my life but never in a place like this. I have never seen so much drinking and drunkenness in my life. It is just outside the city limits and no one seems to want to do anything about it. Some nights it sounds like all the demons of hell were turned loose.[1]

Taylor was the fourth woman to be officially employed to supervise Indian domestic service in Tucson since 1914, and she was destined to be the last. Her incipient nervous breakdown would hasten the abolishment of the position in Tucson, but similar programs were already being wound down elsewhere, and Taylor was, already, one of the very last women to be employed in this capacity across the United States. Encountering this letter in the federal archives of the Bureau of Indian Affairs held in California, I was immediately intrigued. Taylor's unexpectedly passionate outburst, written at the end of both her career and the occupation and bringing into sharp relief the paradoxes and tensions of these outing programs, drew me into the search to learn more about the histories of the women who carried them out.

During the early twentieth century, outing matrons were employed by the Office of Indian Affairs (as the Bureau of Indian Affairs was then called) to oversee young Indian women "working out" in white households. Classified as field matrons, they were part of that special corps of women engaged by the Indian Affairs administration to "uplift" and "civilize" Indian women. However, the outing matrons' role was quite distinct. Unlike the field matrons proper, the outing matrons worked in urban areas rather than on reservations. Their charges were the students from the Indian schools placed out in white homes to work (virtually all girls) and other young Indian women, and sometimes men, who worked in towns. Their duties often overlapped with those of the matrons employed in the Indian boarding schools who arranged placements for their students in white homes, designated at times as "outing agents" themselves.

In the 1920s and 1930s, the day-to-day work of an outing matron entailed locating places for Indian girls or young women to work as domestic servants, arranging the placements—which included providing the employer and the young worker with a statement of their respective obligations—and making inspection visits to the homes in which they were employed. Outing matrons might collect wages from employers and bank them for the girls, a condition of outing in some places. They were also required to be on-call for the girls "working out" if these girls got into strife or fell ill, or required any kind of assistance or intervention. They could be required to go to court in police matters. Some matrons made a point of hosting gatherings and recreational outings, such as picnics, for groups of girls in service, to give them opportunities to be together under supervision and chaperonage. Sometimes, they provided their homes, which were both residence and office, for the girls as places to stay when between jobs or in transit or as places to give lessons in cooking and sewing. The outing matron was, also, typically the person that the families of the young women in service contacted to find their daughter and get a message to her.

Tucson's Indian domestic workers were mostly girls and women of the Tohono O'odham (the "Desert People" or, as they were called by outsiders, the Papago) from the Indian village on the southern outskirts of Tucson, from the old San Xavier mission nine miles south of the city, or from the large swath of desert lying to the west of Tucson, known as "Papago Country" and, from 1916, as the Sells reservation. A sizeable minority were from the Sacaton reservation or the Gila River reservation north of Tucson, and they were of the closely related Akimel O'odham (the Pima or "River People") who traditionally farmed along the Gila River. There were the occasional women from other Indian tribes—the Yaqui from the Mexican Sonoran desert, and the Apache and Maricopa—but it was the O'odham girls and women who dominated domestic work in Tucson in terms of numbers and visibility, and who were considered the proper charge of the matrons. A number were O'odham students released from boarding schools for the summer, but the majority were older girls and unmarried adult women, aged between seventeen and twenty-five years.

The O'odham were historically regarded as friends and allies of the white Americans in Tucson, a tradition inherited from the Mexicans and the Spanish before them, who had relied upon the assistance of the O'odham not just for supplies but also for alliance against the "hostile" tribes to the north and east, especially the Apache. The Milgahn (as the O'odham called the Anglos who moved into the region beginning in the mid-nineteenth century—literally, "American"[2]) had claimed the region under the Gadsden Purchase from Mexico in 1854; this acquisition of territory, extending the southwestern border of the United States, had followed the Treaty of Guadalupe Hidalgo that ended the war against Mexico in 1848, and brought a massive slab of the Southwest under US control. As frontier wars against the Apache and other tribes intensified throughout the second half of the nineteenth century, the O'odham maintained their reputation as friends to the colonizers.

This did not translate into any legal recognition of their land title, however. Cattle ranching and mining interests increasingly encroached on O'odham territory in the last quarter of the century, causing major friction between the O'odham and the colonizers, and serious disruptions to the O'odham way of life, the Himdag. The O'odham had incorporated a folk form of Hispanic Catholicism into their spiritual practices, but they were beset, now, by both Catholic and Presbyterian missionaries, who offered religious instruction for their children alongside education. Catholic schooling had been intermittently provided at the old Spanish mission at San Xavier since 1873, the year before it was established as a reservation. Presbyterian missionaries started a school for Indian children in Tucson in 1888. In the 1890s, the Office of Indian Affairs, which had first appointed an Indian agent for the Papago at Tucson in 1871, began enrolling Tohono O'odham children in the new government boarding school at Phoenix, as well as at the Pima boarding school on the Sacaton reservation. In 1905, the federal government authorized the purchase of a parcel of land from a German settler couple on the edge of Tucson's Indian village.[3] Three years later, the Tucson Day School for Indians began operation, under the supervision of the San Xavier superintendent (the Indian agency at Tucson having been abandoned by then).[4]

A field matron was appointed for Tucson in 1911, and then in 1914, Tucson's first officially designated outing matron would take up the responsibility for overseeing the girls and young women who worked as domestics in private Tucson households. The outing matron's key responsibility was to ensure that the presence of these young women was monitored and contained. The same process involved keeping a watchful eye on those who would employ them also. As they managed and negotiated cross-cultural relationships, the outing matrons functioned as agents of state surveillance and control. Positioned as both agents of federal Indian policy and mediators between white and Native American women, they would be obliged to grapple with the application of federal policies at the very local level.

The story of Tucson's outing program and the matrons who ran it provides a remarkable opportunity to see and to understand, at the micro, everyday level, the impact of the twentieth-century government policy that was known, curiously to the present-day ear, as "outing." Outing in Tucson has, however, escaped the attention of historians, perhaps because the program here was largely disconnected from the Indian boarding schools, which are the subject of a substantial and important body of scholarship on Native American history and are customarily associated with the larger policy of outing.

Historians have tended to approach outing in terms of its integral connection with the first major off-reservation boarding school, the Carlisle Indian Industrial School in Pennsylvania, and with the major southwestern boarding school in Phoenix, Arizona, the Phoenix Indian School. To a lesser extent, outing has also been considered in connection with two other boarding schools that were key sites for the program: the Haskell Institute in Lawrence, Kansas, and the Sherman Institute in Riverside, California. A handful of smaller studies focus on the Berkeley outing center in the San Francisco Bay area, too, where students from Sherman were put out to work. The consensus would seem to be, following the groundbreaking work of Arizona historian Robert A. Trennert, that a strategy originally conceived as an almost philanthropic way of assimilating Native American school students into Anglo-American society devolved in the harsher conditions of the American West and Southwest into a method of forcibly extracting and exploiting Native American labor. For some, the boarding school outing programs here were an integral part of a broader strategy of racial extermination and genocide embodied in Native American education policies.[5]

Army officer Richard Henry Pratt, founder of the Carlisle School in 1879, is acknowledged as the original architect of the outing program. Pratt first experimented in a small way at Fort Marion in Florida, with Indian prisoners-of-war under his charge, and enlarged the idea when they were transferred to the Hampton Institute in Virginia (a training school for African Americans) in 1878. Pratt enthused that his scheme of placing Indians in white homes to work for small wages was "the best method possible" for breaking down racial prejudice on both sides, with both Indians and whites thus witnessing the "usefulness" of Indian people.[6] It was at Carlisle, however, that Pratt was able to fully develop and refine his outing system, beginning with his first placements of students in the homes of neighboring Pennsylvanian farmers in 1880. Pratt's ideal model entailed their placement with families—preferably pious Quakers—over one or two years, attending public schools during the winter months, and receiving small wages, held for them in accounts at the institution.[7] Due to Pratt's unflagging publicity efforts, the outing system at Carlisle became very well known to the administrators of federal Indian policy, and the Indian Office soon moved to utilize his system in the various large new off-reservation boarding schools opened west of the Mississippi from the same time.

The Phoenix Indian School became a second major base for outing in the first two decades of the twentieth century, and there were other boarding schools running outing programs. But it is not so widely known that large numbers of young Indian men and women were also placed out to work by field matrons from the reservations in this period, while in certain urban centers, including not only Tucson but also Carson City, Los Angeles, San Francisco, and Albuquerque, the Indian Office employed specialist outing matrons to place and manage the domestic placement and employment of young women.

Although the outing matrons could and did make work placements for young Indian men, their energies and strategies were focused upon girls and young women, and particularly upon curtailing their mobility and regulating their behavior. Their responsibilities would extend well beyond female pupils' assimilationist training in domesticity, to controlling and invigilating Indian girls and women's work generally, and managing their relationships with their employers. Their records detail the everyday and quotidian matters of domestic service, revealing that the matrons sought to take an active role in all aspects of Indian women's working lives. The gendered and interventionist nature of outing in the Southwest is the context for the role of the outing matrons in Tucson.

Four outing matrons lived and worked in Tucson between 1914 and 1934—Minnie Estabrook (1914–1915), Janette Woodruff (1915–1929), Libbie Light (1929–1932), and Gracie Taylor (1932–1934). Their personal narratives form the organizing structure for this study of the role of white women in indigenous cross-cultural histories. Native American women scholars have drawn attention in their critiques of contemporary white feminisms to the failure to address white women's stakes in and complicity with the colonization of American Indian land, resources, and peoples.[8] White women in colonial situations occupied an interstitial position, embodying at once racial privilege and gender exclusion, a position that has sometimes resulted in an expectation, or hope, that they might have crossed racial borders in the interest of gender solidarity, to challenge racial privilege. Instead, white women have not only been used as strategically deployed symbols to buttress racial domination but also have themselves acted to construct and sustain racial hierarchies and privilege. Racial power could in fact offset, to some extent, gender disadvantage. Given this offset, combined with the weight of colonial regimes' prescriptions for white femininity in colonial contexts, it is the more remarkable that historically, certain individual white women and some white women's organizations made efforts to contest racial domination at all. (Arguably, such efforts were ultimately about challenging white men's power over white women, and so tended toward enhancing white women's power over colonized people.[9]) The outing matrons, whose role it was to patrol racial boundaries, and who were invested with power over not just Indian women but also the privileged white women who employed them, provide a clear insight into the very material yet complex role white women had to play as custodians of colonization's racial order.

In recent years there has been growing interest in the history of the white women who worked for the Office (or Bureau) of Indian Affairs. Both the field matron program and the employment of white women as teachers in the Indian schools were based on the idea that white women might train Native American women in Anglo-American domesticity. The presumption that they could and should do so, as numerous historians have observed, emerged out of the nineteenth-century ideology of "true womanhood." This Victorian idea, that innately virtuous and domesticating white women were central to the progress of "civilization" and could ably lead "uncivilized" peoples and white men alike in an ever-improving project, might be seen as a strategic deployment of white womanhood during the period of the high imperialism of Britain and other European colonial powers and the frontier expansion of English-speaking settler nations. It prevailed in the United States when the field matron program was implemented in 1891.

Correspondingly, a number of historians explain the demise of the field matron program in the 1930s in terms of the program's obsolescence as "a relic of nineteenth century Victorian Indian reform," when professionalization took over from the belief in an innate female capacity for moral improvement. Trennert, depicting the career of Phoenix outing matron Amanda Chingren within this analytic framework, extended the principle to the outing program as a whole, concluding that it was "a dead-end from the beginning, based as it was on an outdated ideal of womanhood held by the matron but not by her subjects."[10]

In her study of the field matron program, historian Lisa Emmerich noted there was always an undercurrent of ambivalence in the program concerning the unregulated interaction between white women and Indian men, and suggested that such sexually charged "uneasiness" might account for the particular kind of selection process that went on for the field matrons. Indeed, the white female employees of the Indian Service continued to be characterized by the performances of propriety, even prudishness, that Gracie Taylor was in some ways enacting in her 1933 letter to Assistant Director of Education Mary Stewart. Yet the same effect could be a product of the specific role these employees were required to play—of monitoring the moral behavior of Indian women and restraining their sexuality. With a long and continuing missionary tradition of celibate or chastely married white women controlling and reforming the sexual mores and behavior of women of other ethnic and racial groups (not to mention working-class white women), the federal Indian Office essentially conscripted the same kind of women to manage and repress troublesome Indian sexuality. Even when the selection process ended after 1897, when the Indian Service came under the authority of the Civil Service Commission and became subject to its regulations for recruitment based on examinations, such a sexually repressive role continued to be required of the female employees.[11]

Noting that contemporary accounts depicted Chingren as "an overworked, confused, and bitter woman," Trennert posits the contradiction between her sympathetic ideals and her repressive actions as the source of the matron's difficulties.[12] Other historians have further problematized the conflicts that women working in the Indian Service faced, to suggest ways of unravelling the discontent that so many seemed to display. White women had diverse reasons for entering the Indian Service, but they often experienced the same disappointment in their expectations. Patricia Carter argues that the apparent personal inadequacies of the teachers in the schools provided the Indian Office with a useful excuse for the failures of the system—and the same might be said of the matrons. Carter's suggestion that we might read their complaints as a form of workers' critique that could develop into counter-hegemonic resistance to Indian policy (admittedly, "limited, intuitive, often egocentric, indiscriminate, and unproductive" resistance) is a provocative thought to bear in mind when considering the outing matrons' role and experiences, as not just white women but also workers.[13]

An ideological maternalism representing white women as loving mothers to childlike natives, based on a presumed racial inequality between women, pervaded cross-cultural interactions between women and informed early feminist interventions in indigenous policies in settler-colonial nations.[14] Maternalism was paradoxical in its effects. In her study of white women and indigenous child removal policies in Australia and the American West, Margaret Jacobs has noted the "politics of maternalism" that mobilized white women in the late nineteenth and early twentieth century. The valuation of motherhood was deployed against indigenous women and communities, white women's maternalism intersecting with and reinforcing the most oppressive government policies separating indigenous mothers and children. With regard to the outing matrons who worked in the San Francisco Bay area, Jacobs finds the source of their difficulties in the contradictions inherent to the structure of such maternalist racial interventions.[15]

Tensions between the maternalist ideals that underpinned the rationale for women's employment in the Indian Service and the "coercive power of the national state" that they actually wielded are pointed to by Cathleen Cahill as the source of female Indian Service employees' frustration and confusion. These paradoxes enlarge the classic ambivalence of white women's position in colonization, holding distinct racial power coupled with gender disempowerment. Intrinsically subversive then, constructing a clear and authoritative role for themselves was deeply problematic for the white women working in Indian Service. As Cahill further argues, they found it as difficult forging acceptable and stable identities amongst local white communities as within the Indian communities. White women in the Indian Service were not so much aligned with one or another grouping, but rather, as female agents of the state, marginalized and distrusted outsiders to both.[16] Work addressing the transgressive experiences of those who married Native American men, and of Native American women working in the Indian Service, direct us toward even more complicated readings of the kind of conflicts inherent to such intermediary positions.[17]

A further aspect to keep in mind when considering the outing matrons' conflicted intermediary position, and indeed the women who worked for the Indian Service generally, is class. While the handpicked women selected for field matron positions in the early years tended to be upper-middle-class, bourgeois women,[18] there were many others—possibly the majority—who came from less-affluent and rural backgrounds. A number were furthermore from first- or second-generation migrant families (not surprising given the importance of migration in the second half of the nineteenth century), including Amanda Chingren, who was born in Sweden, and Janette Woodruff, one of the outing matrons at Tucson, whose family migrated from Scotland.[19] Marginal class and cultural backgrounds would affect when, how, and where female employees aligned themselves, or didn't, with the Indian and surrounding white communities. As historical actors in a colonizing process, we can recognize that in class as well as gender terms they were a dominated fraction of the dominant group: white women in the Indian Service were located in the fissures of a class structure undergoing reconstruction. The field matrons and teachers occupied the least secure reaches of colonial power and privilege, and people in such a position, as John Comaroff has observed in the South African colonial context, tended to subscribe to ideologies of personal self-improvement, and to cling tenuously to their precarious social position.[20] If we consider the gendered inflections, we might account for the particular emphasis the women who worked in the Indian Service put upon morality, genteel femininity, and performances of maternalism.

Such attentive approaches to the conflicted and paradoxical nature of the work of field matrons and teachers can help us to understand the position of the outing matrons. What has been written about them tends to be subsumed under broader histories of the field matrons, ignoring the distinctive significance of their role. The field matrons proper resided on the reservations and had little contact with the Anglo-American communities outside; even the school matrons tended to live on-site, in the boarding schools and amongst the relatively enclosed world of the Indian boarding school. The outing matron, however, was more likely to be inspecting a white woman's residence, or inviting Indian women into her own house, than she was to be going into any Indian woman's home (although of course she did so at times). As the outing matrons moved back and forth on a daily basis between the Indian and the white communities, they experienced a kind of muted version of the isolation from Anglo-American society and immersion in Native American communities experienced by their counterparts on the reservations. Only the outing matrons lived and worked quite literally between the two communities, and the role they played as intermediary was foremost.

Confronting similar problems as the field matrons and teachers regarding their identity, the outing matrons were required to win the trust and acceptance of both local Indian *and* Anglo-American communities in order to be effective. Their central challenge was to calibrate a fine balance between their role as both bridge and boundary between the two groups, while exercising the coercive powers of the state in that regard. In relation to those white women in the community who employed Indian girls and women, the outing matrons' role was particularly delicate. They represented and expressed state authority, yet were required to demonstrate a certain level of deference toward their "patrons," and at the same time uphold their distinction from the Indian domestic workers they supervised. Bringing Indian workers and white employers together, while ensuring that inappropriate and subversive interracial mingling was prevented at the same time, the outing matrons occupied a particularly liminal and fraught position.

We might well consider the outing program in the Southwest, and in particular its manifestation as a system of placing Indian girls into white homes as servants, to be one of the ironies of assimilation that historian Frederick Hoxie described. In the twentieth century, wrote Hoxie, "assimilation had come to mean knowing one's place and fulfilling one's role."[21] K. Tsianina Lomawaima's observations that the domestic training of Indian schoolgirls was a social engineering project geared toward fitting them to take a place of submission within Anglo-American society, rather than preparing them for paid employment as such, are particularly pertinent.[22] If outing was about constructing social relations, it is similarly clear that the outing matrons had a role to play that went well beyond simply providing local white women with the domestic labor they sought. They were more deeply implicated in the consolidation of national power, when the outing program they administered is considered as a distinct policy and practice of governmentality by the nation-state, aimed at producing a subject or citizen population capable of being governed. As such, outing was a way of producing a society (or attempting to produce a society) in which the various unruly individuals and affiliations were reconstituted as distinct and hierarchically organized groups who each knew their "place" in relation to each other and to/within the nation-state.[23] The process furthermore was not simply "top-down," but entailed local dynamics and political contests, played out on the ground wherever outing policies were in operation. In their intermediary role not only between Indians and whites but also between local communities and federal authority, the outing matrons were a crucial part of the machinery of this process.

More so than any other Indian Service employees, these women might be considered as "cultural brokers," living and negotiating between Indian and white communities, and between the state and both groups. As "go-betweens" on cultural borders, they were human pathways that linked people and communities rather than separated them.[24] Their duties simultaneously were to demarcate the boundaries of colonization, to contain and monitor Indian women, and to patrol the unregulated and potentially subversive cross-cultural relationships that were produced in the urban situation.

There were men, also, employed in the Indian Service—including the occasional Indian man—to oversee the employment and hiring out of Native American male labor in the West and Southwest. However, it was the female-designated occupation of domestic service that attracted the most concerted attention and surveillance, and correspondingly, many more women were employed to manage outing programs than men. Why, we might ask, would the work of women have become so significant to the Indian Office in the Southwest?

It is important to recognize the gendered significance of cross-cultural employment relations for colonization. The successful establishment of nation-state power in a colonized country entailed managing everyday relations and dynamics between settler men and women and the people they were dispossessing. This was especially true after the initial wave of frontier expansion, when efforts had to be made to consolidate control and entrench the dominance of the settler state if the colonial project was to succeed long term. Recent postcolonial analyses have shown, particularly in the work of Ann Stoler, that the home was the critical arena in which interventionist colonial regimes sought to create the "affective ties" for both subjugated and colonizer populations that supported the colonial project.[25] The home, or household, was effectively defined during the Victorian period as a female domain insulated from the public world of employment, despite all evidence of the continual blurring of such a dichotomy. It continued to be seen thus, even as close and sustained public management of such intimate ties intensified well into the twentieth century for colonizing settler nation-states such as the United States.

Domestic service was perhaps the preeminent site and arena of intimate cross-cultural relations—after sexuality—and considerably easier than sexual relations for the state to manage and manipulate on a day-to-day basis. The significance of domestic service as a way of structuring female class and race relations on the basis of who did the "dirty work" and who was thereby released from such visible labor has been explored in a range of colonial contexts. Native domestic service was virtually ubiquitous to colonization, and despite a general dearth in the literature on Native American domestic service, the American West and Southwest were no exception.[26] By actively intervening in such domestic relations between women, however, the modern nation-state announced its intention to actively manage and shape such relationships, and even in some cases to generate them as seemed most suited to the purposes of consolidating government power.

In the Southwest, and particularly in Tucson, the outing program was, at its root, a policy about managing cross-cultural relations through managing women's lives, work, and bodies, in order to reshape and perfect not just Indian people but also the broader settler society. As we will see, the O'odham women involved were not passive victims of a sudden infliction of state control. They engaged with and negotiated the system to utilize it, as best they could, to maintain their independence. At the same time, the white women who employed them, and who did demand such provision of their labor, were themselves a target, not always compliant, of the government effort to shape race relations in a way that supported, rather than undermined, the national colonizing project.

The maternalism that girded the late nineteenth- and early twentieth-century feminism of privileged white women was harnessed in such reform efforts. Maternalism was also a key feature of women's relationships in domestic service, particularly across race, in the United States and other Anglophone settler societies—honored as an ideal if not so much in practice. Historians of domestic service highlight that figuring the relationship between mistress and servant as familial and maternalist worked to cement racial hierarchies of power between women.[27] The authorities and architects of Indian policy looked to new frontier societies and did not see much evidence of maternalism in relationships between white and Indian women—but certainly, they believed that it held the key to the colonizing project's success.

When it came to indigenous people, as Stoler argues, the focus of state intervention was not so much on extracting their labor but rather on instilling their desire to labor. The "perfected native" required by the colonizing project was a willing, grateful, and thoroughly domesticated worker, not the "mimic" settler promised by assimilation.[28] If the colonizing project required perfected natives, it almost by definition required perfected settlers as well. The complementary aim for the settler population, when it came to the outing program, was to educate them in the desire to engage colonized labor. Or to be more specific, the aim was to educate Anglo settler women in the appropriate maternalist performance of their use of Indian labor, to demonstrate they were motivated by a desire to care for, to "uplift" and to "civilize" Indians through work, and not simply to exploit and abuse them. Indeed, the colonizing project required a perfecting of relationships generally, to transform what was, as the United States set out to consolidate its hold and authority over the western half of the continent, a disparate, motley, and rather imperfect bundling of various collectivities into a well-ordered and civilized "United States of America." Outing was to be a fundamental part of this process—and women were both its objects and, in the person of the outing matron, its agents.

There is a Tohono O'odham legend concerning the emergence of different races of people, recorded in the 1940s, that explains the poor memory of Milgahn as well as their pale skin. Brought back to life by the ancestral hero I'itoi, these long-decayed people were given the power of writing by him, so that they might keep detailed records to help them remember important things.[29]

When it comes to the history of the outing matrons, the legend is particularly evocative. As it turns out, we are almost entirely reliant on the written records created by the outing matrons to reconstruct their history. Some vague memories of the Tohono O'odham women working in domestic service in Tucson are retained today, as I discovered in conversations with both white and Indian residents there, and recollections of domestic service appear in O'odham and white oral histories and auto/biographies. But the organized government outing program has not been remembered. The outing matrons themselves have been forgotten altogether by white Tucson, and we are left with only the merest scraps of recollections recorded by the O'odham. Peter Blaine's short account of Janette Woodruff seems virtually the one sign of any of the outing matrons being remembered at all.[30] While Woodruff made a somewhat more substantial appearance in Tohono O'odham James McCarthy's recollections, there is no mention of her role in the outing program.[31]

We might expect that accounts by Tohono O'odham women would have more details on the outing matrons of Tucson, but this is not so. Maria Chona, the subject of Ruth Underhill's 1936 biography, never mentioned them. Underhill carried out her interviews with Chona between 1931 and 1933, during the time of matrons Light and Taylor. Fourteen-year-old Ella Lopez Antone, who was home on summer vacation from Phoenix Indian School when she met Underhill, assisted her as her translator. There is the distinct possibility that an outing matron was involved in some way, but there is no record if she was.[32] Underhill's published work on the Papago never mentions the outing matrons or the outing program, or even domestic work at all, while Chona made just the one obscure reference herself, recording that she and her second husband went "to Tucson and worked for the white people" in winter, rather than visiting their families as she had done with her first husband.[33] Presumably Chona's working life predated the outing matrons, but several generations on, the life story of Frances Manuel, who started her working life just at the point that Woodruff left and Light took over, barely registered any more details about outing: "Well there was a place where you go to hunt for a job and they place you with people, and [softly] so you work for them," Manuel recalled.[34]

Yet the matrons were prolific record keepers—even the unhappy Taylor left behind a sizeable file of correspondences when she vacated her office. Their official records documenting their day-to-day work are located in the federal government records repository now at Riverside, California (where they were relocated from a site at Laguna Niguel in the same state); these form the basis for my reconstruction of the matrons' history, supplemented by the complementary holdings in the main archival repository of the National Archives and Records Administration in Washington, DC, and the personnel records maintained by the Civil Service at the National Personnel Records Center in St. Louis, Missouri.

There are evident limitations of such records for the historian. In the first place, they were constructed with a weather eye to the matrons' official employer, the Office of Indian Affairs, not to mention the local superintendent through whom these records had to be forwarded, so to an extent they mask or suppress overt expression of what might be the personal opinions of the matrons. We can also presume that events and episodes that reflected badly upon the matrons themselves, especially those showing them to be inefficient or incompetent, might be omitted or misrepresented, where possible. (Taylor was unusually forthright.) As a result, we need to be cautious about the complacency and confidence their records often suggest in their ability to control the situation. To this end, an against-the-grain reading is necessary to elucidate what the outing matrons were doing, the problems they faced, and how they felt about and responded to them.

Secondly, the matrons' records give a peculiarly skewed vision of the Tohono O'odham experience. The matrons' focus upon issues to do with their domestic employment—the matrons' central responsibility and concern—did not necessarily reflect, even approximately, what the O'odham women and their community found important and worth remarking upon and remembering. Furthermore, the matrons' role meant that any cases of gender abuse, drinking, promiscuity, and conflict involving "working girls" fell to them to manage and to report on, so the impression of a community that was apparently largely well functioning and harmonious most of the time, despite severe stresses and poverty, is distorted. (Of course, other instances of disruption might have been hidden from the matron as well.) As with all such official records kept by agencies of government control and authority, we must be attentive to what is absent as much as to what is there. It is important, in fact, to maintain a reading *along* the archival grain, as Stoler recommends, in order to see clearly the preoccupations, obsessions, and anxieties of government to which such official archives attest.[35]

Finally, of course, there is the fundamental fact that these records were created by white women and so reflect, broadly construed, a particular contemporary white female perspective on Indian people and race relations. Based on their own records—records of surveillance over Indian girls and women—obtained, if not by coercion at least without the consent of those they scrutinized, such analysis returns the focus to the matrons themselves. This does not, of course, preclude the possibility of gleaning some insight into the experiences for the girls and women they placed out to work, or indeed for the experiences of those who employed them. A classic against-the-grain reading of reasonable sensitivity can tease out the agency exercised by the Indian women and the efforts of both them and their employers to utilize the outing system to their own advantage, or to evade and resist it, as far as they were able.

But even so, the vision we are able to attain of the Indian girls and women working in white homes in early twentieth-century Tucson is essentially peripheral and fleeting. We see them as vague, moving outlines out of the corner of the matron's eye, so to speak, with individuals coming into close-up, startlingly clear view suddenly, almost unexpectedly, in the records, snatched fragments of their own lives and the life of their families and broader communities recorded on the page of a frantically scrawled weekly diary or in a series of letters with some third person, before disappearing as quickly from view. If anything, the women who employed them are even more peripheral, even when it is possible to trace some basic background details about individuals. We can get a somewhat fuller sense of the kind of relationships that the outing matrons had with the Indian girls and women they placed, and even of those between the employers and the maids, albeit from the matron's point of view. But in the end, the matrons themselves are the only historical individuals whose stories emerge in full, crystalline view. They are, of necessity then, our eyes into this history.

2

"Herein may lie the solution to the servant-girl question—"

Gender, Race, and Outing

IN 1902, A SYNDICATED ARTICLE out of the Chicago press appeared in various southwestern newspapers with the rather startling headline, "Poor Lo as House Servant." Students from the Indian boarding schools in the Southwest were now "being employed very rapidly by those who keep servants," readers were advised. An "Indian girl, once trained, is a fine maid of all work," not to mention "a modish hairdresser," and "endowed with an inborn taste which becomes picturesque when combined with a few civilized touches." The skeptical reader was assured that the school training system was teaching Indian youth "to become servile to their superior—the paleface" and that "the present generation . . . are more than willing to enter the household as servants. Herein may lie the solution of the servant-girl question—for a time, at least."[1]

The arch tone suggests an appeal to the right kind of employer, and those who might not have considered bringing a young Native American girl into their homes before. Indeed, at that very moment, serious questions were being raised about the viability of extending the outing system to the Southwest. This region, relatively recently settled by Anglo-Americans and populated by Indians and the Mexican descendants of Spanish colonizers, was regarded by many easterners as uncivilized and disorderly. Nevertheless, such misgivings would provide the impetus for a particularly gendered government intrusion, targeting Indian girls and women.

In the first instance, the Indian Office's interest in extending the outing system had been triggered by the founder of outing, Captain Richard Henry Pratt himself. Pratt had energetically promoted his scheme to the Indian authorities and the public. Outing, the organized placement of students in white homes to work, was, asserted Pratt, the "practical solution of the difficulties and antagonism separating our Indians from our other peoples," by overcoming prejudice on both sides, as well as nurturing the Indian "desire to live civilized lives." Pratt shrewdly pointed out in his reports that the provision of board and wages by patrons also amounted to a saving to the government of the inmates' support and declared, indeed, that his "planting-out system" proved that government could dispense with policies of segregating and maintaining Indians on reservations altogether. His claims attracted the attention of the Indian Office administrators in Washington, DC, then implementing the General Allotment Act (or Dawes Act) of 1887. Under allotment, the communal reservation lands were to be divided into privately owned parcels that could be sold after a statutory period of twenty-five years. The commissioner of Indian affairs, John D. C. Atkins, decided that Pratt's outing program was an ideal way to prepare Indians (and their white neighbors) for the breaking up of their reservations. Atkins's successor, Thomas Jefferson Morgan, was even more enthusiastic about outing, describing it as meaning "complete emancipation" for the Indians and urging its expansion.[2]

Original plans for a more extensive outing system outlined by Morgan's new superintendent of Indian education, Daniel Dorchester, in 1889 envisaged the wider distribution of Indian pupils among white households in the "older" eastern states, rather than its extension to the West.[3] Yet outing had actually begun formally in the West that same year, with the introduction of an outing scheme for both boys and girls at the Haskell Institute in Lawrence, Kansas, one of the four new western off-reservation boarding schools opened in 1884. There had also been an experiment with boys' outing at Carlisle Indian Industrial School's sister school in the Pacific Northwest, the Salem Industrial Training School in Chemawa, Oregon.[4] But outing in the West would not begin to take off until the end of the nineteenth century.

"You and I know that frontier 'outing' is and must be a flat failure," Pratt stated dourly to his old associate from Hampton Institute days, General Oliver Otis Howard, in 1895. Relying upon the long-established farming communities of the eastern states to provide "the refined environment and the personal touch" he needed for his outing program, Pratt conceded outing might work at Haskell, where there was a Quaker community nearby.[5] He was not the only one with misgivings. Despite various tentative experiments with outing elsewhere in the West, the last decade of the nineteenth century was characterized by the authorities' continuing anxieties that the white population of the West was not able or ready to provide an appropriate environment for training Indian youth.

Such distrust was reflected in Commissioner Morgan's shocked response when the first outing project at the Genoa Indian Industrial School in Nebraska (putting boys to work on sugar beet farms) had to be cancelled in the face of organized labor opposition in 1891. White Nebraskans were just not "sufficiently civilized" to recognize the importance of such efforts to educate Indian youth in habits of industry, Morgan railed, unlike the white community at Carlisle.[6]

Dorchester was particularly opposed to utilizing outing in the Southwest. "Young Indians from the schools cannot be safely located among such people; they had better go to the wildest reservations and take chances there," he commented somberly, returning from a six-month tour of investigation in Arizona and New Mexico in 1893. In Dorchester's opinion, the frontier communities were "pulpy endogens . . . not the intelligent, substantial municipalities of a strong nation," and he called for a "stronger infusion of moral sense and even of intelligent sentiment, on all the frontiers," to help Indian "advancement" in these regions: "Red men will take their cue from the neighboring populations."[7] William Hailman, Dorchester's successor, similarly concluded that prevailing attitudes towards Native American people in the midwestern states were simply too hostile to countenance their placement in white homes, and that white communities in these areas required a reform and uplift program of their own. Hailman urged philanthropic and missionary organizations to set up posts where Indian reservation lands were being broken up by allotment, in order to enlighten the white "invaders" on their "duties . . . towards these new citizens." Such organizations should find employment for the returned students amongst the white community, acting "to overcome unworthy prejudice against Indians on the part of the white settlers, as well as the stolid fear and distrust of the Indian in his intercourse with the whites." Hailman believed that private organizations could do much to dissipate racial hostility, in ways impossible for government officials.

Hailman did note, however, that outing programs recently introduced in California, Arizona, New Mexico, and Nevada seemed to indicate that government-initiated programs could be successful.[8] Indeed, while outing never really took off in the Midwest, it was in these southwestern states and territories, the former Spanish colonies taken over from Mexico by the United States in the mid-nineteenth century, that outing programs would flourish in the early decades of the twentieth century.

A history of Indian slavery and local systems of Indian indenturing arguably predisposed the Southwest to accept federal policies regulating Indian labor. Deeply entrenched customs of taking war captives, especially women and children, to be servants and slaves had not been shaken by the United States' takeover from Mexico in the mid-nineteenth century. Even before the war with Mexico, Anglo-Americans moving into the Southwest had perpetuated and refined Indian labor exploitation and slavery (actually abolished by the Mexican government in 1829).[9] In the Compromise of 1850, the newly annexed territories of New Mexico and Utah (encompassing the present-day states of Nevada, Utah, Arizona, New Mexico, and parts of Wyoming and Colorado) were allowed slavery on the decision of popular sovereignty, and California was admitted as a "free" state to the Union, balancing Texas, which was recognized as a "slave" state. Unlike Texas, where Anglo settlers had brought in significant numbers of African American slaves, these new entities had continued to rely upon Indian labor.

The new Californian state constitution outlawed slavery, but its new legislature simultaneously enacted Chapter 133, "an act for the government and protection of Indians," which provided for the indenture of Indians, regulated their employment, and defined a special class of crimes and punishments for them that resulted in the spectacle of weekly auctions of Indian prisoners, and "fierce competition" between free Indians for domestic work. Amended in 1860 to allow for the indenturing of Indian prisoners of war, and extended terms of service, the Californian indenture law took control of the many young Indian children orphaned in the wars against the settlers. Black slavery was legalized in Utah in 1852 along with a separate act providing for the "Further Relief of Indian Slaves and Prisoners," which allowed for the purchase of young Indian workers under indenture until they reached maturity. In the Territory of New Mexico, then encompassing what is southern Arizona today, Indian slavery and peonage continued largely unmodified. It took two years from the passage of the Thirteenth Amendment abolishing slavery and involuntary servitude in 1865 for federal law to force New Mexico to end the institutions of debt peonage and Indian slavery.[10]

Arizona, meanwhile, had been carved out as another separate territory in 1863, to counteract Confederate claims to the Southwest. This was just as the New Mexico legislature raised eyebrows by demanding compensation for its six hundred Indian captive-slaves, due to be liberated by the abolition of slavery.[11] The desire to distinguish the new territory from slavery-tainted New Mexico was prominent in the preparation of a new code of laws for Arizona. The Arizonans—still dependent on the labor of Indian captives as well as of the "friendly" O'odham peoples—chose the Californian solution. The new code that came into effect in 1865 contained provisions based on the Californian codes allowing captured Indian children and "any minor Indian child of other than hostile tribes" to be bound under indenture.[12]

There had been early colonial precedents in the eastern states for very similar schemes for indenturing Indian children to domestic service in the wake of violent contests over land,[13] but it is ironic to think that Pratt's first subjects for outing, being war captives, could have been subject to indenture had they been taken prisoner in the Southwest. At any rate, given the longstanding tradition in the region of utilizing Indian captives, especially women and children, for domestic service, and the continuing provisions for indenturing young Indian workers that continued into the second half of the nineteenth century, it is not surprising that outing in the Southwest should have assumed the form it did.

As outing was extended and adapted in this region, it quickly took on a distinctive gendered patterning. Boys were typically placed out in groups or gangs as contract labor on farms, with little immediate contact with any white family, while the placement of outing pupils in individual white families instead targeted girls. Furthermore, the girls' outing programs would overtake the boys' in significance, especially in Arizona and California.

While Pratt had endorsed outing for girls, even arguing that the benefits for girls under the care of "kindly housewives" outweighed those for the boys, at Carlisle girls were no more likely than boys to be placed out in white households and, in the beginning, much less likely. In terms of absolute numbers, more boys than girls were always placed out in any given year at Carlisle. Some hesitation over "planting-out" girls was due to the concern that they might thereby "drop" into the servant class and run all the risks associated with that occupation.[14] But mainly, the gender bias was because as a way of demonstrating the usefulness of Indians through their employment, outing was not considered relevant to girls—Pratt's presumption being that Indian women would not need or want paid work outside their own homes. Indeed, the instigation of an outing program for girls at both Carlisle and Hampton was driven by the lack of accommodation facilities for them, while the introduction of an outing system in 1886 at the privately run Lincoln Institute in Philadelphia, the one other eastern Indian institution at the time, catering to girls only, might well have been largely due to similar issues over the summer.[15] In the southwestern outing programs, however, working placements for girls quickly and clearly became predominant.

At Phoenix Indian School, in Phoenix, Arizona, girls were first enrolled in 1892, nine months after the school opened. From the outset, the school was promoted as a training institution for Indian labor. The superintendent originally envisioned that outing girls should join the boys in the fruit-growing industry, but it was in the field of domestic service that he found the first placements for female students. Supplying less than half the requests he had received for them, he explained the school had been "careful to send out only those girls that were sure to do well, as we could not afford to have any failures at the beginning of this 'outing' business." Within three years, the majority of pupils working out from Phoenix were girls, employed in domestic service.[16] In the 1890s, girls were also being placed out as servants in significant numbers from Haskell in Kansas and Genoa in Nebraska, while an outing program inaugurated in 1899 by the former Phoenix superintendent at the Perris Indian School in Perris, California, had assumed "rather extensive proportions" when it came to the girls' placements by the following year, and would be carried over when the school was officially merged with the new Sherman Institute at Riverside in 1903.[17]

We might surmise various reasons for the relative importance of the girls' programs. Demand from surrounding white communities was one—as the superintendents at both Phoenix and Genoa schools reported, from the outset demand exceeded supply.[18] Furthermore, girls' outing did not pose the same threat to organized white male labor and did not meet with the same opposition. (By the same token, the success of boys' outing programs in the Southwest, which involved contract gang labor on farms, could be due to the fact that they competed largely with Mexican American rather than white labor.) But clearly the superintendents themselves found sending girls out more convenient. The Haskell superintendent, reporting in 1900, highlighted that placing girls was much easier than placing boys, because farmers wanted boys only for short periods, and the work involved in organizing the "changing-about" was "very laborious." Long-term placements of adolescent girls relieved the school equally long term of their responsibilities to them, while sending them to work at a distance—as Phoenix's superintendent found—kept difficult parents away from the school.[19]

The central administration in Washington, DC, also looked favourably on the domestic outing of girls, despite having qualms about frontier society. In his press to expand the outing system in 1889, Dorchester chose a somewhat salacious example of young Indian women being traded into polygamous marriages on the reservations to make his point. When Dorchester advocated the "constant, wise, and helpful supervision" provided by "respectable white families" embodied in outing, he was focusing not on how the boys' usefulness as workers might be demonstrated, as Pratt had done, but on the protection and control of young Indian women.[20]

Dorchester, of course, only imagined that girls and young women should be placed in homes in the eastern states. At the end of the next decade, the then superintendent of Indian schools, Estelle Reel, recommended that Pratt's system should be put into effect in "every" non-reservation school, but like Dorchester, she emphasized the protective and uplifting aspect of outing for girls. Approvingly, Reel would quote the Carlisle girls' matron's paper on the outing system for girls, delivered at a Minneapolis meeting in 1902: "A savage nation brought into contact with a civilized one is always elevated by this contact."[21]

Yet serious questions remained about how "civilized" the white nation west of the Mississippi really was. Even Reel, by 1902, had retreated from her original position that outing should be introduced everywhere, cautioning that the "best localities" for the outing system had large, settled rural populations in the vicinity, and recommending instead that outing be introduced "wherever possible" and wherever such conditions existed, "as it is one of the most efficient civilizing agencies."[22] Outing was a civilizing project only effective if white society was civilized enough already. Even more telling was Commissioner of Indian Affairs William Jones's report for 1903 in which he reflected at some length on the outing system. The system was "brought to perfection" at Carlisle, Jones stated, where the school was located amongst a community of "thrifty farmers . . . where local prejudices are not brought into play, and the ratio of the Indian population to the white is relatively infinitesimal." In the West, however, results were "somewhat problematical and experimental." There was always "an element of danger as well as of good," as it could not be known with complete certainty whether the families with whom the students were placed were, in fact, "honorable, upright, and kind."[23]

Ironically, the dangers to which Jones alluded had arisen at one of the more "civilized" sites in the Southwest, the large and bustling city of Phoenix. The Phoenix Indian School's outing system had recently come under intense scrutiny. Investigation soon disclosed that white Phoenicians were in no way hostile to employing Indian labor, at least not female labor. In fact, the domestic employment of Indian girls and young women was widespread in that city, altogether independently of the school. Increasingly vocal concerns about their behavior and the lack of employers' control over them would be directed towards the Indian Office to address. Eventually, the solution chosen would be the appointment of an officially designated outing matron at Phoenix, to oversee both the school program and the independent workers and ensure that domestic service was a "civilizing" agent after all.

In 1900, the superintendent at Phoenix, Samuel M. McCowan, had successfully sought approval for the employment of a matron (probably his wife) to supervise the girls' outing program, having stated frankly that the families taking the girls cared for nothing but the work they could get out of them. With similar observations being made by an inspector for the Indian Office, Reel personally reviewed the outing program at Phoenix. But after interviewing some of the leading Phoenix citizens who engaged the girls, Reel assured Commissioner Jones that she could not "speak too highly in praise of the civilization that these girls receive" by their contact with such "good" families. Two years later, in April 1902, a review of the program by the new school superintendent Charles W. Goodman pointed out again the lack of supervision of those working out. He was quite possibly, like McCowan, angling for a matron to supervise outing.[24]

Goodman was advised to cut back the program to a few selected families, and reminded that he would be held responsible for the conduct of the girls placed with them.[25] A new head matron had arrived at Phoenix by the end of June, Marie Schach, but in September she startled the Indian Office with her resignation on the grounds of her opposition to the outing program. Declaring her refusal to "be made instrumental in the moral downfall of the girls," Schach complained that most employers neither knew nor cared what became of the girls, and that the outing girls were "scattered about" the town "with little or no restraint." The eruption of a minor scandal at the same time, over the "immoral behavior" of young Indian people at a school event in town, compelled decisive action. Despite Goodman's protest that the offenders were not pupils themselves, and that the schoolgirls needed the experience (as much as the mothers of young children in Phoenix needed their assistance), the commissioner directed the outing program be discontinued.[26] If outing was intended to highlight the "civilizing" effect of contact between the races, it was clearly failing to do so in Phoenix.

But complaints about the conduct of young Indian workers in Phoenix did not abate with the end of outing, by any means. At the end of the year, the superintendent of the Sacaton agency, James B. Alexander, forwarded the commissioner a long letter he had received from a Reverend McPhee of Phoenix. Writing on behalf of a number of "citizens," McPhee's chief grievance was that the young Indians working in Phoenix refused to heed their employers' control, instead changing employers as they chose if subjected to any unwanted discipline (such as being ordered to stay in at night). The reverend called for "some systematic supervision" of all Indians off the reservation that would teach them to "respect the rights of those who employ them" and prevent "this child population of ours" from working for lax and careless employers.[27]

The disgruntled reverend highlighted one of the major sources of friction in Phoenix—competition among employers for Indian domestic labor—and the ability and willingness of Indian workers to manipulate the situation to their best advantage. The reverend was outraged that Indian servants should be so headstrong in their determination to work where they were allowed their freedom—indeed, that they should expect freedom in the first place. No doubt he would have been horrified by the suggestion that his attitudes and those of the respectable citizens he represented could be traced to a deeper tradition of Indian slavery and indenture. Paradoxically, the increasingly vociferous demand by Anglo-American citizenry in the Southwest that a federal government authority, namely the Indian Affairs Office, control Indian workers actually expressed a growing self-consciousness about the national image and status of the Southwest. Indian boarding schools were welcomed not just because of the ready labor they promised but also because of how they reflected upon the community that supported them—a "civilized" community, on a par with the best in the old eastern states. Proof of their own civilization required that southwesterners should be seen to be able and willing to "civilize" unruly and childish natives, and cultivate within them the proper spirit of obedience and gratitude toward their benevolent civilizers.

We cannot overlook the significance of repeated deprecations, made by those representing the government's authority, concerning unsuitable, "uncaring" employers. This was both a provocation to the local white community and an injunction for government intervention. Implicit in the call to properly supervise Indian female workers was the demand that improper people be restricted from employing them, and that others be made aware of their responsibilities. While Reverend McPhee tended to defend white employers generally, arguing that if they attempted to exercise "greater care" over their workers, they "invariably" lost them, Goodman made it quite clear in his response on the matter that he saw recalcitrant employers as being as much a problem as renegade workers. The Phoenix superintendent explained that the problem was that the young workers' employers also resisted the school's interventions. As an instance of this, he cited a recent case where a runaway from the Presbyterian Indian mission school in Tucson (known as the Tucson Indian Training School and later as Escuela) had been traced to a home in Phoenix where she was working as a servant. Her mistress (who "thought nothing of her frequently being out all night") baldly denied all knowledge of the girl and put her up in a boarding house to conceal her while the school authorities were searching for her. "To such lengths will some people go in this country to secure Indian domestics," wrote Goodman with disgust.[28]

Goodman's choice of example indicates that the anxiety underpinning the lack of regulation was profoundly gendered and revolved around the sexuality of young Indian women and the inability or unwillingness of certain female employers to control their sexuality. Specially selected white women, the outing matrons, would be installed to control the Indian girls and help prevent such patently unsuitable women employing them. Superintendent Alexander had suggested appointing a "special outing agent," or a field matron, for Indian workers in Phoenix. Goodman was enthusiastic about the appointment of what he envisaged as a "competent, middle-aged Christian woman" to secure "the co-operation of the best people of the town in caring for them." She could see to it that those Indians who persisted in "living disreputable lives" were forced to return to the reservations and that those who defied territorial or federal laws against polygamy, bigamy, and cohabitation were prosecuted.[29] Goodman's ideas about the role of this new appointment in enforcing marriage laws highlight that fact that the concern about Indian domestic employment was at heart a concern about controlling Indian women's sexuality. As with the example he gave of the runaway girl in the boarding house, the allusion to prostitution was always somewhat veiled, but indigenous prostitution, together with the continuation of traditional Native American common-law and plural marriages in the midst of a major urban center, was an affront and challenge to the conceit of Anglo-American civilization.

But the full extension of outing as a system of regulating Indian girls and women's domestic labor, requiring the commitment of government resources for such a position, was still to come. Commissioner Jones wrote confidently in 1904 that as "high a type of civilization" had been developed in the West as in the East, now, and so there was no longer any need to take Indian children to eastern schools: "Civilization is around him in his western home. He will soon find natural contact with this civilization." Jones's use of the male pronoun was telling—at Phoenix a new industrial cottage had been set up to train Indian girls in housework, as an alternative to outing.[30]

With the appointment of an enterprising new commissioner, Francis E. Leupp, in 1905, outing programs for boys across the West received a major boost. Leupp stated in his very first report that white easterners were mistaken in their belief that Indians wanted to live and work like white Americans. Rather, Indians believed their ways superior to the white ways, were suspicious of whites generally, and resented government efforts to make them work. But the Indian had to be made "an active factor" in the "upbuilding of the community in which he is going to live." "The theory, too commonly cherished on the frontier," Leupp went on, "that he is a sort of necessary nuisance surviving from a remote period, like the sagebrush or the giant cactus, must be dispelled, and the way to dispel it is to turn him into a positive benefit."

Leupp's new plan was an "employment bureau" for the Southwest region, "designed to gather up all the able-bodied Indians [from the reservations] . . . and plant them upon ranches, upon railroads, in mines." This was a "policy of shrinkage," because every Indian thus stricken from the tribal rolls "by his emancipation reduces the dimension of our red-race problem by a fraction." Its intent was not assimilation, but the perfecting of the Indian population for colonization. As Leupp argued, "Our proper work with him is improvement, not transformation."[31]

The commissioner's attitude at this time was a kind of willful misrepresentation of Indian economic engagement over the previous century. Indian wage labor, unknown prior to European arrival (as opposed to trade and reciprocal labor exchange), was largely a historical product of the original Indian and European encounter; as Knack and Littlefield have pointed out, it is a fallacy to conceive of Indian wage participation as having been instigated by federal policymakers in the twentieth century. Wage work had been critical to

Indian survival in the nineteenth century, individuals and communities actively crafting their engagement with the non-Indian economy in ways that allowed them to maintain their own cultural traditions and values.[32] By casting labor participation as an alternative to Indian dependence, to be forced upon an unwilling people, rather than as a longstanding Indian strategy for survival and autonomy, Leupp in fact indicated that the proper position for Indians was as a subordinate, dependent, and controlled labor resource for the settler economy.

Leupp set to work establishing his new Indian employment bureau, headed up by a Carlisle graduate, Charles Dagenett, and directed toward coordinating the contract employment of large groups of boys and men as laborers in railroad construction, irrigation, and beet farming. Because the kind of employment this service offered was practical not philanthropic, Leupp argued, it had the goodwill and support of the public. White settler communities were now regarded as being "intelligent enough" to realize that Indians were a "permanent element" amongst them and that it was wisest to direct the Indians' energies toward "the upbuilding of the country." In 1907, Leupp announced that he was developing outing "on a vastly bigger, broader, and more practical basis" than ever before, and explicitly disclaimed its connection to any school curriculum.[33]

Two years later, Leupp resigned in favor of his assistant commissioner, Robert G. Valentine. He promptly wrote a book in which he described Pratt's outing system "as the great monument of his life work" and "an inspiration."[34] It was Valentine, however, who would really push the expansion of outing in the Southwest. One of Valentine's first acts on taking office was to approve the appointment of Amanda Chingren as Phoenix's new outing matron, a question that had been up in the air over the past year. Chingren was not the first appointment directed to oversee girls' outing programs specifically (that was probably Carlisle teacher Annie S. Ely, listed as "agent for out pupils" at that school from 1889 until 1906[35]), but her formal appointment and designation as outing matron were significant in marking a new importance accorded outing for girls and women, and the start of a systematic approach to their employment and supervision.

In a letter to Commissioner Leupp in 1908, Chingren stated that the Sacaton agency superintendent, Alexander, having "detailed" her to look after the Pima girls working in Phoenix over the summer, had promised her the position for the coming year, contingent upon its reestablishment. The matter had been left in the hands of Dagenett, and she had had no further advice. After the McPhee complaint in 1903, Alexander had arranged to have somebody from his staff look after girls from there working in Phoenix, his sister-in-law Mary Nott. Chingren had been working as a matron at the Pima Indian School since 1905. Before that, she had been at the Phoenix Indian School, starting as a domestic science teacher there in late 1902, before being made an assistant cook. Perhaps her Phoenix experience explains why Alexander selected her for supervising the girls from Sacaton in the summer of 1908. Chingren now told the commissioner that she would like the position of outing matron at Phoenix, but if it was not to be reestablished, she desired a transfer elsewhere.[36]

Unbeknownst to her, Alexander had actually recommended that the matron's position at Phoenix should be discontinued and the supervision of the girls from Sacaton should be left to Dagenett's local representative in Phoenix, a Mr. Colegrove. Alexander had also requested Chingren's transfer. Any decision was left in abeyance for months. Then in May 1909, just before the start of the summer, Alexander's recommendations were approved by the acting chief clerk in the Indian Office.[37] Whether Chingren protested, or someone in the Washington, DC, office raised an alarm, it was not long before a female inspector in the Indian School Service appeared in Phoenix to investigate the situation.

Inspector and Special Agent Elsie E. Newton would go on to be very important for the broader field matron program. She headed the program from 1911 to 1918, and played a leading role in all facets of designated "women's work" in the service until her retirement in 1922.[38] In the process of securing Chingen's appointment, she would be instrumental in establishing a defined outing matron position within the field matron program, with different and more extensive responsibilities than those of the "outing agents" and "girls' matrons" in the schools. Reporting back to the Indian Office in 1909, Newton expressed her cautious support for Chingren: Alexander was personally biased against Chingren, she observed, and Colegrove did not value her work highly. Newton advised very firmly against shifting Chingren's responsibilities to Colegrove. Being in charge of the men's employment outside of town, Colegrove could hardly provide "satisfactory supervision" for Indian women and children in Phoenix, she felt. Newton had also discovered a consensus among various employers of Indian domestic workers. The outing matron was a "necessity," those she had spoken with agreed—"without one, the girls become demoralized, flitting about from place to place and becoming careless of their work and habits."[39]

Privately, Newton dismissed Colegrove's objections to the formal institutionalization of girls' employment: "But he has the Carlisle-outing idea, which isn't applicable to Arizona."[40] In Newton's view, the outing program here was inevitably going to be different from the scheme conceived and operated by Pratt. Pratt registered his opposition to placing girls in cities to work in 1900, but Pratt was now in retirement, having been forced out of Carlisle in 1904, just as Commissioner Jones announced that the western regions were now as "civilized" as the eastern states.[41] At Phoenix, where girls and women had been working and living in the city for years, outing would be directed toward urban female employment from the outset.

Newton recommended no change for the present, which meant leaving Chingren responsible for supervising the girls from the Sacaton reservation only, but she clearly foresaw the establishment of an outing matron position with a wider compass. Acknowledging the "freedom" of Indian people to come and go as they wished between reservations and towns, Newton suggested that such independence should not be curtailed to the extent that they became dependent on government assistance. An outing matron could act only in an "advisory capacity," but nevertheless this would be an important role:

> The more independent of the girls dislike to be under strict control while they are earning their living, and any attempt to assert too much discipline would result in their avoiding rather than seeking the help and advice of the outing matron. Her very presence, if she is a woman of tact, judgment, and firmness, and her acquaintance with white employers and Indian employees, even though she has no jurisdiction, cannot fail to be a restraining influence to both parties.

She should then hold a similar position in relation to the Indian women as the Young Women's Christian Association did in regard to the young white women who came to work in the cities, although as a government employee, the outing matron would have "a firmer footing."[42]

In June 1909, Chingren was informed that her position as outing matron was to continue, but under the supervision of Dagenett, instead of the Pima superintendency, giving her a much wider ambit. The statement of duties she then received highlighted that her role was to keep close account of all Indian women working in town and to ensure smooth relations between them and their employers. Her first duty was to find places for Indian girls and women to work. Having placed such workers, she was to inspect and report on their working conditions and "their associations" and to "keep in touch with the employers" so as to keep herself informed as to the girls' conduct, both at work and after-hours. She was to make herself available for consultation by employers and also "give the girls counsel, avoiding any attitude which may antagonize them" and encourage them in "as great a degree of independence in personal matters . . . as is compatible with their protection." Such protection involved organizing health certificates for the girls before placing them in situations (this constituted a check for pregnancy as well as contagious disease) and advising them on the spending of their earnings. Finally, she was "to act as arbitrator in any difficulties between employers and girls which they may bring to you."[43]

Chingren was expressly directed not to find employment for boys, out of the concern to minimize potential conflict with Colegrove. Tensions between the two nevertheless meant that by the end of the year she was not under Dagenett's supervision but came more directly under the school's administration. Although Chingren worked from private lodgings in town, her salary was apparently paid out of the school budget, and would be increased in 1911 to cover the cost of her quarters.[44]

In his report for 1910, Commissioner Valentine announced his intention to see the outing programs enlarged under the aegis of Dagenett's Indian employment bureau. He had appointed a Miss Emma Johnson to assist Dagenett in June that year. A Pottawatomie woman from Oklahoma who had held teaching positions in Arizona and New Mexico (including a stint as principal of the Pima Indian School), Johnson presumably had responsibility for coordinating girls' and women's employment.[45] Together with Chingren's new appointment, these appointments signalled that outing was to be more seriously extended for girls.

Circulars were now sent out to all boarding school superintendents, requesting detailed information on the operation and the extent of their outing programs, and statements outlining their plans in connection with outing. This enquiry revealed active programs at a number of schools, including Phoenix, where roughly even numbers of male and female pupils were reportedly being placed out now, the girls' program having re-started there with Chingren's official appointment in 1909. Likewise, outing programs for both boys and girls were operational at the Stewart Indian School in Nevada, Sherman Institute in California, Wahpeton Indian School in North Dakota, and, of course, Carlisle. Boys' programs dominated at five schools, these being Flandreau Indian School in South Dakota, the Fort Hall Indian boarding school in Idaho, Grand Junction Indian Industrial School in Colorado, and Santa Fe Indian School and Albuquerque Indian School in New Mexico. Girls' outing predominated at the Fort Mojave school in Arizona as well as at the Genoa and Haskell schools. Outing was not operating at all, or to a very limited extent only, in many other schools, including some of the Southwest ones. But superintendents reporting little or no outing programs in operation received follow-up exhortations to "make an earnest effort" to place students out to work.[46]

At the end of the first decade of the twentieth century, outing was uncritically endorsed as the cornerstone of federal Indian education policy in the Southwest. Despite continuing misgivings about the placement of girls in domestic service, at least in the town and city environments, the outing programs for girls focusing upon their employment as household workers had been reconsidered, as a way of managing the kind of racialized gender anxieties then circulating. The appointment of specialized employees to deal with this kind of employment, marked by Chingren's appointment as outing Matron for Phoenix, point to the authorities' central concern to regulate and manage preexisting patterns of Indian female employment. The role of these outing matrons would become critical in recasting Southwest race relations. In Tucson, their story was about to begin.

3

"The good an outing matron can do"

The Start of Outing in Tucson, 1913–1914

IT WAS 1913, THE YEAR AFTER ARIZONA became a state, when the push began in earnest for the appointment of an outing matron in Tucson. Henry J. McQuigg, the Indian Service superintendent of the San Xavier agency, had been asked to supply the numbers of girls and women working in town by Elsie Newton during her recent inspection visit to Arizona. Newton was now the Indian Office's supervisor of field matrons. There were at the time some sixty girls and women who worked in town, McQuigg reported. Half of them were married women who took in washing or came in to town to work during the day, and the other half were younger single women living and "work[ing] steadily" in town. It was these younger women who particularly concerned McQuigg. A "capable woman," he argued, could "do a great deal for these young women, who should in time be good mothers of Indians [*sic*] families, and can assist them to obtain and keep fair wages and stay [on] the right path."[1]

McQuigg had just that very day brought two Indian domestic workers before a county court. The judge committed them both to a state reformatory at Benson. Cousins Minnie P—— and Clara A——, both about seventeen, had been at the Phoenix Indian School before returning to their parents in "Papago country," as McQuigg termed it, some two years earlier. On their return, Minnie and Clara came in to Tucson, where they quickly found work as domestic servants.

According to McQuigg's account, they had "got going in such bad company that their people came after them and brought [them] home." Shortly afterwards, one of the girls made it back to Tucson "walking in nearly the entire distance of 65 miles," an incredulous McQuigg reported, and despite several more times being sent back to the country, he stated, the pair persisted in returning.

Had the girls been prepared to conform and go about their work quietly and invisibly, that may have been tolerated. But three times the cousins were placed in the city jail for being drunk and, on one occasion, arrested for "creating a disturbance with some low Mexicans," were found to be armed with a shotgun. Justifying his actions in having the girls hauled before a judge, McQuigg stated that it was "plainly shown that nothing could be done with these Indian girls to have them lead a good example and life." Sending them away to an institution was "their only salvation," he argued. "It pained me exceedingly to be forced to do this as I am afraid that even this will not benefit them any and as I believe a competent outing matron could have saved these intelligent Indian girls in time."

The cousins' overt insubordination was the issue, it seems. They confounded his expectations of the appropriate behavior for young Indian women working in Tucson, and then persisted in returning to Tucson against instruction, defying all efforts to contain them. Most outrageously, the irrepressible cousins had managed to break out of the city jail and had escaped, "very cleverly," from the agency jail at San Xavier prior to that. For the agency superintendent, these quick-witted and rebellious young women were setting a very bad example indeed to the other young Indian women working in town.[2]

From the turn of the century, it appears increasing numbers of Tohono O'odham families began coming in to live in the village to the south of the city, rising from a population of several families consisting of about 40 people in the early 1890s to 344 people in the 1902 census. The desert people had long lived with other O'odham and in villages at the river springs (as Tucson was) on a cyclical basis, particularly during winter.[3] A proportion of these villagers, however, were returned students from the new boarding schools. The subversive influences of female faith healers within this community were a source of complaint to the Indian Service farmer at San Xavier at the time. These women, he claimed, were "educated Indians" who allegedly preferred to make their living by "preaching and baptizing." They were probably connected with the Tucson Indian Training School, established under the direction of the Women's Executive Committee of the Board of Home Missions near the present-day site of the University of Arizona in January 1888, and the farmer blamed them for a major confrontation in 1903, when the village families refused to allow their children to return to Phoenix Indian school after the summer vacation.[4]

By then, Indian girls and women were in high demand in Tucson as domestic workers. Peter Blaine, born in Tucson in 1902, recalled his mother cleaning different homes in Tucson and taking in washing. "You might say they were the washing machines," Blaine described the hardworking O'odham women of that time. Blaine's pride in his mother and in the contribution of the Indian women is clear. "My mother was a working lady," he recounted. "My mother, she was a real lady."[5]

Before the arrival of the Spanish, the Tohono O'odham had been semi-sedentary farmers, supplementing their seasonal crops of corn, beans, and squash with hunting and gathering. Cattle, horses, wheat, and legumes arrived with the Spanish from the early 1700s, and by the time the Anglos arrived, the Tohono O'odham had developed a semi-pastoral economy based principally on stock-raising; additionally, they worked for their Akimel O'odham neighbours to help harvest the River People's wheat farms. As the century wore on and their ability to continue to raise stock was undermined by the expropriation of their land and water resources, the Tohono O'odham worked for Anglo and Mexican American farmers and ranchers as well.[6] "It is the boast of the Papago that they have always worked," recorded the anthropologist Ruth Underhill in the 1970s.[7]

In 1871, a century earlier, the superintendent of Indian affairs for the Territory of Arizona reported that there were "a large number" of Papago living in the vicinity of that town, "self-sustaining, industrious, and well-behaved people; their women are virtuous, and their general character is commendable in every way." An Indian agent in Tucson, appointed that same year, noted that many Tohono O'odham were "in the habit" of coming to Tucson during winter. They lived in jacals, daub huts of saguaro ribs or ocotillo branches, and worked for Tucson residents and sold hay. Four years later, reporting that Indians living in or near Tucson "find employment from the citizens which affords them a pittance for support," the agent described how between late fall and early spring "trains of women can be seen daily coming from the [San Xavier] reservation, packing hay and other products of their toil to this market." In the late nineteenth century, the Tohono O'odham women with their long skirts and towering burden baskets, the conical carrying nets they wore on their heads and shoulders, were a familiar sight in Tucson, if exotic enough to be the subject of photographs.[8] As the situation deteriorated during the 1880s, with the people out on the desert farms being continuously "harassed, cheated, bulldozed, by lawless whites and Mexicans," there were warnings that the Tohono O'odham would soon become dependent upon government support, or even become extinct. With the market for the women's longstanding trade in woven baskets and earthenware jugs, ollas, in steady decline (due, in the case of the latter, to the establishment of ice factories), the women of Tucson's Indian village were inevitably pushed to look for paid domestic work just as the men found casual employment working on the railways.[9]

At the turn of the century, Tucson's diverse ethnic makeup included, in addition to the Tohono O'odham, the Akimel O'odham (Pima), Yaqui people from Sonora, and Apache people, as well as Mexican, Chinese, Jewish, African Americans, and Anglo-Americans. Many were relative newcomers from the West Coast or the eastern states, while Hispanic-speaking people from across the new southern border continued to join the existing Mexican American community of Tucson. In 1864, the first territorial census had counted 1,500 residents, the majority of them Mexican Americans. From that point the Anglo population began steadily climbing. Tucson remained "a haven for upper- and middle-class Mexican society in the southwestern United States" throughout the late nineteenth century,[10] but between 1900 and 1910, white Tucsonans gained the numerical advantage, and *los Tucsonenses* became increasingly marginalized and their culture despised by the new majority as second rate. The much-heralded arrival of the steam train that connected Tucson to the eastern states in 1880 had split the city in half, demarcating the southern barrios—described as populated by "Papagos" and "lower-class Mexicans"—from the Anglo-dominated north and east.[11]

The O'odham women in Tucson at the turn of the nineteenth century often worked for Mexican employers, and may well have preferred to do so. The Tohono O'odham name for the Mexicans was Chukham, or "smarties." They shared a common language (Spanish) and sometimes formed long-term quasi-familial relationships—some Tohono O'odham took their surnames from their Mexican employers.[12] The Milgahn (Anglo-American) employers seemed to consider that the Chukham should be servants rather than employers of servants, although they themselves "like[d] the Indian girls better than the Mexicans," according to the superintendent of the Presbyterian Indian mission school in 1905. The school had been supplying white Protestant families with Indian servants, boys and girls, from at least 1897 when a summer outing program was reported, and it had always had more demands than it could accommodate.[13] Other would-be employers relied on their own personal networks to secure the services of Indian girls and women outside the school system. Mrs. Ethel Drachman, an Anglo woman who had married into one of the leading Jewish families of Tucson, sent her husband a note in 1910 for "the Indian girl" working for another family they knew, asking her "to try to find me a good Indian girl—So please don't neglect to give it to her. When you go down in the morning you can stop in & leave it with her," she anxiously directed her husband.[14]

High demand and competition for Indian women's domestic labor did not mean that Indian girls and women wielded real power in Tucson. Their options in the non-Indian world were certainly still tightly constrained, and they in turn were compelled by economic necessity and the expectations of non-Indian society, and possibly often their own communities also, to take such employment. Nevertheless, the employer demand for their work did allow enough flexibility and freedom of action in the negotiating process to give these young women a sense that at least when it came to their working lives, they could make their own decisions. Minnie and Clara were clearly resistant to attempts by both the superintendent and, it seems, their families to control their behavior in Tucson, and the demand for their labor meant that they could find the paid work they needed there.

The superintendent was confronted, however, not only by rebellious young women like Minnie and Clara but also by his field matron based in Tucson, who "strenuously" resisted taking on responsibility for the conduct and care of the girls working in Tucson. Lydia Gibbs insisted she could not manage this work as well as attend to the needs of the older Indians resident in Tucson, and she declared "the work in looking after the older Indians to be the more necessary."[15]

By the time McQuigg penned his plea for an outing matron, the field matron program, in place since 1890, had undergone some changes. In 1896, the field matrons, along with other employees of the Indian Service, came under the supervision of the Civil Service. As historian Lisa Emmerich states, this had a far-reaching impact on recruiting procedures and the field matron corps. Under Civil Service supervision, candidates for field matron appointments were no longer handpicked by the commissioner of Indian affairs, typically from philanthropic associations with an interest in Indian issues. Now they were selected by standardized examinations and eligibility lists. As women who were senior domestic workers (housekeepers) or professionals, looking to earn a better living or to build a career, joined the altruistic women of the initial program, the class basis of the field matron corps was shifting downwards.[16]

Lydia Gibbs, born at the end of the Civil War in a small Ohio township, joined the Indian Service in 1905 alongside her husband, taking a job as housekeeper at Day School No. 5 on the Pine Ridge reservation, South Dakota. She passed the Civil Service examinations to qualify as a field matron in 1910, the year that McQuigg arrived in Tucson. For the previous two years, she and her husband Frank had been working as the teacher-housekeeper couple at the Tucson Day School on the farthest southern city limits of Tucson, on the edge of the Indian village. According to McQuigg, the couple was bitterly disappointed by his appointment, Frank having hoped to take the position of superintendent himself. Gibbs's stab at promotion to field matron was perhaps designed to enable her to accompany her husband at San Xavier, had he been given the superintendency. Instead, she was made field matron resident in the Tucson Indian village in 1911, possibly at McQuigg's suggestion.[17]

He probably did not want her at San Xavier, where a Catholic nun, Mary Doyle, employed as the housekeeper from March 1910, acted and was treated as the field matron well before her official promotion to that position (on a "half-time" basis) in October 1914. Doyle's

Catholicism was an anomaly in the largely Protestant demographic of the field matron corps, but so was that of McQuigg and his wife.[18]

McQuigg had noted in his first summer at San Xavier that there were some eighty young Indian girls working in Tucson, most of them, he reported, outing placements from the Presbyterian Indian mission school, and unsupervised: the school used to keep one of their "lady teachers" in residence at the school over the summer break, but that had ended when the school relocated in 1907 several miles south of Tucson. Around the same time that Gibbs was made field matron for the town, the Presbyterian school (now known as Escuela) managed to secure church funding to keep one of their school matrons in town over the summer. The Escuela superintendent there had argued successfully that without such protection the parents would not condone their daughters working, and the school would have to return them to their families' care instead and "run the risk of losing some of our girls."[19] As a Catholic himself, McQuigg possibly felt pressured by expectations upon him from his largely Catholic Indian constituency to provide similar custodial care to that offered to the students of the Protestant mission school. But Gibbs seemed unhappy about the whole thing, and her position was only made the more uncomfortable when Frank was transferred to Oklahoma in 1912, and another couple was installed as the Tucson Day School's new teacher-housekeeper team. Mrs. Philipson took on many of the duties of a field matron in the Indian village, while Lydia remained in a three-room rented cottage with her two "half-grown" sons on Tucson's outskirts, several blocks from the day school, hoping for an opportunity to arise for a position elsewhere for both herself and her husband together. Disgruntled and lonely, she was "in harmonious relations" with neither McQuigg nor the Philipsons.[20]

McQuigg's chief frustration was the lack of any effective disciplinary control over the young unmarried Indian girls working in town. As he pointed out to Newton, unlike outing students working in service in Phoenix, the girls in Tucson had already come home from the off-reservation schools, and there was therefore no place they could be sent away to, other than "home to their parents." In the case of Minnie and Clara, it seems the parents were unwilling or unable to control the girls (they were "incorrigible with parents," according to McQuigg), and in any case, returning home was not, as McQuigg recognized, the kind of effective threat that might "hang over the heads" of those who would not behave. Nor did he have the power to insist they go to particular employers or places of work. The girls often would "not tolerate any instruction" as to where they should work, he complained, and not much could be done if those who employed them wished to continue to do so, "unless it can be shown that there is a deleterious atmosphere for the girls." In such a situation, "the only means of correction a Matron would have and her greatest support and authority in dealing with the girls here would be her personality and persuasive powers and the good will of the girls." Gibbs was quite inadequate for the job. McQuigg's ideal was somebody "exceptionally competent and capable," because (as he explained in his ponderous way) "one not greatly interested in the girls or who would not set the example or take the responsibilities, would incur the ridicule and ill-will of the girls and do more harm than good."[21]

Newton's report of her inspection of Tucson in April noted that while there was a high demand for their labor, conditions for the young unmarried women employed in Tucson were "somewhat demoralized": workers did not "keep their contracts, and they have too much freedom of action when off duty," she suggested. Only the girls from the Presbyterian Indian mission school who worked during their vacation had any supervision. Yet Newton was not convinced of the need for a government-funded, full-time outing matron. Recommending a transfer for the unhappy Gibbs, she suggested that the field matron position should be retained, to oversee "outing work" in Tucson, or the position relocated to the main village, Indian Oasis, on the Tohono O'odham country to the west of Tucson (the lands that would become the Sells reservation in 1916).[22]

McQuigg, dismayed, replied to the commissioner of Indian affairs that he believed that if Newton had "closer knowledge" of the young women working as domestics around Tucson, she would have been more emphatic about the need for "a suitable woman to look after them":

> I am more convinced each day that there should be a capable woman to look after the material and spiritual interests of the Papago young women working around Tucson. There are many worthless Mexicans and Whites who drift in here for a time; and

> with the pleasure resorts, the wide-open policy of Tucson, etc. the temptations in the way of the Indian girls are pronounced. The Indian girls, as a very general rule, wish to do right but as the white families in many cases are careless there should be some one to confer and advise with them and look after their interests. . . . This subject of an outing matron here is a subject I feel deeply about lately on account of having the conduct of these girls brought to my attention and the knowledge of the good an outing matron can do.

The young women changed situations as they pleased and went back and forth from their family homes in the country. They "never save a cent and send very little of it to their people," complained McQuigg, "but squander and waste it on silk hose, millinery, pleasure resorts, etc. to the scandal of the white people." Indeed, the lack of control over the working girls was "the cause of more adverse criticism towards my administration and that of the Indian Service in general than any other thing that I hear of."[23]

With statehood fresh in their minds, many of the newly enfranchised good citizens of Tucson probably *were* scandalized by the young Indian workers' exuberance. Complaints about domestic servants squandering money on finery and changing employers on a whim have been part and parcel of domestic service relationships wherever and whenever workers have had any extent of freedom,[24] but the white community in Tucson at this time had a particular desire to see the O'odham girls behaving meekly or, rather, not to see them at all. Racial and class boundaries were hardening in this period, and increasing racism was an integral part of that process. Historian Eric Meeks has shown how Tucson's permeable racial lines began to close up in the course of Arizona's struggle to become a state. The leaders of the Anglo-American urban communities argued for an end to territorial status on the grounds that the majority of residents were "white, educated, and civilized." The once wild frontier town was subjected to determined measures to stamp out openly renegade behavior in the saloons: private rooms for prostitution were prohibited in 1906, gambling in 1907, and all-night opening in 1908. But as the statehood campaign gained momentum, non-whites and non-English-language speakers became increasingly disenfranchised in territory politics. In 1912, women attained the state vote, making Arizona the first state for female suffrage. Indian women were notably excluded. The new state constitution of the same year explicitly denied suffrage to all Native American residents under a "guardianship" clause.[25] The Indian girls who spent their earnings on the fripperies and worked for whom they pleased were testing social boundaries, and the limits of their power, just as these were being consolidated. And outright rebels like Minnie and Clara, the gun-toting, jail-breaking cousins, exemplifying the "uncivilized" Indian woman, were disturbing reminders of the town's "Wild West" past.

Tucson's lawless reputation was long established: "a paradise of devils" one Anglo traveller famously described it in 1864, its "best view" the one taken when departing.[26] But Tucson had been an Indian town first. Predating not only the United States' Gadsden purchase of 1854 but also Spanish colonization by untold centuries, it first appeared in historical records in the late seventeenth century, when Spanish missionaries encountered the Indian community of Stjukson, on the bank of the Santa Cruz River. In 1775, the Spanish Presidio San Augustín del Tucson was established, a ten-foot-high adobe wall built in a square around the village, "fitted with loopholes or small windows for outlooks, and for firing on raiding Indians or other enemies."[27] Remains of an ancient indigenous village have been found under the foundations of that walled city, the shadow of which endures in contemporary Tucson's city center. In 1916, O'odham leader Jose Alvarez reminded a commission investigating the establishment of the large Sells reservation on the O'odham lands southwest of Tucson that the Indian settlement had been the original township. "Tucson was an Indian village many years ago and when the white people came in they lived in our town and later adopted our name for the new white man's town." Now the white people would "have us live in the air like birds," he exclaimed.[28] His voice of protest was an insistence upon a history that an Anglo-dominated Tucson preferred to forget.

As nineteenth-century historian Hubert Howe Bancroft remarked sardonically, and with some foresight, in his 1889 history of Arizona, the "principal fault of the Pápagos has been their possession of so much valuable land near the city." When the Indian village on the southern outskirts started to increase in the early 1900s, it was apparently "to the great annoyance of everybody," according to the Indian Service farmer. It certainly competed with the growth of white Tucson. Peter Blaine, whose mother's family had moved to Tucson in the 1890s from Mexico, explained that in the early days the southern edge of Tucson was Seventeenth Street. "South from there was mostly just scattered houses. The streets were all dirt. . . . No whites lived there, just a mixture of Mexicans and Indians." As Tucson grew, Blaine explained, Mexicans and Indians were pushed "farther and farther" south. The 1910 Mexican Revolution resulted in an influx of Mexican nationals across the border into Tucson, who were confined to the segregated southern and western barrios by the suspicious white Tucsonans.[29] At the dawn of statehood, young O'odham women who cavorted with Mexicans and behaved as if the "white man's town" were their own were an affront.

McQuigg, it seems, was personally embarrassed by the spectacle the Indian girls were making, at least in the opinion of Tucson's respectable white citizens. Such criticisms, he felt, reflected badly on himself as a representative of the federal control of Indian people. But the implication of his stance was that the Indian Office should be clearly seen to be exercising a wise authority over Tucson's Indian population, an authority notably lacking in those who employed them. The "good" an appointed outing matron could bring to Tucson was not simply in terms of helping the young women stay on the right track, but her solicitous care of them in fact would stand in place of their employers who, despite being white, were neglectful, while her very presence would make Anglo-American state power visible in the town.

Unperturbed by McQuigg's warning about growing local criticism of the administration of Indian affairs, however, the Indian Office told him no new appointment could be made until a vacancy was found for Gibbs elsewhere and directed him to order the matron to look after the girls working in town, "unless there are good reasons to the contrary." McQuigg soon renewed his efforts to have somebody else appointed, reporting that Gibbs had "complained bitterly when instructed that her work was to watch after the Indian girls doing housework in Tucson. . . . I do not believe that this work should suffer contingent upon a suitable transfer for her."[30]

McQuigg hinted now that he was feeling under pressure from parents of Indian girls working in town. Having explained that several young Papago women were "becoming loose in their morals and a scandal to the other girls," he went on to elaborate that the Indian parents looked to him to protect their girls in Tucson, and held him responsible for any lack of care over them when working.[31] He was also being heavily leaned upon by the then superintendent of the Sacaton agency, Frank Thackery, to acknowledge his responsibility for two recent cases where girls from that reservation had fallen pregnant while working in Tucson.

Alice E——, an Akimel O'odham girl from one of the Sacaton villages who had attended the Presbyterian Indian mission school at Tucson, was working as a "house girl" in the town when she became pregnant. There was another servant girl, Lolita S——, a former Tohono O'odham pupil of Sherman Institute who was born at Sacaton agency while her parents were there working for Akimel O'odham farmers, in a similar position. What complicated matters was the racial transgression these two cases entailed. Alice identified her boyfriend as "half white and half Mexican," while the father of Lolita's child was a white railroad worker.[32]

Thackery was determined that the Tucson community "which had been so indifferent as to allow several cases of this kind," as he put it, "should bear the burden" of caring for the two young mothers and their mixed-descent babies. While McQuigg insisted that Lolita, an orphan, was virtually a stranger to the Tucson Indian community, had not mixed with the local O'odham girls while she was working there, and had certainly not had "her conscience warped" among these "most moral and virtuous" Indian people, Thackery reported to the Indian Office that there were in fact very bad influences around the girls in Tucson, and that "a number of Indian girls who have been house servants in Tucson have left there in the family way." In the face of McQuigg's objections, he arranged for Lolita's return to Tucson where her betrayer could be brought to justice and asked the governor of Arizona to assist in bringing about legislation to cover such cases, should it be found that there was no such law at present.[33]

Thackery's and McQuigg's efforts in these two cases point to the connections between anxieties circulating about the young Indian women, the rapidly evolving legal machinery of interracial sex regulation, and the call for regulation of Indian domestic labor in the Southwest. "The theory apparently of Arizona laws at present," McQuigg lamented, was "that a girl over 19 years should look after herself and the laws then withdraw their refuge." He hoped that the revised codes to come into effect the following month (October), compelling the father of any child, legitimate or not, to support the mother and child, would mean that such cases would be taken care of in future, but at this stage he had no avenues of legal redress.[34]

Amongst those legal avenues McQuigg had considered was to prosecute the men involved under the "White Slave Law." The federal 1910 Mann Act (also known as the White-Slave Traffic Act), originally intended to suppress interstate traffic in prostitution, was so loosely framed that it was used to punish interracial relationships, most notoriously in the sensational case of the celebrated African American boxer Jack Johnson, sentenced earlier that year. McQuigg was not able to do this in Lolita's case, however, as he could not show that the father of her child had arranged for her transport for "immoral" purposes as such—he had paid Lolita's fare to go to her friend's family at Sacaton to have her baby—and McQuigg did not consider that option in Alice's case.[35]

Alice said she was willing to marry her boyfriend, and McQuigg may well have seen this as a reasonable outcome. He learnt, however, from the girls working in Tucson, that Alice's lover had left town (perhaps Alice, who could give only the young man's first name, knew this too).[36] And even if McQuigg had found him, under current Arizona law barring intermarriage, their marriage would have been technically illegal.

Prohibitions against racial intermarriage between whites and other groups dated back to the start of the territorial period. Mexicans claiming Spanish and therefore European lineage were legally treated as whites; theoretically, this meant that Mexicans were also prohibited from marrying people of other groups. But while rates of Mexican-Anglo intermarriage declined steeply from the late nineteenth century, common-law unions, at least between Mexican Americans and Indians, had continued.[37]

In 1913, however, major changes were afoot, all of them in the works even as McQuigg worried about what to do with Lolita and Alice. In that year, legal recognition of common-law marriage was abolished in Arizona by the outlawing of cohabitation. As legal historian Sonya Garza suggests, this development was linked to growing hostility to interracial unions, whether formalized or not, in the early twentieth century. At the same time, the existing laws against intermarriage were extended by a carefully worded amendment prohibiting marriages between "the descendants" of people of "Caucasian blood" with "the descendants" of any of the other groups. As would be argued in at least two later court cases in Arizona, the amendment meant there were no lawful partners for anyone of mixed descent. While the new law was obviously not practicable, together with the anti-cohabitation laws, this development can be read as an official public disavowal of the complex ethnic mingling that existed in the genealogies of Arizona families and communities, and an indication of the hostile attitudes that must have surrounded girls in Alice's and Lolita's predicament.[38]

McQuigg decried anti-miscegenation legislation as "a most unjust and idiotic law and one that is bound to work many hardships." Nevertheless, the social interaction between Indians and Mexicans was a key concern for McQuigg (recall the cousins' crime of mingling with "low Mexicans") and Thackery. Alice had mentioned a "part Mexican girl named Dolores" as somebody in Tucson who might be able to help locate her baby's father. As a number of other Indian girls apparently knew this Dolores, Thackery suspected she might also be connected in some way to Lolita's case. "It seems probable to me," he speculated to McQuigg, "that it may develop that this woman Dolores and possibly others in association with her are responsible for the downfall of these Indian girls." That a friendship between an Indian and a mixed-descent Mexican girl was considered "an apparently bad situation" is another sign of the racial and social anxieties that were triggered by the young Indian workers in town.[39]

By now McQuigg hoped he might engineer the transfer of a female employee from Santa Ana Pueblo in New Mexico for an official outing position. But he was still waiting for his new appointment a month later, writing in response to an enquiry from the outing matron at Phoenix Indian School that he had just had a white man charged for seducing a sixteen-year-old and that the girls "certainly need a good outing matron." He invited Amanda Chingren's suggestions as to how he might get "a competent sensible woman" appointed.[40]

The idea that a "competent sensible woman" was the solution to the problem of young Indian girls being seduced by white men was a direct expression of the maternalist assumptions about white women's role. In such a construction, the maternal figure of white womanhood was the embodiment of the sound common sense and capability needed to ensure the establishment of a virtuous and orderly society. She was to stand as a guardian of civilization between the vulnerable Indian girl, whose own culture and race were seen to be able to offer limited guidance, and the lustful, predatory white man unable to control his innate sexual urges. Such a figure offered the kind of moral suasion for both Indian women and white men that a white man himself, regardless of his position of authority, could not hope to. It was not surprising that McQuigg should seek Chingren's help in the matter, for the same notions about white women had underpinned the establishment of the original outing matron position in Phoenix. But without strong support from Newton, the instrument of Chingren's appointment, who evidently saw no reason why the current field matron in Tucson could not fulfil this role, McQuigg's efforts were fruitless.

And so the new year arrived without any further developments. Gibbs continued working from the room McQuigg had rented for her work in town, trying "to do the best she can," McQuigg reported gloomily.[41] Then, in early February 1914, McQuigg's campaign received an unexpected new impetus.

No less than three petitions concerning the Indian girls in service were received in the Indian Office, forwarded by Miss Sarah Chapin from the Presbyterian Indian mission school. Chapin, a former field matron in the Indian Service, was presumably the school employee assigned to look after Escuela's outing students. She explained that in her work with the young Indian domestics, she found "our young women exposed to city conditions, for which they are poorly prepared coming from the restraints of school or from their homes in the country far from the glare and excitement of the city with its manifold temptations":

> In their off hours from domestic service, there is no place for them to gather where the influence shall be for honesty and purity and healthful social enjoyment. When Government and Mission schools close there will be added numbers to those already here. They have many afternoons and evenings with most of Sabbath afternoon or even later if they do not see fit to return home. During the last month, two of our girls have fallen in the snares set for their undoing.

> I have talked with the men and women whose names are on the enclosed petition and with one accord they urge this attempt to put the Government outing matron [i.e., Gibbs] in shape to help them, as she cannot while she boards and has but her one room at her disposal. The city of Tucson has not Y.W.C.A. or any organization where these or any other girls are having safe influences thrown about them during their hours of relaxation, so that we cannot turn to what does not exist for help. You are our only hope. I could have lengthened this list to take in all the public men of the city, but is not this sufficient?[42]

Indeed, it was not the public men of the city but their wives who were the driving force for this new campaign. Chapin's longest petition bore some thirty-four signatures, most of them by the spouses of leading Anglo-American businessmen. Declaring themselves as "We, the undersigned ~~women~~ citizens of Tucson, some of us employing Indian girls as domestics," their petition emphasized the "great dangers" that these girls confronted in the city, their evenings "largely spent at moving picture shows or on the streets till late hours." Having "seen results which alarm us for their moral integrity," the petitioners asked that the Indian Office arrange for a room "where these girls will be free to come for social intercourse and recreation" under the care of the government outing matron. Their petition highlights the importance to the white women who employed Indian workers of securing control over their sexuality. It demonstrates, also, the limitations they felt they had in terms of their own ability to provide moral protection for the young women and girls who worked for them, and their expectation that the government body responsible for Indian affairs provide more practical support.

The citizen women's petition was accompanied by a petition signed by eight "Clergymen of Tucson," representing the various Protestant churches in Tucson. The clerics endorsed the appeal for a room for Indian girls, adding that this provision was "vitally necessary to save many of them from becoming girls of the street." As with the Reverend McPhee's representations some years earlier concerning the Indian workers in Phoenix, it seems "respectable" employers had sought an alliance with the clergy to strengthen their protest.[43]

But most interesting of all was the third petition, bearing the signatures of nineteen "Indian young women, working in Tucson."

The petitioners stated that they had "no place" to meet for recreation and social enjoyment, other than at the moving picture shows and on the streets. "We want closer relation [*sic*] with the Outing Matron, and a room with her where we can go for our afternoon leisure or for evening socials, with all respect to you, Mr. Commissioner, we entreat for such a room equipped in any way you see fit for such conveniences." The signatories to this petition included Lolita, although not Alice E——. Presumably, they were all working for the women who had signed the original petition and were connected to the Presbyterian Indian mission school. Their motives in signing the petition, which we must presume was at the encouragement of their employers or the clergymen, are difficult to ascertain. While it mimicked some of the arch language of the citizens' petition, the grammatical structure suggests that the petition could have been a genuinely combined effort. Unlike the two other petitions, the workers' petition did not raise the issue of moral protection. Rather, the Indian girls stressed the opportunity of having a place where they might relax and socialize together in Tucson, out of the public—and white-dominated—space.[44]

Their expressed desire for such a place to meet suggests that the young workers themselves felt vulnerable and exposed on Tucson streets, and that they were, indeed, at real risk of harassment and even attack in the town. The outing matron, with whom they wanted "closer" relations, was perhaps in their eyes, then, a useful authority figure to deflect dangerous and unwanted white attentions. Furthermore, as such a government representative, she provided the endorsement for the establishment of their own social center in Tucson. The workers' petition suggests that discourse of maternalism could be appropriated by Indian girls to assist them in their own purposes and needs. As the forerunner to future petitions in relation to outing matrons, the young Indian women's petition suggests that they were sensible to the use of writing as a political tool and were in the process of developing their own culture of petitioning to negotiate their world.

The petitions succeeded where McQuigg's efforts had not. Within a few weeks, the Indian Office found a vacancy for Gibbs at the Zuni agency in New Mexico and offered her a transfer. It must have been intensely frustrating for McQuigg when Gibbs, after consulting with her husband, declined to take it, unless Frank could be given a "satisfactory transfer" to the same place. Increasing pressure was brought to bear on her by the Office, with Commissioner Cato Sells in the end directing McQuigg to tell Gibbs that if she did not accept the transfer she would be furloughed. Under protest, Gibbs finally accepted the transfer.[45]

McQuigg, meanwhile, had been notified that his recommendation that an outing matron be installed in place of the field matron had been "carefully considered," and that the Office was looking at transferring a Mrs. Minnie M. Estabrook from the Hoopa Valley Indian Reservation in northern California for the position. He was directed to secure, for her use, either a suite of rooms similar to those maintained in cities by the YWCA for young white women or a small cottage. "This Office desires very greatly to make this establishment of a rescue home in Tucson work to the greatest advantage in establishing a home for these Indian girls, and you will devote to this project your utmost personal effort, referring to this Office without delay any requests necessary for the completion of this project." At the same time, Assistant Commissioner Edgar Meritt wrote to thank Chapin for her interest and express the hope "that our labors may result in a beneficial uplift and improvement of environment for these unfortunate people for whom we labor."[46]

It seems that the Indian Office was finally swayed by the evidence that there was, in fact, a genuine public issue that demanded response. McQuigg, however, was not a signatory to the petitions, and there is no sign he knew anything about them until after they were sent in. He may have looked upon Chapin's campaign as yet another criticism of his administration, and his feelings about the forthcoming outing appointment were no doubt somewhat mixed.

There were certainly signs that the plan envisaged by the Office might be a little different in approach than McQuigg had imagined. Explaining the situation to an aggrieved Gibbs, the assistant commissioner had told her the Office intended to appoint someone who not only had the requisite training in "domestic economy" but also was, additionally, "especially fitted for the work by reason of experience in settlement work in one of our large cities." This was a reference to the settlement movement, by which progressivist reformers, many of them energetic middle-class women, established residential homes among communities of poor and immigrant people in the urban centers, in the hope that by modelling middle-class behavior and values they could improve these people's living conditions. Beginning in Britain in the 1880s and quickly becoming popular in the United States, the settlement movement was flourishing in 1914. By chance, the Office had just received a letter of recommendation for Estabrook's promotion from her district senator and, looking into her slim file, as Estabrook had only recently joined the Indian Service, no doubt considered her a likely candidate for such work. She was, quite evidently, of an educated background, she came from the right area (Lowell, Massachusetts), and she had already demonstrated some reformist inclinations at the Hoopa Valley Indian Reservation, where she had set about finding supplies for the so-called hospital at the school. There is, however, no evidence in Estabrook's surviving Indian Service record of any settlement movement experience as such.[47]

McQuigg's main motivation in pushing for an outing program had been to find a means by which the troublesome behavior of young Indian women in the town could be curtailed and controlled, thus bringing to an end the vexing criticisms of his administration. The Indian Office had not been easily convinced of the necessity for an outing matron appointment, however, when there was already a field matron there, and with no large government boarding school placing out girls to work in large numbers, there was no sizeable student worker cohort to oversee. But now, Chapin's three petitions had galvanized the Office to take action.

The appointment of Estabrook, like that of Chingren at Phoenix several years earlier, marked a new orientation in Indian policy toward managing cross-cultural contact and relationships between Indian and non-Indian people. Centering on women's work, it was virtually inevitable that calls for such an intervention were cast in the settler-colonial discourse of maternalism that underpinned the broader programs of female employment in the Indian Service. Yet it is also interesting that the Indian Office responded by emphasizing the progressivist work of urban reformers in explaining their decision to appoint a specialized outing matron to manage the Indian domestic workers of Tucson. As Minnie Estabrook held herself "in readiness to report" at Tucson,[48] what an outing matron program would be like in that place was still very much unknown.

4

"Naturally a trouble-maker"

Minnie Estabrook, 1914–1915

MINNIE ESTABROOK ALIGHTED FROM a Southern Pacific Railroad carriage to take up her appointment as Tucson's new outing matron on May 8, 1914. In her mid-thirties, well built, stylish, and animated, she made a striking figure. She wasted no time in making her presence felt, either. Finding the quarters that San Xavier superintendent Henry J. McQuigg had organized for her not at all satisfactory, Estabrook immediately had McQuigg telegram the central Washington, DC, office to advise that she "prefers better house at thirty five dollars monthly unfurnished for her ambitious work and energy . . . please wire authority." Similarly, the horse McQuigg had arranged for her use was "utterly unfit and unsafe for a woman to use," and within a few days Estabrook asked that the horse and buggy used by the San Xavier field matron be given to her for her work. "Only yesterday I could have placed a girl with a baby if I had any way to reach her and these things will be constantly coming up," Estabrook rebuked him sternly. "We cannot afford to start in a hit and miss manner on this undertaking and I ask your response to my request." Two weeks later she wrote to McQuigg again, in her large, sloping, flowery hand. "I must try to impress upon you the *real necessity* of my being provided with some way to make a complete round of calls upon my Indian girls and the ladies who employ them," McQuigg's new matron wrote. "Until I am provided with some means of working effectively I am at a standstill."[1]

Tucson's outing program would be established under Estabrook's firm hand as a decided means of controlling the young Indian women who worked in Tucson, and controlling their sexuality particularly. Tellingly, Estabrook herself, years later, explained that the central purpose of her position was to "correct the condition the newspapers had given unpleasant notoriety to as 'THE RED SLAVE PROBLEM.'" She did not mean the exploitation of Indian girls and women as household workers. Estabrook referred to the prostitution or concubinage of Indian girls and women, and interracial sex, as in the sensational media coverage of the time. Estabrook personally held that "contact with the white race" had degraded the morals of the Papago. Her duties as she saw it then were to manage and, as far as possible, restrict such contact.[2]

How this would play out when it came to the work of placing Indian girls in private white households as servants was a complicated matter. Key, in Estabrook's eyes, were the women who employed them. The new outing matron called upon Tucson's leading women to help her to "uplift" the girls they employed in their homes, appealing to them to take on the maternalist role expected of women of their status and position. She would seek their assistance, as far as she could, to press charges under the new anti-cohabitation laws against those girls who had relationships with men, of any race, including their own. And with the help of such "ladies," she tried valiantly to establish her own home as a site for the Indian girls' moral advancement.

What Estabrook lacked in experience she made up for in passion and persistence. She would confront McQuigg's lack of enthusiasm, and his growing fear that she was out to destroy him, as she antagonized Indian parents and stirred up scandal—as McQuigg saw it at any rate—in Tucson. The Indian Office, too, looked somewhat askance upon the live wire they had dropped into Tucson and her ambitious plans. Estabrook did win the admiration of Elsie Newton, who described her as "one of the most efficient, intelligent and forceful women we have in our Service."[3] But despite this and other strong endorsements by those sent to inspect her activities, in the end Estabrook was simply too controversial for the role.

Estabrook had come with explicit and detailed instructions as to her duties from the Indian Office. While she would have no "actual jurisdiction" over the Indian women and girls working in private homes in and around Tucson, she was responsible for their oversight, and her success in this endeavor would depend "upon the exercise of tact, sympathy and discretion in securing the confidence of both the employed and the employer." The two "important problems" she was told she would be required to deal with were, firstly, "the disposition of the Indian girls to laxness in habits and morals, resulting from lack of restraint, which condition is often conducive to scandal," and secondly, to "settle amicably" differences that might arise between the girls and their employers about their "wages, environment, treatment, etc." She was additionally required to keep a record of the Indian workers, enabling her to "classify and identify" them. The Indian Office advised her to stop at Phoenix for a few days on the way to consult with Amanda Chingren on that regard, which she did.[4]

Estabrook was the only daughter of a well-to-do manufacturer, a self-made man who was the son of a Scottish migrant laborer. After a short-lived marriage to a man whose occupation was listed as "conductor," divorce left her with a son and daughter to support. She worked as a secretary to the mayor of Lowell, Massachusetts, before sitting the Civil Service examinations that would qualify her for appointment as a field matron in the Indian Service. The offer of a probationary field matron's position in November 1913 came at a cost. Estabrook had to agree to relinquish the care of her two children to be considered for any field matron position because, the Indian Office pointed out, most places where such matrons were stationed were isolated and so not appropriate for leaving children unattended. Although Estabrook expressed her preference to take her two children with her if possible, and did request accommodation for them when she arrived at Hoopa Valley, California, there is no evidence that the children in fact accompanied her. They probably remained with her parents in Massachusetts.[5] When the recommendation for her promotion came through, the Indian Office had offered her the choice of three positions—two of them field matron appointments on reservations, and the other the new Tucson appointment. Perhaps Estabrook decided upon the outing matron position in the hope that she might have been allowed to bring her children to live with her in this urban-based position.[6]

Any plans she might have had for the future, however, would be confounded by the intense acrimony that quickly developed between herself and her superintendent McQuigg. In August 1914, Estabrook complained about him to the Indian Service clerk at Sacaton, Herbert Marten. A former trading post manager for a Phoenix company on the Sacaton reservation, Marten had lost his position when taking up the cause of aggrieved Indians there against the superintendent, James B. Alexander. He had gone on to lead a damning investigation into Alexander's administration in 1911, supported by the reformist organization, the Indian Rights Association (IRA). Described by the IRA's recording secretary, Matthew K. Sniffen, as an "idealist with high principles, and ready to lend a hand to the oppressed,"[7] the clerk was now surreptitiously gathering information about McQuigg's administration. And so Estabrook became embroiled in a complex, long-brewing fight against the San Xavier superintendent.

McQuigg was a beleaguered man who made matters worse for himself by his gracelessness and paranoia. Described by Marten as "small, suspicious, inordinately jealous," McQuigg was being criticized from all directions—including other Indian Service workers, powerful Tucson land developers, and members of the "progressive" Tohono O'odham Good Government League—and the central Indian Office would ultimately hold a formal investigation into his administration in mid-1915. Intimidated by the outspoken Estabrook (who was a few years his senior) and soon convinced that she had been sent to "spy" on him by his enemies, McQuigg lost no opportunity to obstruct and annoy her. Estabrook, for her part, adopted a "carping frame of mind easily critical of everything the Superintendent does" and made no secret of her scorn for him. Confident and energetic, she was the polar opposite of McQuigg, a taciturn fellow who did "not look you in the eye and always has his head lowered." Estabrook considered him an incompetent man whose longstanding neglect of the Tucson Indians was a "burning shame"; McQuigg saw her as "high strung and impulsive," attacking him for her own career advancement.[8]

Their conflict, however, had both roots and ramifications extending well beyond personal incompatibility. There was a divergence between the matron and the superintendent over her quarters at the very beginning, and the issue of the appropriate accommodation and provisioning of the Indian girls would become the centerpiece of their conflict. As the symbol of her endeavor, the question of whether or not Estabrook should be permitted to host Indian girls in her quarters went to the heart of white ambivalence about Indian women. For all her highhandedness and cultural chauvinism, when it came to day-to-day interactions, Estabrook put assimilation into practice and expected the same standards and treatment for Indian girls as were allowed young white women. This flew in the face of the casual disregard for their comfort that was held by virtually everybody else in authority and, it seems, in Tucson generally, and it was a question that would not and apparently could not be resolved during her tenure.

The establishment of a "rest and rescue home" for the girls working in Tucson was Estabrook's first priority, and she soon selected a six-room brick bungalow at 317 South Sixth Avenue, some twelve streets back from the city's southern limits at Twenty-fifth Street, where the O'odham village lay, and three blocks from the railyards that lay to the east. It had been left "in very bad condition by the former tenants who were Mexicans," Estabrook noted disapprovingly, and she had the old kitchen floor taken up and a screened porch installed.[9]

Her next challenge was getting supplies. Lydia Gibbs had handed over her own meager list of government property, and the schoolteacher provided a supply of basic household goods from the Tucson Day School, but Estabrook had little else with which to start her new enterprise. She now reported to McQuigg that she required chairs, a "washing machine," a garbage can, a clock, and three bedspreads—the latter "needed at once."[10]

Having inherited just "1 worn red blanket" from Mrs. Gibbs, her most pressing need was evidently bedding. "Would you kindly hurry along the supplies which you have in hand to fill my requisitions?" Estabrook wrote to McQuigg a week later. "I most particularly need blankets and some provision for washing. I have only one blanket and there has been some girl here nearly every night so that on nights like last night I have had no covering for my bed when it was needed."[11]

A couple of weeks later McQuigg sent through ten blankets for her use, along with a small washtub to clean them in. All were dirty, three seemed to have been used for horse blankets, and, even worse, another two were "putrid with dried vomitus." Estabrook was incensed. She put the offending items aside as evidence of McQuigg's maladministration, borrowed another blanket for herself from a "Tucson housewife," and used the rugs from the floors "to cover girls who stayed with me through the night" until McQuigg, eventually, purchased three blankets for her from a store in town.[12]

The dirty blankets became symbolic for Estabrook of McQuigg's neglectful attitude, and indeed his disrespect for both her endeavors and for the Indian girls themselves. To Herbert Marten, who had written to her asking her opinion of McQuigg just at that time, she replied with a strongly worded letter of accusation. Complaining about McQuigg's failure to provide her with supplies, she gave a vivid depiction of the shocking poverty she had witnessed in Tucson's Indian village—dying women and children "lying on the desert floor [of their homes] . . . with thousands of flies crawling over and about them all the time"—which she attributed to years of neglect and penny-pinching by McQuigg.[13] At the same time, Estabrook sent a report to the commissioner of Indian affairs, Cato Sells, via McQuigg, complaining about the "lack of provision for the maintenance of Indian girls who stay at my house for various reasons."[14] Evidently confident that the Indian Office would support her, Estabrook's appeal and the correspondence that followed revealed instead the conflicting and contradictory views of the Office, the superintendent, and the matron regarding what constituted appropriate care of Indian women and what exactly her role was supposed to be.

From Estabrook's view, her role was clear. She was there to prevent "immoral" sexual relations between the young women working in Tucson and men, especially non-Indian men, and the way to best do that was to establish her residence as a place in which they could be so protected, while coming under her moral guidance and uplifting influence as a white woman. She was to provide an example for them and inculcate in them the values of white female domesticity and respectability. Although McQuigg had drawn upon maternalist discourse in his call for the appointment of an outing matron, and was galvanized by various scandalous cases that led to criticism against him, he envisaged a more down-to-earth and practical role for the new appointment in ensuring the young women were under restraint while working in town. The Indian Office, likewise, seemed to be after a woman who could take charge of the situation with a minimum of fuss, and of expense. The maternalism evinced by Estabrook, instead, required considerable resources and attention and, if realized as she had wished, would have given her a prominence and power in Tucson that went far beyond what was evidently deemed appropriate.

In his reply to the commissioner's request for an explanation of Estabrook's first report, McQuigg spelled out his objections to Estabrook's plans for a girls' home, making it clear that this was not at all what he had in mind for an outing matron. His central opposition was to her hosting the girls in her home overnight.

"When Mrs. Estabrook first entered into these quarters we saw the possibility of different Indian girls desiring to stay there during a change from their different positions, or for other good reasons," McQuigg began. "These times when the girls should stay there should be very infrequent, if the work is run in the best manner, in my opinion. I will say that personally I do not like to see these girls kept as boarders there often or for long periods, as it dulls their sense of self reliance and their spirit of need for self support." As far as he was concerned, the matron's job was to protect the Indian girls in service from temptations and to find appropriate employers for them. She was "not to hamper them in their own uplift."

McQuigg claimed Estabrook had agreed that all girls working in Tucson should contribute to the maintenance of the home, so that those who were stranded or otherwise in need in Tucson might board there when necessary. Instead, it would seem that the government was expected to supply their food, and if this was indeed necessary, McQuigg went on slyly, then he was anxious this should be done without delay. Unfortunately, Estabrook had not provided a list of requisitions and a justification he could submit to the Office for approval. Having apparently just learnt that she had written to Marten before, McQuigg concluded by declaring himself unsurprised that she should now make unjustified complaints against him.[15]

McQuigg's suggestion that Estabrook's plans would breed Indian women's dependency might seem to clash with the assimilationist impulse to remodel Indian women as the dependent wives of Indian men. Nevertheless, it struck a nerve in the central administration. Commissioner Cato Sells wrote then to Estabrook, reiterating and endorsing McQuigg's contention that the boarding of girls should be only infrequent, for "it would dull their sense of self-reliance and the desire for self-support" otherwise. Estabrook promptly replied. Certainly, "keeping the girls as boarders would be a very bad thing from every point of view," she agreed, "but there are cases which it is necessary to care for in some way. If the morals of the outing girls are to be bettered the girls cannot be allowed to stay on the streets when changing from one place to another; they must be cared for when they arrive in Tucson without money, and there has been one case where a girl was saved from a jail sentence by my being willing to keep her here until other arrangements could be made." She reminded the commissioner that there was no boarding school to facilitate her work and there was nowhere girls might be placed "in any case of emergency." Defending her original plan to provide facilities to afford "safe and sane amusement for the Indian young people," Estabrook complained that under the present conditions her house "cannot afford amusement of any form, nor can I even keep a girl over night as I have no government bedding, even for my own use."

It had been very hard for her in Tucson, Estabrook continued, setting up her work with "little or no co-operation from my Superintendent." She reckoned he spent less than half an hour a month with her discussing her work, and had met her only infrequently and briefly in the time she had been there. With a horse available to her in the mornings only, she did not have time to make the trip out and back to San Xavier before noon, yet McQuigg came into town "nearly every day," she wrote, "and if the proper interest were taken in the work he could easily come to my office to keep in touch with it."[16]

McQuigg's indifferent attitude to Estabrook's efforts evidently perplexed her, and does seem to beg some questions about what he had expected from his outing matron. An investigation into the field matron program conducted by Newton back in 1910 had found that "good work" was not always appreciated and ineffectual work was the result of either the superintendent's lack of interest, or because care had not been taken to find a suitable incumbent.[17] Given that McQuigg had pushed so hard for the appointment of an outing matron in the first place, and had been so critical of Gibbs for her lack of enthusiasm for the job, one might have expected him to have shown more interest in Estabrook's project. It is difficult to escape the conclusion that McQuigg had simply sought to shift the blame for any faults in his administration to Gibbs's failings, and that his hope all along was simply for somebody who could keep the Indian domestic workers under control with minimal trouble or time for himself.

It seems that for McQuigg, at least, "uplift" for Indian girls equated to paid work in white homes, nothing more and nothing less. And in a sense, the role that McQuigg envisaged for the outing matron in Tucson paralleled the role that was being imposed upon the young Indian women working in the town. Maids and matron alike were to carry out the grimy, mundane labor of keeping house and city clean and civilized, quietly, efficiently, and without visibly drawing or requiring any attention: they were to be submissive, obedient, and deferential, and to know their place. But McQuigg soon found his demanding, supercilious new outing matron more trouble than he could have imagined.

Estabrook certainly had expectations for the project that could have seemed preposterous to McQuigg. She had initially sent him an itemized list of the papers and magazines she had selected for the girls to read—nine periodicals totalling $11.60 when provided at a special "club" discount by a local proprietor. In addition to setting up a reading room in her house, she wanted a tennis court and open space for relay races in the yard. In November 1914, she began discussions with University of Arizona faculty about starting up a dance class for the young women employed in town. In Estabrook's view—as she had argued to Sells—offering these "amusements" to the Indian girls was "both excellent and necessary," being the means of keeping them from the corrupting effects of interracial relations: "These Indians have never had any good influence in Tucson, and were thrown entirely with the Mexican and railroad elements, with bad results already known in Washington." Her strategy aligned with the conventions of the urban settlement social reform movement of the time. But such leisurely pursuits were also strong cultural markers of both upper-middle-class status and whiteness, and her plans clearly had McQuigg perplexed, not to mention the Indian Office leaders in Washington, DC.[18]

McQuigg's lack of support virtually compelled Estabrook to rely on the assistance of the white women of Tucson for her project, privileged women who did not find her or her ideas threatening—"the ladies of Tucson who realize that better morals mean better maids," as she put it. One woman in particular had given Estabrook much encouragement, a "Mrs. Soloman," who "recently offered me the use of her beautiful home in which to entertain the young Indians, saying at the same time that she thinks other ladies will follow her lead."[19]

How genuinely enthusiastic the Tucson ladies were about Estabrook's campaign to make "better maids," as opposed to simply wanting to be sure they could get the servants they wanted, is a matter of conjecture. The numbers of girls being placed out from the Escuela school had been in decline since the school relocated out of town, and soon a new superintendent there would decide to give up the summer rooms in town for their matron to save money, on the grounds that only a very few girls now worked out from that school.[20] Yet demand for domestic labor was still very strong, and within the first five months of her appointment, the new outing matron had placed some forty-five to fifty young women in situations in Tucson.[21] Without doubt, many had gone into the homes of those who had signed the citizens' petition, and probably the homes of their friends, the prominence in Estabrook's records and correspondences of the petitioners' names suggesting the special attention paid to these particular individuals. The philanthropic Mrs. Solomon, however, was not one of the signatories to the citizens' petition, and as a Jewish American woman might have had a special interest in cultivating Estabrook's favor, and in encouraging Indian girls into her home.[22]

Estabrook's letter to Sells with its assertion of support from Tucson's well-meaning ladies failed to impress the commissioner, who possibly judged that support to be self-interested. From the Office's point of view, it seems that Estabrook's campaign rather overstepped the mark. A week or so later, McQuigg told Estabrook to use no more electricity or gas services at her residence, saying that he had been advised by the Indian Office that they sought to "economize wherever possible," and that they believed that "oil light" was "more in keeping" with Indian practices.[23] Whether that meant primitive tallow-burning lamps, or the now old-fashioned kerosene lamps, either way, modernity was a privilege not to be extended to Indian women. It was a pointed response to Estabrook, as well, considering that Estabrook could have been seen as grooming and fitting the girls she hosted for work in well-off white households, where such conditions would be the norm. It was not assimilating them with "amusements" or even making better workers of them that was required of Estabrook, but straightforward control and discipline.

And the superintendent was expected to discipline his matron, as Assistant Commissioner Edgar Meritt indicated in his response to McQuigg's querulous reports on Estabrook. He was to "say to her that this Office expects, so long as you and she are retained in the Service at Tucson, that she will render to you hearty and earnest cooperation to the end that the best results may be obtained from the appointment of a field matron at Tucson," Meritt directed, with faint impatience.[24]

Such results did not in the Office's view necessitate electric reading light. McQuigg, no doubt, was somewhat niggardly, but he answered to the Indian Office, and those authorities themselves were unquestionably concerned by the expense. As a witness in the investigation against McQuigg would point out, McQuigg could not be entirely blamed for Estabrook's problem getting supplies, "owing to the fact that . . . the Department did not seem disposed to grant them until full inquiries had been answered." Every itemized request from Estabrook sent through by McQuigg was met by requests for further report, the Indian Office demanding that McQuigg explain "why, if these girls have positions in the homes of the white citizens of Tucson, they should be subsisted by the Government."[25] The Office's point of view seemed to be that if the Tucson ladies wanted "better maids," they should look after them better themselves.

Yet McQuigg's response was surely calculated to undermine his new matron's project. Halfheartedly explaining that Estabrook wanted to teach the girls in service "better house-keeping if possible and more cleanliness," the superintendent asked the Office to meet her requests, but only "so she may not be able to find any excuse for not doing this work." Some months later, Estabrook still without supplies, McQuigg irritably reported that now she believed that he, personally, did not want her to have them. However, McQuigg made it quite plain to the commissioner that he despised her project. "The plan of work has changed somewhat since Mrs. Estabrook came, due to her apparently more up-to-date and efficient ideas of such work," he wrote with sarcasm. "I thought her requests should be placed before your office on their merits, for I still believe your office takes the sanest and most reasonable view on all such matters, and can be trusted to give the wisest decision."[26]

In March 1915, Newton visited Tucson and was dismayed to find the "deplorable" relations that existed between the two, although McQuigg was inept, she felt, rather than maliciously inclined towards

Estabrook. Newton called for the Indian Office to fully support Estabrook: "She has had New England training; she is familiar with social settlement methods; she knows how to approach persons of all classes. She has a high ideal for the work at Tucson, and I would like to see her have a free hand to carry it to its highest efficiency." Newton recommended that Estabrook's project be extended further, with the provision of extra beds and two "tent houses" in the yard, for the care of girls who were sick, and a housekeeper hired from the Indian village, as well as the various supplies she had requested. While the Office might consider something like a tennis court to be unnecessary, wrote Newton, there "must be some means of attracting the girls, of keeping them interested." The "outing work is still new in Tucson," she explained. "The girls have grown careless, even lawless, and it will take time to get them into line." Newton's intercession and support must have been gratifying to Estabrook, especially as McQuigg was then directed to implement all that Newton had recommended, and to forward Estabrook's requests for supplies to the Office.[27]

It all sounded promising, but it only took McQuigg a week to locate a city ordinance prohibiting tent houses in city limits, and so the "entire plan" had to be withdrawn, and henceforth, McQuigg told Estabrook, her requirements were to be "only for a home for Indian girls when they are out of work, or otherwise in need of temporary care." This obviated the need for an assistant, in McQuigg's view, and for much of the recreational facilities. He refused to submit her requests without detailed estimates, and he bombarded the Office with copies of correspondences fired back and forth between them. In June 1915, the assistant commissioner rebuked Estabrook for the tone and manner she adopted toward her supervisor when asked for details. Stung, Estabrook declared that she inferred that she was not to be reimbursed for her expenditure for the home and that "in the future I cannot do this and I have learned that I am not expected to even tho [*sic*] the work suffer."[28]

But Newton had touched on a critical issue—attracting the Indian girls to Estabrook in the first place. Without supporting legislative powers, Estabrook relied on persuading young Indian women (and their parents) that coming under her supervision and care was to their own advantage. Unlike Estabrook's white ladies, fiercely competing among themselves as well as with Mexican families for the services of Indian workers, the workers themselves could find the work they needed when and where they chose. There was no particular reason why they should seek out Estabrook nor, if they did want help getting a place in a white household, that they should bide her advice or instruction once there.

In the absence of tennis courts to coax girls to her, Estabrook chose the sterner option. By March 1915, probably around the time of Newton's visit, Estabrook had been made a deputy sheriff—perhaps not the very first female deputy sheriff in the United States, as she thought, but certainly one of the first. Much to McQuigg's aggravation, she had also secured Newton's support for her refusal to wear the uniform designed for the field matrons, arguing instead that street dress was "much more appropriate for city work" and enabled her to be inconspicuous when carrying out her duties. With police powers to intervene in Indian women's interactions, Estabrook had unprecedented authority for an outing matron and would exercise it eagerly to carry out her duties.[29]

In June 1915, the official investigation into McQuigg exonerated the superintendent of all of the charges against him, but found that his inexperience and poor judgment had resulted in a lack of discipline and loyalty amongst his staff. But the investigator, Inspector Traylor, was glowing in his estimation of Estabrook. She was the "most competent matron I have ever seen . . . and extremely courageous."

Traylor described with awe how she was prepared to stand "in an alley, side street or backyard all night in order to catch some seducer of the Indian girl," and had secured the cooperation of the city and county officials to help her "break up these unlawful and illicit intercourses," seeking jail for white and Mexican offenders and forcing Indian couples to marry "at once." She paid the upkeep of the matron's home herself, and although she took care of too many Indians, for days and weeks at a time, to bear this expense, she had told him "it is necessary to do this or permit these girls to lie in the most filthy jail in the United States." Estabrook's "high ideal" of providing an uplifting home environment for girls working in Tucson had given way to a much more prosaic reality—providing an alternative to jail. In the process, the outing matron had become a jailer.[30]

From the outset, Estabrook had been called to a number of court cases concerning O'odham domestic workers. Some of these involved allegations of theft of employers' property, including one dating from Gibbs's time that concerned parties who had both been signatories to the petitions concerning Indian girls in service forwarded to the Indian Office by the Presbyterian Indian mission school's matron Sarah Chapin. By October 1915, Estabrook had brought at least another three such cases to court herself, under her own police powers. Of these, the one girl found guilty was put "on probation" under her care. Estabrook reported to the commissioner that she was holding the young woman "virtually a prisoner and at my personal expense."[31]

As Traylor's observations suggest, however, Estabrook's decision to secure police powers in her own right was more directly related to her duties patrolling and policing the domestic workers' sexual lives. Near midnight one night in February 1915, Estabrook had accompanied a police officer to the home of an employer in north Tucson to surprise Eliza P——, the Indian "house maid," "in bed with a white man." The pair were arrested, and the next day they pleaded guilty to "a charge of illicit cohabitation," the man admitting he had been staying regularly with Eliza. They were both convicted and offered the choice of a fine or jail, Eliza paying a fine of $30 and her partner taking sixty days' imprisonment.[32] Estabrook apparently gained her deputy sheriff credentials following this incident. Having such powers of her own removed the need for police assistance to enter the premises of the white employers where the girls lived and worked.

At this time, Indian girls employed by white families were typically accommodated outside the walls of the employer's own dwelling, usually in a small one-room structure in the yard, perhaps in the family's garage if they had one or, at best, on the porch. As a way of symbolically cordoning them from the family's inner life, this exclusion was a major source of concern for Estabrook's counterpart Amanda Chingren in Phoenix. Chingren saw it as a reflection of the primitive conditions of a "new country," but also an indictment of white employers who could or would not provide their workers with "even the comforts of living the reservation represents."[33] The Indian girls, in whose own culture sleeping and much of day-to-day living outside under open-air ramada shelters was the norm, might have resented the segregation and substandard, isolating conditions. We can acknowledge, however, it would have given them at least some privacy and time away from the demands of employers and their children. Certainly, the outside room allowed them to go out at night unobserved, if they wanted, and to have visitors stay.

Eliza and her white lover were charged under Arizona's new anti-cohabitation legislation. There was also a new provision allowing the prosecution of fathers of illegitimate babies for maintenance, on the complaint of the mother,[34] and combined, these laws could be used to intervene in personal relationships between Indian men and women. Estabrook's efforts towards compelling Indian couples into marriage by using the two pieces of legislation would receive amused coverage in the local press.[35] But the matron's records indicate that it was the less-publicized cases, where white and Mexican men were involved with Indian servants, that actually drew most of her attention.

Her records also indicate that it was difficult to make charges against white men stick. In June 1914, Estabrook reported on the four illegitimacy cases she had taken up "in justice to Papago Indian girls who have been delivered of bastard children within one year" (and before her arrival). They included Lolita S——; Angelita C——, a seventeen-year-old former pupil of the Presbyterian Indian mission school who had given birth to the daughter of another white railroad worker at Gibbs's home in December 1913, and who had been a signatory on the 1914 Indian girls' petition requesting a place for them to meet; and another young woman who had delivered her child by a Mexican blacksmith in January 1914. The fourth case involved a girl from the Escuela school, who gave birth to a white man's child shortly before Estabrook's arrival. This last case never went to court. Angelita's case had failed because the father could not be found. Lolita's case also failed, although Estabrook had got the father on trial, because the evidence of her employer was "against the girl." The other case—the only one of the four involving a Mexican rather than an Anglo man—resulted in a conviction against the man and a payment of $10 a month for the young mother.[36]

The Indian Office strongly endorsed these activities, in notable contrast to their ambivalent response to Estabrook's other efforts. The matron should continue to "keep track of Papago Indian girls who are in service with white families," Meritt repeatedly directed McQuigg and exhorted him to "continue your efforts in this direction as this constitutes one of the most vital problems in the uplift of the Indian." This official support was a harbinger, in some ways, of more extreme proposals by the Indian Office during World War I to give "social service workers" police powers over returned students.[37]

But for McQuigg, Estabrook's juridical zeal was as much a problem, if not a greater problem, as her plans for tennis courts and reading rooms. In the following year, they locked horns over the issue of care for two vulnerable young women who had the misfortune to be as pawns in the now openly venomous battle between superintendent and matron. The two girls, one of them Eliza P——, the girl charged with cohabitation in 1914, were being held as witnesses in a second case Estabrook was preparing against Eliza's former partner. The other girl, Marie A——, was apparently prepared to testify against the white man on a charge of rape, although we might wonder what kind of pressures were on both young women. Sick with venereal disease, allegedly, the girls were tossed back and forth between the town's hospital, Estabrook's home, and the jail, where they had to "sleep in the public corridor only a few feet removed from the general lockup of the men" while they waited for the case to come to trial. McQuigg, fearing that Estabrook was representing him in a poor light to the white citizens with whom she dealt, warned the commissioner that she was creating an atmosphere detrimental for the Indian Service in Tucson.[38]

Hot on the heels of this confrontation came a complaint from an angry father of another young woman working in Tucson, who told McQuigg that Estabrook had thrown his daughter Elena into the county jail. Writing to Estabrook to admonish her, McQuigg told her that he had known the girl for years and did not believe that Elena would have stolen her employer's property: the employer must have been mistaken, as others had been in his experience. Elena's father was "convinced that it is a trumped up charge," fabricated by the employer to avoid paying Elena the wages she was owed. Apparently, the father, along with other relatives, had tried to get this employer to pay the girl, but the employer refused and claimed instead that she owed them for an ornamental pin that was missing. Elena's father had then taken his daughter to work for a family that had employed her previously. "He says the next he knows of the case is when you came out yesterday with a police officer and Elena to his home [on the San Xavier reservation] and searched it," wrote McQuigg to Estabrook. Elena's father "protests strongly" about having his home searched "without authority" and on a "malicious unfounded charge," and had demanded to know "if this is the usual method of the Government."[39]

McQuigg was evidently upset himself that Estabrook used her police powers on the reservation without consultation or permission from him. By her highhandedness, she undermined his own authority with the O'odham. Furthermore, as he pointed out, her actions were likely to have a counter-productive effect. It was important that the parents of girls working in town were satisfied that they "will at least receive the rights of due process of law."[40]

According to Newton, it was due to McQuigg's attitude on the matter of Eliza's and Marie's accommodation that Estabrook did not "even report" Elena's imprisonment. Elena had indeed been put in a cell with "a case-hardened Mexican woman and a dope fiend," Newton recorded, but only because Estabrook, though willing to keep her in her home, "had not sufficient bedding, and moreover she had no authority to subsist Indian girls."[41] In her deposition before the investigation into McQuigg's administration, Estabrook stated that Elena was declared by the magistrate to be "simple-minded" and incapable of standing trial, whereupon she took the girl to the doctor's office, where he found she had gonorrhea and should be placed in the town hospital for treatment. However, McQuigg insisted there was nothing wrong with the girl, claimed Estabrook, and had her returned to the reservation. That was a damning claim against McQuigg and, if Estabrook was telling the truth, reveals him to be out-of-step with the prevailing white anxieties about Indian women as sources of contagion.[42]

But what was actually going on? It appears that Estabrook had gotten into a contest of wills with the girl and her father. Elena had gone to work for a former employer with her father's encouragement just before Estabrook had Elena arrested—this act of defiance, rather than the employer's claim, may well have triggered Estabrook's intervention, especially since the employer never seemed too concerned to press the charge. We might assume that Estabrook had arranged Elena's placement, and we know that she did not assist Elena or her father to reconcile the wage issue. Perhaps she was not even aware of the conflict, learning of it only when the employer, perhaps, complained to her of the girl leaving. The employer may indeed have made a false allegation, as the father suggested, perhaps to spite Elena for having left as much as to justify not paying her due wages. When Elena's father then helped his daughter get work with another employer—quite clearly without Estabrook's permission, and possibly an employer of whom Estabrook did not approve—Estabrook deliberately set out to show her authority by throwing Elena in jail, while simultaneously manipulating the situation to embarrass and annoy McQuigg. McQuigg's intervention on the father's side might be seen, in turn, as his attempt to shore up his own authority with the O'odham on the reservation. Whether Estabrook's rather belated claim that the girl was suffering from disease was just a red herring and a concoction to further damage McQuigg's credibility, we cannot know, but we might suspect.

Not surprisingly, the investigation into McQuigg's administration had concluded that the superintendent and the matron could not work together. "She detests and despises him and the breech is now so great between them that I see no chance for any future loyalty and cooperation between them," Traylor wrote. McQuigg should be transferred to a smaller reservation where his duties would be less demanding, Traylor recommended, but if the Office should decide to retain him at San Xavier, then Estabrook by necessity must be transferred elsewhere.[43]

The Indian Office, however, took no immediate action. Estabrook took leave immediately after the investigation and went back East, presumably to visit her children and parents; as soon as she came back, McQuigg took his leave. Returning to Arizona in September, McQuigg forwarded a sworn statement by one of the San Xavier agency's Indian policemen, declaring that while he was away Estabrook had told the policeman that she and others, including the Escuela superintendent, were going to "get [McQuigg] out." According to the policeman's statement, the outing matron wanted him "to sign some reports and be witness to others," and when he protested that he did not want to be "mixed in it," she threatened to see that he was fired if he refused to support her.[44] The reports Estabrook wanted the policeman to witness doubtless included references to some of the incidents she detailed in a report to the commissioner written during McQuigg's absence, including an alleged murder at a recent Indian dance and her complaint that McQuigg refused to stop the Indian dances because there were no regulations against them.[45] But a separate and much more explosive matter that Estabrook was now raising would be, as it turned out, the catalyst for her own transfer out of Tucson.

"Mrs. Estabrook is naturally a trouble-maker," wrote McQuigg in his letter to the commissioner. "I am told that since she has returned from her vacation that she has tried to work up more immoral cases against the Mexican and Yaqui girls. She spent nearly one whole day at least in the home of a Mexican girl who later swore out a charge of seduction against Mr. Reginald Kensey, a deputy Sheriff and a regular city peace officer. Mr. Kensey was at first suspended and then reinstated and the friends of Kensey say it is a 'frame-up.'"[46] Kensey, it seems, had actually been tried on a charge of raping the girl, but had been acquitted in the Supreme Court. This white policeman had previously assisted Estabrook in catching Indian men and women violating the miscegenation and cohabitation laws, which McQuigg implied was further reason enough to accept his innocence.[47] But whether Kensey was culpable or not, McQuigg continued, Estabrook's "activities in such lines do not do the Indian Service any good," and even if she was not "laying traps for me," as people kept assuring McQuigg, she was putting the reputation of his administration in jeopardy.

People were saying that the outing matron was "wasting her time" looking into the Yaqui and Mexican girls' affairs, a job she was not being paid to do, wrote McQuigg. But as she had "needlessly driven many of the Papago girls from working in Tucson," she no longer had enough work to keep her busy there, and she should be transferred.

In her "delight in dirty and smutty cases," Estabrook had stopped the Indian parents from wanting their girls to work in Tucson, being concerned about possible scandal, the superintendent complained. "The Papago tribe holds the morality of their women very high and any suspicion on a girl injures not only herself but her family." And the matron had created "the wrong impression of these hard working girls among the housewives in Tucson." Estabrook, he accused, had in fact deliberately set out to turn "all the Indians and the citizens of Tucson" against him.[48]

Apart from highlighting his own personal paranoia, McQuigg's letter points to more widespread and persistent ambivalences and anxieties about the very presence of the Indian domestic workers. In the course of Traylor's investigation, both McQuigg and Estabrook declared their earnest belief that O'odham living in Tucson should be actually living on their lands in the country. This belief was evidently shared by the investigating inspector, who did not approve of Indians being in the town vicinity at all. Traylor's final report declared that "moral, sanitary and physical" deterioration of Indians was "very rapid" in the city, with girls, especially, being affected "with veneral [*sic*] diseases, laziness and indifference," and he recommended that McQuigg and his staff should "exert every power and influence to have these Indians leave Tucson" and return to their desert allotments. "In a few years time Tucson could be emptied of all Papago Indians," Traylor argued. "I am sure from my investigation that the condition of the Indians would be bettered and that Tucson would lose nothing by having these Indians removed from its citizenship."[49]

Estabrook was in an inherently contradictory position. Appointed to regulate Indian domestic workers in town, her efforts to uplift and assimilate the young women had been met with indifference, if not outright opposition, while her efforts targeting their sexual behavior were strongly endorsed, at least by the central Office. By her actions, however, she had generated local scandal and criticism from both the O'odham and the white community, which militated against the urban employment of young women. One might think this was not an altogether bad thing in the view of the authorities. And yet her superintendent thought it a strong case for getting rid of her.

At McQuigg's request, then, Estabrook presented a list of the Tohono O'odham girls working in town in October, together with a list of the names of those who were working in Tucson when she arrived but were not now and the reasons for their withdrawal. The latter list of forty-two names was twice the length of the first, although Estabrook provided the disclaimer that "the girls do not consult me always [when changing employers] so that I cannot be sure that all the facts are as I have stated them nor am I sure that I have the list complete." As to the reasons for their withdrawal from employment, the largest group she claimed left to be married. Other than McQuigg's assertion, there is no evidence that Indian parents were stopping their daughters from taking work in Tucson. Still, the numbers of girls working in Tucson for white families had indeed halved in the two years she had been there. There is no doubt that mutual distrust between the white employers and the Indian workers and their families existed, while Estabrook's activities could not have failed to stir an already rather volatile mix of racial and sexual antagonisms.[50]

In November, McQuigg sent through a letter he had received from a Mrs. R. Kensey, presumably the policeman's wife or mother, in which she had accused Estabrook of "persecuting Mr. Kensey for some pollitical [*sic*] purpose in place of attending to her own business as Indian matron" and demanded an investigation of Estabrook herself. McQuigg reiterated his previous recommendation that for the sake of the Indian Service's reputation, Estabrook should be transferred.[51] By then the Indian Office had already decided on a plan to have Estabrook switch places with another field matron, based in Nevada. Matron Janette Woodruff, described by her current superintendent as an "excellent employee" and "a power among the Wadsworth Indians where she is located," doubtless seemed a safe choice.[52] As there were already plans to abolish the field matron post at Wadsworth, and to establish an outing program at the city of Reno, Nevada, instead, the question of what to do with Estabrook, so ringingly endorsed by Traylor and Newton and yet so difficult, could be left to stand over for the time.

On October 16, 1915, Woodruff was informed that instead of being relocated to Reno as she had expected, she was now assigned to the Tucson field matron position in Arizona. Provided the same outline of duties that was provided to Estabrook, she was told to report for duty at the San Xavier agency office on December 1, 1915. Notice of Estabrook's transfer to Wadsworth "for administrative purposes" was sent to Estabrook via the superintendent's office at the same time, with the advice that as soon as funds became available she would be expected to establish an outing matron position at Reno.[53]

One might imagine McQuigg's glee on receiving this notice. The superintendent wasted no time in informing the newspapers of Estabrook's impending departure, even before Estabrook had heard the news. Estabrook herself replied to Commissioner Sells a week later, with careful dignity, that "the public" and the Indians both seemed reluctant to have a change, but that she was willing to accept the transfer.[54]

By that time, the commissioner had received two petitions in response to Estabrook's removal. One was a handwritten petition from the "ladies of Tucson employing Indian girls in our homes." It was signed by nineteen women and requested simply that Estabrook be allowed to remain as matron. The second "petition" was actually a telegram bearing the names of thirty-four Indian people, describing themselves as "outing girls and others." The telegram petition appealed to the commissioner that "you allow her to remain here as our matron we are just beginning to get acquainted with her and to appreciate the value of the work she is doing for us."

In both cases the numbers of signatories did not come close to the matron's October tally of employers and workers. Only seven of the employers' names matched those on Estabrook's October list, suggesting that the majority of employers either did not want her to stay, or did not care. The Indian "petition" suggested much the same, with only eight of twenty-five women's names on the telegram corresponding to her October list of girls currently working, and another three to those formerly employed. And while the employers' petition was somewhat cool, the careful wording of the O'odham telegram is particularly interesting.[55]

We can only imagine how the Indian girls and their community viewed their zealous, argumentative, interfering matron—aside, of course, from Elena's father, who was clearly not at all impressed with her. Traylor, who claimed to have spoken informally with the local Indian people, believed that Estabrook was "very popular and greatly respected" by them. Some conservative sections of the O'odham community both in Tucson and on the San Xavier reservation, as well as out in the "Papago country," were concerned by the girls' activities in town and might plausibly have approved of Estabrook's efforts to guard them from white men particularly.[56] However, the cautious and reserved tone of the Indian petitioners suggests not endorsement of their current matron so much as trepidation about what might be in store for them. Having only just started to get accustomed to Estabrook's ways and, possibly, having worked out a way of dealing with her, the Tohono O'odham domestic workers and their families may well have been worried about what might be coming next.

Another appeal on Estabrook's behalf would make a much stronger statement in her support. The Pima County superintendent of health, a Dr. T. Pratt, wrote to the commissioner explaining that he had heard in the local papers of her transfer, and that petitions for her retention were circulating in Tucson. Estabrook was "a live wire," wrote this eminent doctor. Liked by "all of Tucson" and "loved by the Indians," she was being transferred away from Tucson "because she is a 'trouble maker.'" Estabrook had "made it hot for officials in making them prosecute dirty cases" and had "gotten behind other officials in making them attend to their job." Pratt concluded by saying that he hoped that if the petitions then circulating in Tucson were sent in to the commissioner that he would "look into why they are sent."[57]

Such investigation would not, of course, be forthcoming. The commissioner assured the O'odham petitioners that Estabrook's appointed successor had years of experience among Indians and they would not "suffer" from the change. The Tucson ladies were advised the change was "in the interests of good administration"; they would find in her successor, wrote Sells, "a woman of unusual ability and one to whom I feel sure you will accord every assistance in carrying out the effective work already begun." Dr. Pratt received a similar reply. Having finally made its decision, the Indian Office was prompt to implement it. By the time the commissioner's replies reached Tucson, Estabrook had gone, and Woodruff had taken her place.[58]

Estabrook's appointment as Tucson's first outing matron arose out of a complex interplay of anxieties surrounding those young Tohono O'odham women working as domestic servants in Tucson in 1913. A formidable person with energy and ambitions for the project of moral improvement and guardianship, Estabrook's visions were constrained by the rather more prosaic requirements of her role, and the urge to enforce and invigilate tightening social and racial boundaries. Her clash with McQuigg made her efforts in any direction virtually impossible to sustain. Yet in McQuigg's defense, Estabrook was no easy person to deal with. Where even an angel might have hesitated, Estabrook's actions were incendiary. No doubt McQuigg would have felt vindicated that Estabrook's new superintendent at Wadsworth quickly decided that given a chance "she would be a trouble maker" and, before she could be transferred to Reno, engineered her transfer to the Salem Industrial Training School in Chemawa, Oregon, and out of his jurisdiction entirely. Turning out to be even less suited to work in a boarding school than she had been to the outing matron work—her superintendent at Chemawa, shocked when she brutally whipped a girl with a hose (for wearing a ribbon in her hair) and concerned that she was undermining him among the other staff, soon moved her along in his turn—in the end Estabrook would find a new career at the end of World War I as a federal investigator for the War Department, policing the morals of young white women. After the war she would hold similar positions with a variety of other federal administrative bodies, and was probably well suited to such investigative roles.[59]

The gentle, caring maternalist role envisioned for white women in the Indian Service never sat easily on Estabrook's ramrod shoulders. It is ironic that it was she who set in motion the development of a systematic program designed principally to smooth race relations between women. But the truth is that in her attitude, approach, and methods—and indeed in her obsession with illicit sexual relations and disease—Estabrook embodied the moralistic and controlling aspect of progressive reform that underpinned the pressure to regulate the Indian domestic workers in the first place.[60] The central authorities, if not her own superintendent, had supported her heavy-handed and even punitive tactics, and the decision to transfer her to Nevada, where she was going be required to institute an outing program there, suggests that they saw such an approach as in fact useful and strategic. While the Indian Office had stressed the need for tact, diplomacy, and sensitivity in the work of outing matrons, perhaps its establishment did require a certain measure of sheer force. But it would be Estabrook's successor, the much more congenial Janette Woodruff, who would oversee the full flowering of Tucson's outing program in the 1920s.

5

"I try to keep the girls from going to the dances"

Janette Woodruff, 1915–1929

TOHONO O'ODHAM PETER BLAINE recalled Janette Woodruff as the person who helped his wife and other girls and women find work. "I remember her because all the young Papago girls used to go to her place to have their gatherings," Blaine told his biographer Michael Adams. "She checked the town after eight o'clock to see that the Indian girls were away from the city." In Woodruff's own recollections, however, she was there to bring the young women closer to white Tucson and believed she was helping the O'odham along the "steppingstones" of employment with the white people, to lead them toward a "a more comfortable life."[1]

A studio portrait of Woodruff, taken at the time of her entry to the Indian Service in 1900, shows a schoolmarmish woman of indeterminate age, with an upswept Edwardian hairdo, a high-necked Victorian lace collar, and light eyes beaming kindly from behind round rimless spectacles. Six months after her arrival, Superintendent McQuigg described her, doubtless with relief, as "sympathetic and motherly" toward the girls working in Tucson and "doing much good among them." Woodruff was the model of deference to McQuigg, and by March 1916, the Indian Office advised him that there was no longer any need for him to submit the outing matron's reports to the central Office, a measure instigated after Elsie Newton's investigation of his dispute with Minnie Estabrook. Not long after, McQuigg was transferred himself, making way for a new superintendent, Jewell

Martin. Both Martin and his successor in 1918, Thomas McCormick, acknowledged that the outing matron had "a difficult position," but—as McCormick wrote approvingly—"she never complains."[2]

Indeed, Woodruff had proved herself at Wadsworth, on the Pyramid Lake Paiute Indian Reservation in Nevada, where she had replaced a particularly miserable and discouraged field matron, a Miss Sparks, in 1908. Reports on Woodruff's work thereafter had been consistently admiring. She was "remarkable," "excellent," and hard-working to the point that she had to be cautioned against overwork; she put her "heart and soul in the work for the betterment of the Indians," and they in turn demonstrated "the greatest confidence in her." Perhaps most importantly for the outing work in Tucson, she had "succeeded in bringing about good feeling between whites and Indians in the town."[3]

Janette Woodruff, the eldest daughter of Scottish migrant farmers in Wisconsin and a sensible sort of woman, entered the Indian Service at the turn of the century. She had been a dressmaker and milliner before the birth of her only child, a son, in the early 1880s. By 1899, when she took her Civil Service examinations, she was divorced, had just turned forty, and was living all on her own at Sisseton in South Dakota. She had been an assistant postmistress there for the past five years or so, but had recently returned to dressmaking.[4] An occupation favored by aspirational working-class women, dressmaking offered a genteel if rather precarious route to economic independence in the nineteenth century, but at the start of the twentieth it was an occupation in steep decline.[5] Woodruff decided to enlist in the Indian Service.

Her decision, taken against the advice of her "well meaning friends,"[6] reflected the constraints upon white women at the time and the opportunities that Indian Service employment provided. The Indian Service at that time was one of the most prominent employers of women among the various federal agencies, and the importance of women in the Indian Service was underlined by the very high-ranking positions that well-educated individual women, like Estelle Reel, could attain in it.[7] Woodruff required some means of supporting herself, and the work of a school or a field matron for the Indian Service would provide not just security and a position of respectability but also a sense of purpose and the possibilities of advancement.

Woodruff started out as an assistant matron at a reservation boarding school in Montana in October 1900. Ten years later, the Indian Service field matron's salary she earned, $720 a year, was not lavish. But at a time when a "comfortable" urban family's annual household income ranged between $1,000 and $3,500,[8] it was not inadequate for a single person without dependents, especially when additional bonuses and payments were factored in. It also remained one of the higher-paid rank and file positions for women in the Indian Service.[9] Undoubtedly ambitious, in 1911 Woodruff sought appointment as an agency superintendent herself. For a single woman this was a forward move. Women occasionally did achieve positions as superintendents of boarding schools in their own right, but agency superintendents were typically men, whose wives were appointed in lesser positions alongside them, exempt from the requirement to sit the Civil Service examinations to do so.[10] Woodruff, instead, was allowed to sit examinations for the position of assistant clerk, but did not get a high enough score to qualify.[11]

At that time, she seriously contemplated leaving the Indian Service. But she listened to her "better judgment": "Stay with Uncle Sam, and your future is secure." She was not enthusiastic about being transferred to Tucson in 1915, either, having hoped to take up the promised new outing matron position at Reno, and for quite some time after her move to Tucson, Woodruff toyed with the idea of returning to Nevada. In 1921, approval was finally given for her transfer to take up the Reno outing matron position. At that point Woodruff changed her mind and decided she preferred to stay in Tucson after all.[12]

In Tucson from the end of 1915 until her retirement in 1929 almost fourteen years later, Woodruff was by far the longest serving of the Tucson outing matrons. She held her tenure during a critical time period for the Tohono O'odham, stretching from the start of World War I to the onset of the Depression. On March 1, 1919, the Indian agency headquarters were officially moved from San Xavier to the new reservation that had been created out of what had long been known as "Papago country," and was now called the Sells reservation in honor of the commissioner of Indian affairs, Cato Sells. Having secured official recognition of their rights to live on a section of their traditional lands, the O'odham were soon fighting to get back portions of the original Sells reservation that had been excised. The Indian Citizenship Act of 1924 giving citizenship to all Indians not yet citizens was meaningless in Arizona, where Indians would be refused the state franchise until 1948. Tohono O'odham politics were characterized by a rift between the "conservative" and traditionally minded people living on the reservations, and the "progressives" who identified as Presbyterians and embraced Milgahn culture, even as they too sought rights and recognition for their people. Throughout this entire period, the O'odham confronted an increasingly obtrusive government effort under first the Sells and then the Burke administration to enforce conformity to Anglo-American culture.[13] In this respect, the outing matron's role was crucial.

Under Woodruff's charge, the outing system in Tucson developed into a system that looked very much like a specialized employment agency—indeed her superintendent would describe it so in his report for 1920.[14] In contrast to Estabrook, Woodruff tended to orient herself toward the needs of the Indian girls and women in employment—or, at least, what she believed to be their needs—rather than catering so much to their privileged mistresses, with whom Woodruff seemed to have had little to do in any social sense. She did not necessarily have any more success in her endeavor to control or assimilate the young women than had her stern predecessor. She did, however, have a notable success in shifting white perceptions of Indian women's domestic service. During Woodruff's time all talk of moving Indians out of Tucson ended; as historian Eric Meeks points out, it was the sustained government focus on recruiting Tohono O'odham women for domestic service that created the perception amongst Tucsonans that they were particularly suited for such work, resulting in a distinctly racialized and gendered pattern of domestic employment.[15] The work of the outing girls was central to the O'odham economy by the time Woodruff retired, and their presence in town was not a source of controversy to the white community, but instead an everyday and unremarkable sight.

On her arrival, Woodruff had taken residence in Estabrook's former house, where she soon discovered a large room set aside "for the working girls." Straightaway, the new matron unwittingly raised the issue that had so vexed relations between the former outing matron and the superintendent, innocently asking McQuigg in January 1916 if there was any provision for boarding girls at her house when they were out of work, as she had two young girls staying with her while she looked for positions where "the employer was willing to teach them."[16] One can imagine the look on McQuigg's face when he read that letter, but if he made any written response, it has not survived.

But Woodruff managed to secure the approval of the central Office to keep girls with her even, remarkably enough, when they were employed. At the start of 1917, she wrote to Commissioner Sells, explaining that she boarded six girls who worked in Tucson homes, and that she intended to keep them with her until she could find positions for them where they could have rooms inside the house. "The most of the women here have a room in the back of their yard for the girl to sleep in," she explained. "(The room looks very much like a whitewashed chicken coop.)" It was much too easy for the girls to sneak out after their work was done, wrote Woodruff, but those girls housed inside their employers' homes knew that they would be "reported" to her if they stayed out late. The commissioner, never persuaded by Estabrook that there was any good reason why the outing matron rather than the employer should be provisioning the young women who worked in Tucson, was won over by Woodruff's imperturbable conviction. He wrote back warmly applauding her aim to place girls "where their environments will be of an inspiring nature."[17]

Woodruff's success depended, however, neither on McQuigg's nor the commissioner's support, but on the support and assistance of the Indian people. Her first long-term houseguest, a young married woman who was only after "company," according to Woodruff, certainly more than earned her welcome. Mrs. Tiger quickly began filling Woodruff in on all sorts of valuable information about "which women kept maids, which ones kept them the year round, which women were liked by the girls and which were not, with the reasons pro and con," not to mention the kind of wages the girls were taking in. Impressing Woodruff no end, Mrs. Tiger—as a sign of respect Woodruff never gave her first name—seems to have set out on a reconnaissance mission to meet the new outing matron. Something of a trailblazer in the sense that her Indian husband was an outsider (he was from Oklahoma), Tiger might well have been acting as a kind of spokesperson or cultural broker for the group of girls then working in Tucson. She undoubtedly wanted to acquaint Woodruff with the outlook of the young women. Mrs. Tiger stayed for some time with Woodruff, during which time another three girls moved in to the matron's house, making up the four she reported living with her more or less permanently at the end of 1916.[18]

They "had got to be street walkers at a late hour," Woodruff had explained, but she used the term literally.[19] Woodruff's three new houseguests were out of a job, for different reasons, and therefore needed a place to stay. Sally, who left a husband behind in Papago country to come to Tucson for work, had quit because she believed she could get higher wages elsewhere. Molly had been thrown out by her employer, after staying out all night on a drunken carouse. Jane had told her employer that she was going away to attend a fiesta. "And Missis got a mad spell about that little thing," she said to Woodruff, "and told me not to come back." Allowing for some embellishment in Woodruff's memoirs, and for the strategic considerations that might have shaped her contemporary reports, we might still see that the young Indian women working in the Tucson of 1916 had limited options for accommodation, and that employers might use their dependence to their own benefit. If so, then young women like Sally, Molly, and Jane might have appreciated Woodruff's place for the leverage it gave them. For Woodruff, their willingness to quit work and come to stay with her was that of "irresponsible children," but it seems rather a pragmatic and practical decision on their part.[20]

By February 1918, Woodruff was no longer living at Estabrook's old address. She had not gone far—only a few doors south down the same street, in fact—but her new residence, which Superintendent McCormick leased on her behalf, was apparently quite an improvement. It was likely that this was the home that made her heart "glow with pride" when she moved in: "It was just a modest cottage, but compared with what I had known before, it seemed like a corner of fairyland. Vines climbed lovingly over the back porch, and lights illuminated every room. Electric lights—the first I had known in the service! Truly I was advancing with the times."[21] Throughout her years in Tucson, Woodruff's home would always be open to O'odham houseguests. These included not only girls out of work or waiting to be "rightly placed" but also girls who were sick or pregnant (including one emergency childbirth), girls waiting for their families to take them home to the country or to arrange somewhere for them to stay in the village, and, sometimes, whole families in transit. Like Estabrook, she used her home in place of the jail to hold girls in trouble with the law, considering it "a disgrace to put even men into such an unspeakable place." But she also sheltered the occasional wife and children from an abusive husband and rebellious girls from their parents, such as the girl whose father threw her out "because she bobbed her hair . . . her father came to try and have her return home, but she would not." And she hosted girls overnight, returning to town from the Indian village, who may not have wanted or been able to go back to their familes' homes or their employers' homes.[22]

Woodruff's home in essence became a way station between the Indian village and the northeastern suburbs where they worked, across the railway line. Woodruff had, like Estabrook, the use of a horse to make her calls to the village, but as she observed sympathetically, it was a hot, two-mile walk each way for the village women who worked in Tucson. Not until 1928—just as Woodruff neared retirement—was a bus service established between the edge of the Indian village and central Tucson.[23]

Woodruff succeeded where Estabrook had failed in making her home a place for the girls to get together, away from the curious and sometimes hostile gaze of white Tucson, and perhaps, for some, from the demands of their families in the village. Woodruff organized a sewing circle in the afternoon, where the girls made dresses with material sent to them by "Eastern ladies," followed by a reading circle in the evening. In her memoirs she recalled that she did most of the cooking on these "Girls' Days," not liking to ask the young women to do any work on their one afternoon off. She wanted them to see her house as "a place they could call home," though her reluctance to ask the young women to assist her because she felt they would expect to be paid suggests that the girls probably still saw her home as a white work space.[24]

Partly in an effort to change that attitude, Woodruff hosted parties in her home for the young women, "which pleases them very much." They danced to records played on a Victrola record player and, according to Woodruff, did not like to leave in the evenings until they had played them all. However, her guests were reticent, even suspicious, when Woodruff first urged them to invite young men to come along. Eventually, one of the young women summoned up the courage to ask her whether she planned to arrest the boys when they came over, and Woodruff then discovered from them that Mrs. Estabrook had been in the habit of having courting couples thrown in jail, in her attempt to force them to marry. "When the girls found out that my policy was vastly different," declared Woodruff, "they gave me their confidence and their warmest friendship."[25]

But Woodruff had other reasons for encouraging these parties at her place, and like Estabrook, they revolved around monitoring and controlling the young women's sexuality. Obliged to justify her mixed parties to her supervisor, she did not hesitate to claim that the "morality" of the girls was much improved under her careful chaperonage. These quiet and respectable "courting bees" gave Woodruff the opportunity to meet the young men and act as an advisor and counsellor to the girls, gently nudging them in the direction of marriage with those she thought suitable, and away from those who she thought rather less so.[26] But equally importantly, they provided an alternative, and in Woodruff's opinion a much superior one, to the gatherings the girls organized themselves in the Indian village.

Woodruff had been deeply concerned when she discovered that Indian dances were being held in the village on Sunday evenings. When only two of the outing girls attended church on Easter Sunday in 1917, Woodruff's interrogations disclosed that the rest were in bed at their employers' houses, sleeping off a dance they had organized among themselves in the Indian village the night before. Displeased, she told the girls (as soon as she could rouse them) "that at those dances that they so much desire to attend without a chaperon or myself is just where a lot of my trouble arises," and she forbid them to arrange any more dances without permission from the superintendent: "So what did they not do but on the 22nd have the boys to get up a dance at the home of Romon Tigers. They all went to church on sunday and danced all sunday night until morning. The girls were so sleepy and tired their employers were wondering what was the matter with them."[27]

Relatively early on, Woodruff had arranged with "my Indian policeman" to have him patrol the streets of Tucson on Saturday and Sunday nights, making sure that the girls returned to their employers' homes before late. But although she complained that the village parties made the girls too tired to work the next day, it was the drinking by the men in particular that Woodruff said most concerned her. Drinking, of course, was the one thing that could be actioned against, with federal as well as state prohibition in force. Her efforts to stop the dances included arranging for an Indian policeman and a judge to ambush some of the young men on their way to the dance and threaten to fine them if they were caught with alcohol. But the dances were not illegal, and the outing matron could not stop them.[28]

Woodruff's tenure as outing matron was during a period of severe, even tyrannical government repression of Indian culture, symbolized in an uncompromising attack upon traditional Indian dancing. Under the new commissioner, Charles H. Burke, superintendents were instructed to dissuade dancing on the reservations. Burke published his notorious "Letter to All Indians" in 1923 that ordered the tribes to do away with their dances and hold none without the permission of their superintendent. Burke's anti-dance policies would not be reversed until January 1934 when the then commissioner John Collier issued a circular on "Indian Religious Freedom and Indian Culture."[29]

In the Southwest, the anti-dance policies were especially deeply entwined with anxieties about the "debauching" of young women. For the Tohono O'odham, however, the significant impact of these restrictions concerned their central rain ceremony, the *naiwat*, which required the drinking of cactus wine, and without which the seasonal rains for their desert crops would not come. At a conference held in 1923, a number of the O'odham participants, speaking on the importance of this ritual, declared with ire that "the white people ought to leave us alone." With Superintendent McCormick determined to follow Burke's instructions and prohibit the naiwat ceremonies, however, the Tohono O'odham would be forced to hold them in secret throughout the 1920s. Along with other grievances concerning the taking away of their children to boarding schools and the construction of wells, the suppression of the naiwat galvanized resentment and political protest among the O'odham on the reservation.[30]

In such a tense atmosphere did Woodruff try to stop the girls' village parties. But her capacity to prevent the girls' dances was actually limited. The social fiestas about which Woodruff complained, called *wailas*, were not religious ceremonies. People danced to polkas—played by fiddles, guitars, and drums—in pairs in a circle lit up by a fire, while in the darkness around them, others watched and socialized. They continued all night and into the next day. But these "chicken-scratch" dances did not attract the same intense official opprobrium as the naiwat. In February 1924, McCormick instituted a curfew that ended all village dances—on the reservation as well as in Tucson—at 11 o'clock in the evening during school term. Woodruff had to be content with that.[31]

Perhaps in an effort to reassure her, one of the outing girls invited her to a dance the girls had organized in the village in 1924. Woodruff was not reassured. "The Indians would have had a very nice time among themselves and no drinking," she recorded afterward, "but when the Mexicans and Yaquis heard the music, they came from all around lining up from three to five rows and more around the yard, venturing in after a dance was over they would elbow some of the Indian boys out into the dark and get them to take a drink." Woodruff stayed until after 1 a.m. (the dance must have been held out of school term), by which time there were "so many drunk men that some of the girls were glad to come home with me." The drinking "was worse than I expected to find," Woodruff wrote unhappily. "I try to keep the girls from going to the dances, while some do not care to go there are others that do."[32]

Woodruff insisted that the Indians living out on the reservation wanted the dances stopped too.[33] Though we could question how she knew this, as her contact with the people on the reservation seems to have been quite limited, there might have been some truth in her claim. Organized by the young women themselves, the Tucson Indian village dances were important for the construction and maintenance of a new and close-knit young Indian women's urban culture, revolving around wearing the fashionable clothing and jewelery the girls could buy with their earnings and reflecting the pleasure they took in their new social and economic independence. This may not have impressed the "conservative" O'odham out in the reservation villages who supported the traditional dances, any more than the "progressives" who opposed them. Frances Manuel, who came in to work in Tucson just as Woodruff retired, recalled that when she worked for white people and earned her own money as a young woman, she started buying “pretty clothes,” jewelery, and hair ornaments: “I would go to my people’s dances, and the people maybe looked up to me, maybe that’s what I liked, why I wanted them.” Yet Manuel hints at broader community disapproval, “softly” adding, “But I knew it wasn’t me so I changed back to simple things, the way I was raised.”[34]

Yet the young women’s dances were undoubtedly important for the creation and maintenance of their own sense of identity and community. In some ways, the Tucson domestic workers’ dances of the 1920s paralleled a broader phenomenon widely seen across the United States at this time. Young rural women, many of them domestic servants, many from immigrant families, were flocking to a new dance culture in the towns and cities, while urban reformers and the older, traditional elements of the rural communities united to fret about their morals. But the Indian domestic workers’ dance culture, being distinctively Indian, albeit urban, was also an assertion of their distinctively Indian culture. In the face of the government matrons’ repression of both customary marriage relations and dancing on the reservations, continuing the dance was central to the continuation of Native American cultures, as historian Joan Jensen has observed, dance embodying the sacred in Indian life; it might also be said that the secular and social Indian dances in urban Tucson were critical to the cultural survival and vitality of Indian communities in the early twentieth century. It was as a combined expression of the Indian girls’ disturbing sexual and social independence, coupled with the transgressive assertion of continuing Indian culture in the urban environment, that a disapproving Woodruff looked on the girls’ dances. Her heartfelt wish that they could be banned indicates her distinct discomfort with the full implications of young Indian women’s collective engagement with urban modernity.[35]

Ambivalence also continued to mark the Indian Office’s attitude to Indian domestic service in the Southwest at this time. In 1919, the Indian Office had looked very carefully at the question of outing policy in general, on receiving a report on Woodruff’s program that indicated the relatively high wages Indian domestic workers could earn in Tucson. Remarking that a smaller wage in the country was “of greater value than a large salary in town when all is spent for amusement,” Commissioner Sells (or his assistants) drafted a circular intended to go to superintendents in agencies and schools in the Southwest. The commissioner was "anxious" to extend outing work for Indian girls to "as many schools as possible," but girls should be placed out only in small towns or country homes. It was "inadvisable to send Indian girls to cities. . . . The lure of the town and its questionable amusements begets a taste for luxuries and a desire for constant entertainment. Opportunities for association with those of the opposite sex are infrequent and marriages rarely occur. Discontent follows a steady round of city attractions, when the girl goes to a less-stimulating environment, and the OUTING has not prepared her for successful homemaking on her allotment."[36] In the end, however, there would be no definitive policy against outing in the cities. During the 1920s, urban outing programs flourished, with outing matrons employed at Phoenix, Los Angeles, and Berkeley, as well as at Reno, Albuquerque, and Tucson; many young Indian women were placed out from schools or reservations to work out in towns and cities elsewhere, without any further direct supervision. But the outing matrons' role was given a heightened significance, particularly when it came to the selection of families for placements.[37] Under the regime of Commissioner Burke between 1921 and 1929, the entire responsibility for the success of the outing program fell upon the outing matrons.

From a mundane but influential position as an intermediary, Woodruff managed the Indian workers and white mistresses with a subtlety Estabrook had altogether lacked. She was maternal in the most classic sense, sympathetic and affectionate toward the Indian girls and women to the point of infantilizing them (she described one young woman in a report, for instance, as being "just as innocent as a little child"). Woodruff genuinely liked the O'odham girls and admired the respectful, sensitive way they treated each other, their generous natures, and their "handsome . . . dark, exotic beauty." And she may have won the girls' trust and respect in return by her willingness to be their advocate with employers who would not pay their due wages, as well as with others who tried to exploit them (such as the unscrupulous shopkeeper who refused to allow them to try on clothing in his shop or to return ill-fitting purchases).[38]

Every morning, according to Woodruff, there was a regular crowd of young women waiting patiently on her porch, to look at her newspapers for a "good job." In time, the "ladies in town" learnt to leave their names and addresses with Woodruff if they wanted an Indian girl to work for them.[39] Woodruff was rather more circumspect in her relations with the white employers. That she worried about the diseases the employers or their children might pass on to the girls they employed, rather than the other way around, was symbolic of the way she viewed the situation, but Woodruff was always respectful in her dealings with white mistresses.[40] At the same time, she evidently felt that the employers needed some guidance themselves.

In the early days of Woodruff's tenure, she was confronted by the husband of one employer. He was most indignant that a girl who worked in his house had left suddenly, without warning. Woodruff had recently advised the O'odham girls to give a week's notice if they intended to leave—"unless there was to [*sic*] much work to do"—and the young woman told Woodruff that was indeed why she had left without notice. Woodruff did not see it quite the same way. The girl actually went to work for another family "where there are only two," admittedly less work, but not really what Woodruff had meant. However, she was taken aback by the man's strident demand that she punish the girl. "I tried to explain with careful and calm advice they will in time learn all that. It is hard for white people to know and understand the ins and outs of the different characters. He wanted me to take an office here where I would have the power [to] use more authority. I told him I could not do such a thing without the Supt. permission, and I also considered that contrary to the rules of the government."[41] This was of course exactly what her predecessor had done, but Woodruff was averse to such blunt tactics. As her response to this man suggests, her efforts were focused upon educating and disciplining the white employers in their responsibilities toward the young women as well. Woodruff's support for girls who left employers who overworked them and who were otherwise unpleasant toward them continued throughout her years in Tucson.[42] But her main concern when it came to the white employers was to make them understand their obligation to provide appropriate accommodation and supervision for their young workers.

Woodruff considered the failure of many employers to provide "inside rooms" for their workers particularly reprehensible, and she would not contemplate persuading any girl to stay in such places.

Whenever she wrote on this issue, a detectable disdain for these women crept in. Most Tucson employers took no interest in their servant as to what happened to her or where she was after her work was done, Woodruff had told the commissioner in 1917, echoing the Phoenix matron Marie Schach many years earlier. To give a "little sample of this," Woodruff described how five girls working in Tucson hired themselves an automobile to drive out to a dance at the San Xavier reservation, not returning till 5 a.m. "Not one of their employers knew they were gone," wrote Woodruff. "When I found it out and told them they will hardly believe me until they get the girls to own up to the truth." One employer had even "felt sorry" for her worker whom she thought was sick the next day, "and done the girl's work," Woodruff snorted.

Woodruff had no patience with such careless employers. "My earnest endeavor," she went on, "is to keep the girls from working for those families that have the outside rooms. And until the ladies of Tucson can be interested in their Clubs to treat and show the Indian girls they have an interest in them, the girls should not be allowed to work for them, for it causes the downfall of quite a number of the girls."[43] Clearly, Woodruff perceived her duties as being to ensure that the white women employing Indian girls took the maternalist role that was expected, indeed demanded, of them. Like Marie Schach at Phoenix many years before her, Woodruff was confronted by the disregard local white mistresses displayed for the moral care and guidance of the young women who worked for them, and she tried to refuse to be part of a system of simply providing such employers with Indian labor. Woodruff went further, in demanding would-be employers actively and publicly demonstrate their solicitude for Indian girls through their social organizations, and in attempting to wield her position to force them to do so.

Despite her brave words, however, Woodruff continued to battle on the accommodation issue over the years she was in Tucson. Prescriptions for maternalism were evidently not shared by the women who employed O'odham girls, and indeed were actively resisted by them. "Many times [when] I ask a lady to watch over her girl," Woodruff complained in 1925, eight years later, "she tells me very plainly that she don't want that kind of a girl that she has to be responsible for her actions." The matron's only recourse was to threaten to take girls out of such places, and she did so on occasion. But generally it was difficult for her to follow through on such threats. She had no legal grounds or authority for their removal, and there were too many girls who were happy to work for such "careless" employers.[44]

For Woodruff was also confounded by the resolute independence of the young women. "She will deliberately up and leave the people without any reason whatever," Woodruff had sighed about one girl in a letter to Commissioner Sells in March 1917, "and of course there is no law to compel her to stay." The girl had been staying nights with Woodruff for the past three weeks. "It seems to me there should be a place to send girls of this type when they are not capable of managing their own affairs, and not willing to be governed by the matron," Woodruff went on. Evidently she had not been able to get her employer to govern her either, and Woodruff was starting to see the employer's point of view: "It is surprising what some of the white women take from the Indian girls in order to be nice to them so they will not leave." But the commissioner did not reply—after all, it was Woodruff's job to work out what to do—and the following month Woodruff asked the superintendent (Martin) to help her devise a "plan" for dealing with those young women who repeatedly left their places.[45]

At the root of many issues of confrontation was the refusal of the young women to heed the matron, and it was this aspect—their refusal to "mind me"—that most exercised Woodruff. Attending the dances against instruction and, of course, "immorality" annoyed the matron, while drinking, at the dances or elsewhere, was guaranteed to incur her displeasure. But if the offending girl was prepared to endure one of the "long talks" Woodruff specialized in, Woodruff tended to be willing to help find her another place to work in Tucson. As Woodruff was painfully aware, however, most of the young women were perfectly capable of finding their own work through their networks. In fact, when one worker left a position, there was every chance that another, placed elsewhere by Woodruff, would promptly leave her position to take up the position her friend had vacated, much to Woodruff's vexation.[46]

One of the young women who had stayed with Woodruff at the beginning was the young woman in question when Woodruff asked Martin for advice. The outing matron had just found out that Molly had left the "exceptionally nice" employer Woodruff had organized for her—"and she sick in *bed*"—to work for somebody else. Molly told Woodruff, when they met by chance on the street, that she had to leave her position because her family were visiting the Indian village from the reservation and needed her, the "same story" she had told her employer. (A suspicious Woodruff had since learned the truth from another girl.) Woodruff fumed, furiously wishing she could put Molly into a boarding school outing program and then "make her work without pay until she felt sorry for what she had done":

> I do not think it would be any punishment to send her home. I do not know whether she has an inside or an outside room. Mrs. Estabrook used to put them in jail when they done the like of this. If she is allowed to do this others will follow her example. I thought I would not say anything to her until I hear from you. It would be a good come down if the policeman would take her to the Agency, but that is the next difficulty to know what to do with her after taking her there.[47]

In the end, Woodruff asked the outing matron at Riverside to find outing work for the girl in California. Perhaps she was not able to insist that Molly work without pay, but she was gratified by Matron Orrington Jewett's reports back that Molly was "quite a different girl." Woodruff would not see Molly again for many years. In 1926, Molly came home. Quite a different girl, indeed—Woodruff "hardly recognized the healthy, carefree girl I had sent away." Like all too many of Woodruff's outing girls, Molly was dying of tuberculosis. The girl spent all the savings she had accumulated on her funeral, and a stricken Woodruff purchased the silver handles for the coffin at her request.[48]

In terms of a "plan" as such, Woodruff never got very far, and was left to work out a solution to the girls leaving their places without any advice or assistance from either her superintendent or the central Office. She did send other girls away to Phoenix or Riverside, at least in the early years, but most often, it seems, Woodruff took the more persistently defiant girls from their employers to send back to their families' control. This was a strategy that of course required a certain level of cooperation from both the employers and the girls' families.

As Woodruff also was aware, it was not really much of a punishment, and indeed she was directly told so by the one of the girls she knew, that "all the Indians say that they don't mind that, that they are just pleased over it."[49]

A telling anecdote from her reports gives an insight into the complex relationship between Woodruff and "her girls." In July 1921, Woodruff was perplexed to discover that one of the outing girls had been boasting that the matron allowed her to drink liquor. Woodruff called Lupe in for an explanation, and Lupe told her that she and her friend Cecilia, also working in Tucson, had "stole a bottle of grape juice" from Lupe's mistress, Mrs. L——. Downing it in front of the other girls, they then pretended to get so drunk that they could not walk home, or even stand. Woodruff was pained. "I said that was a very nice thing for you to do[,] was it not? [A]nd I went on to tell her [Lupe] how her story has ended, and the trouble she has caused me." After threatening to send Lupe back to her family on the reservation, Woodruff had Lupe promise to stay in every night at her employer's home as punishment, until Woodruff came back from her impending annual vacation and reviewed the situation. It might be that Lupe really had got hold of some alcohol, either from her employer's household or elsewhere (Lupe's mistress assured Woodruff that she kept none in the house, but then she would say that), but the fact that Lupe made a point of claiming Woodruff condoned her drinking is significant. No doubt the prank represented girlish high spirits, but it also tells us that the young women working in Tucson could find the idea of openly ridiculing the matron's authority quite funny.[50]

Some of the girls who worked in Tucson were "at times a little to [*sic*] quick tempered for their own good," Woodruff reported in 1919. "They seem to forget they are servants, and without thinking are trying to run their employer which leads to them leaving, and the starting in a new place is not always easy for them. . . . They seem to think 'changes are lightsome.'" Woodruff saw the girls as fickle and restless, but her own records show that the girls left their positions because they were unhappy with their employers, or because they felt their wages were too low.[51] As David Katzman, an historian of domestic service has pointed out, changing employers represented the only defense for workers otherwise largely powerless to affect their wages and conditions.[52]

There are certainly some odd stories in Woodruff's papers. One of Woodruff's regular employers complained that a girl Woodruff had placed with her "acted so queer" that she was afraid of her, and as the girl wanted to leave, she was more than happy to see the back of her: "She thought the girl was a little Off." Considering the high turnover of servants this particular employer had, however, it is hard not to suspect the girl's "queerness" was a ruse, and that the employer was perhaps "a little Off" herself. Other girls left because their employers' demands offended them, such as the young woman who allegedly marched out in umbrage when her mistress asked her to keep her company in the evening. The girl "was very impolite to the lady," recorded Woodruff.[53] We might imagine various scenarios that would explain this curious incident.

It was not merely unhappiness with employment that led the girls to leave but also their cultural commitments and obligations. "Home-sickness" was sometimes the reason expressed by girls for wanting to leave the places Woodruff found for them, and one that was perhaps calculated to win her sympathy (recall Molly's excuse to the matron about needing to see her family). But in truth, family and community commitments always came first for the O'odham girls, particularly attendances at major religious observances, most importantly the Festival of San Francisco Xavier held in October at Magdalena, Sonora, in northern Mexico. This could be an inconvenience for individual employers, but was a particular problem for the outing matron, who was trying to establish herself as responsible for providing Indian girls. Woodruff found she was obliged to work with the O'odham community in this regard, and although these commitments might have been annoying, she could at least predict when girls would not be available to work and retain some of her credibility. Indeed, she ended up assisting the girls and their families, if she could, to make the annual pilgrimage to Magdalena. Such strategies of negotiation and compromise with the Indian girls and their families, born of necessity but encouraging Indian cooperation, might well have been the key to Woodruff's success in institutionalizing the outing program in Tucson.[54]

From 1920, Woodruff embarked on a new approach that allowed her to maintain the appearance of authority, while acknowledging and even embracing Indian agency. She invited certain young women—those she judged mature and responsible—to go and "talk with the lady first and see what she requires them to do before they decide to take a place, and think it over first." The girls "usually judge for themselves whether they are going to like the lady or not," she reported. "When I do that they stay in the places very much better."[55] Ensuring that employers treated these selected girls with respect at the outset and recognizing their right to choose where they worked and under what conditions they worked no doubt set the tone for more harmonious relations between mistress and maid from the beginning.

Eight years later Woodruff had expanded this system to the girls in general. She explained how it worked: "[They] talk with the lady first, to find out what there is to do, and how many in the family, and whether they want her to cook, or to be a helper, and tell them what wages they want[.] If the girl chooses to work for less that is up to her, but if she wants to wait until we can get another place, she can do so, I want them to be satisfied when they begin work in the home. Some will not work where there are children." Woodruff's only condition now was that if the employer did not provide accommodation at all, whether inside or outside, "then the girl cannot consider that place." With this one exception, essentially the young women were themselves now responsible for the selection of the homes where they were placed, an important shift and one presumably made incrementally over the passage of the intervening years.[56]

Woodruff was always required, however, to be seen to be closely monitoring anything that might tweak white employers' anxieties about having Indian girls and women in their homes. These included instances of violent conflict between Indian men and women. Although these were rare, such episodes highlight the continuing white anxieties around Indian domestic service. One incident occurred in 1919, when an Indian man, known as a problem to both the girls and Woodruff, followed two young women as they were returning to their employers' homes from the Indian village on a Sunday evening and attacked one of them in a Tucson street. The commotion brought a "white man" to the scene. The two girls, who reported to Woodruff as well as the police, evidently sought her intervention, but the eighteen-month sentence their attacker received in court probably reflected not so much Tucson's white residents' desire to protect young Indian women as their outrage at such goings-on on their tidy streets. A second assault occurred not long afterwards, in the same year, when the jealous boyfriend of a girl in service turned up while she was minding her employer's children for the evening and gave the girl "a beating." The employers were out at the time, and although "Mrs. M—— knew nothing about it until this morning," understandably, "She says she can't have him around acting that way." Woodruff, who had been hoping she could get the couple to marry, was "at a loss to know what to do."[57]

Less dramatic disturbances included a discovery that an Indian youth had stolen a girl's suitcase and money from her employer's home and was ringing up other young women where they worked, pretending to be somebody else. Woodruff reported at one point "a number of the ladies" were complaining about the young men visiting the girls during their work hours and demanding that she stop them. The threat employers perceived in the romances of their live-in domestic servants was an obstacle to Woodruff's schemes for getting the girls married, and another reason why she started the mixed parties. Such employer distrust was not of course restricted to Indian domestic service; however, the men in question being mostly Indian, and bearing all the stereotypes and fears concerning Indian men, such tensions were undoubtedly heightened.[58]

Careful Woodruff, however, never raised the more volatile issue of Indian girls and white men. She was less than approving when the girls chose Mexican boyfriends, and she "broke up" at least two such relationships, when she could not talk the girls involved out of them. Although hostile to Mexican-Indian romances, her attitude toward white-Indian relationships was more flexible, and depended on her evaluation of the relative class status of the couple. Thus she recalled advising one Tohono O'odham girl with "an education and some refinement" against marrying her uncouth "half-breed" boyfriend—"Keep on your own level and marry someone of your own race"—but she did not object to a "higher, more cultured" young O'odham man marrying a white girl. But over her entire tenure, Woodruff reported only one case of a "white" baby being born out of wedlock, and this in a very impassive manner. She explained that she had helped the Indian mother, but that the father could not be found. Her temperate, even complacent response was a striking contrast to the approach of her predecessor.[59]

Facing a potentially scandalous incident involving an Indian Service employee in 1918, Woodruff's cautious reaction here was also completely different to Estabrook's pursuit of the police officer Kensey. Woodruff asked a construction supervisor employed to oversee new building works on the reservation to stay at her home and look after the premises while she was away for three weeks. Having felt "safe that every Indian girl was in a good home," Woodruff was clearly troubled to learn that her guest had let in a girl who had turned up from Sacaton, and then later that night propositioned her. But Woodruff did not make much of the situation when notifying the superintendent of the incident: "She says she firmly resented, and he went away back to his own room." McCormick forwarded her letter to the commissioner, asking for instructions. It seems none were forthcoming, and as Woodruff made no further effort in the matter, nothing further came of the girl's complaint.[60]

This was not an isolated incident. A casually abusive attitude toward young Indian women was widespread, even amongst employees of the Indian Service, as evidenced by a similar incident a year or so earlier at the Phoenix Indian School. There, a visiting inspector had boasted to a female clerk working at the school that his position "gave him opportunity to learn at first hand the sexual attractions of Indian girls." The clerk, Estelle Armstrong, made a complaint through her superintendent, John B. Brown, but was even more disturbed to learn from the man himself, later, that no action had been taken against him. "Those men in the Bureau are not a bunch of eunuchs like you field people," he told her contemptuously. He was, nevertheless, apparently engaged upon a vengeful smear campaign against the superintendent and the school's rigidly moralistic "head matron," as well as against Armstrong herself.[61]

Discreet where others were outspoken, Woodruff was considerably smarter at avoiding trouble than her counterpart in Phoenix (who could well have been, in actuality, the matron targeted by the vindictive visiting inspector). In 1923, the superintendent at Sacaton (A. F. Duclos) complained that the Phoenix outing matron was "absolutely without tact and diplomacy" and could not get along with employers or the Indian working girls. The ensuing investigation found

Chingren lacked sympathy for her charges, and was too abrupt with their employers. She was instructed to treat the girls more kindly, while being "more careful in future in her contacts with employers."[62]

The experiences of Woodruff and Chingren highlight the limitations of the maternalist power held by the outing matrons. Expected to exercise strict moral surveillance over the girls working in service *and* to ensure that the girls' employers exercised similar care and control, there was evidently no practical support to back them in such endeavours. Instead, when confronted by unwilling employers or exploitative men, it was the outing matron who ran the risk of being censured. The outing matron was supposed to ameliorate conflict, not create it. It is not surprising that the outing matrons should focus most of their attention instead on the Indian girls and women, channelling their energies into projects for their moral reform, efforts which were not necessarily justified at all.

Janette Woodruff would devote a whole chapter of her memoirs to the "moral problem" amongst the O'odham, explaining that while marriage had been "just as sacred" in traditional culture "as in our own," "Evils seemed to arise from the mixture of the two." The intensity of Woodruff's preoccupation, meshed as it was with her sympathy for Indian women, suggests a projection of her own vulnerabilities as a single woman in a patriarchal society and her frustration, perhaps, at the limitations of her power to protect the Indian girls from predation.[63]

The Indian Office's insistence upon compelling Indian couples into legal marriages was part of the broader gendered thrust of assimilationist policy. Frequently justified in terms of protecting and uplifting Indian women, and presuming that through wifehood along Anglo lines women could lead their families to assimilate, Indian marriage reform was driven, contradictorily, by an intense distrust of Indian female sexual and social independence. This hostility was vividly demonstrated in the implementation of the reform effort generally, which was typically directed against women, and often very punitively.[64]

Arranged marriages were still customary during Woodruff's time among the O'odham, and there was considerable disapproval of those young people who dared to challenge these arrangements. Husbands and wives under Indian law were also free, within the constraints of consanguinity and as long as they ensured their children were cared for, to take "plural" spouses (as Woodruff termed it) which might or might not entail continuing a relationship with the original partner. Families and the wider O'odham community tolerated premarital sexual liaisons, and to Woodruff's confusion, she found that sometimes the girls' families were unperturbed, just as long as the lovers did not challenge their elders by entering into a legal Anglo-American marriage contract. Such contracts may have been reserved only for marriages that were also traditionally condoned, representing an unexpected Indian capacity to adapt and assimilate the Milgahn system to their own cultural traditions. This was especially galling to Woodruff when it came to couples of whom Woodruff approved wholeheartedly, but who could not be convinced to go against their families' wishes by legalizing their union.[65] But she was unwilling to force Anglo marriage contracts on unwilling couples.

From the outset Woodruff was reluctant to use the anti-cohabitation laws. She had appealed to McQuigg for advice in January 1916 regarding the cases of several unmarried and pregnant girls, one of whom she was being urged to arrest by the girl's employer. "I have never done any arresting," Woodruff told McQuigg somewhat anxiously, suggesting he might instead remove the man involved—who had managed to get his wife, who also worked in town, pregnant at the same time—to San Xavier as punishment. Another case involved Lolita S——, pregnant again, "& no one to look to for support." Woodruff was aware that if action was taken against her married lover his wife could have Lolita arrested also. The third case concerned a couple whom Woodruff hoped she could talk into marrying "the right way"—"but she don't seem to want to and he does not say a word, he is perfectly dumb when I talk to him, [though] he can talk and understands every word I say to him . . . I will have to ask you what to do?"[66]

Woodruff believed that the women were particularly vulnerable to abandonment without formal state recognition of marriage, and she would have long debates with them on the subject. She took great personal pride in those couples who did marry, believing it was the power of her persuasion.[67] But others were not convinced. There was Lilly, for example, who was already legally married on the reservation, but who, having begun a new relationship in Tucson, found it "easiest" to "fall back upon the Indian way of marriage," lamented

Woodruff, rather than go through official divorce and remarriage. Woodruff seemed wholly unaware that the couple had both been charged and convicted of cohabitation by Estabrook, Lilly paying a fine while her lover spent ninety days in jail at the end of 1915. Their resistance, then, hardly seemed the "easy" option. As Lilly argued, Woodruff's way was not so much difficult as unnecessary. She told Woodruff "sweetly" that she did not see what difference it would make to her: "The missionary, he spoke words out of the Bible; then we go to live together. Now we go to live together, but without words. What difference? You must not care so much, Mrs. Woodruff."[68]

Lilly became a cautionary tale for Woodruff, after her new lover left her for a younger, sassier girl working in town, and eventually stopped supporting her and their children altogether.[69] There is no denying that life for single O'odham mothers could be horrific. The most heartrending case documented by Woodruff concerned a young woman named Felicita who, becoming pregnant to a married Indian man while she was working in service, gave birth to twins, and then was forced to take day work in Tucson. The newborn babies were only ten days old. The twins' father, who might have offered some practical help, at least, "run away and did not come back until after Mr. Martin left," recorded Woodruff. She did not seem to see the impact of the superintendent's directions to her at the time to investigate the situation, with a view to having the father charged. Felicita left her babies in the care of her older daughter, by her Indian husband on the reservation. Only a child herself, the daughter left the babies unattended; discovering this, the enraged mother beat her when she came home from work, and the child's paternal aunt, horrified by such abuse of a child, then took the girl away with her and demanded an investigation by the matron. Felicita then had to leave the tiny babies in the care of other little girls in the Indian village. Woodruff gave a graphic description of the little babysitters' ordeal, "out in the blistering hot sun jumping up and down to keep them quiet, giving them a bottle of water to drink, trying to hold body and soul together until the mother gets home." Not surprisingly, the twins did not live long.[70]

Always conscious of her own needs for financial security, Woodruff seemed convinced that legal marriage offered this to the young women. It is not certain that marriage would have helped Felicita all that much, even if the father of her twins had not been already married to someone else. Felicita's difficulties, and indeed those of the Indian women workers generally, were the result of endemic poverty caused in turn by colonization and dispossession. The irony, revealed in Woodruff's own records, was that the men were becoming increasingly reliant on the women's wages, even as her outing program became institutionalized.[71]

While the young women earned on average only one-third of what the men brought home, a great many more girls and women were able to find regular work, as domestics, than the boys and men of the village were able to get ongoing employment. Of those men who *could* find paid work, the largest group were taking irregular jobs that earned them a pittance in comparison to the girls' earnings (in 1924, for instance, a measly $10 a year in comparison to $177, the average wage of the girls and women). The relatively high wages that brought up the male average earnings, such as the three lumberyard workers (including Lilly's boyfriend) who brought home a yearly average income of about $770 each in 1924, were only available to a handful of lucky individuals.[72]

During the 1920s, the earnings of the "outing girls" overtook those of the married women in the village who worked on a daily basis washing and ironing. Some older women made fairly good money selling traditional Indian ollas and woven baskets, but they were a tiny minority now. However, the amount of money taken in through laundry work—the mainstay of the women's employment at the beginning of the twentieth century and still the "main support" of Tucson's Indian families in 1921[73]—plummeted from the mid-1920s with the advent of electric washing machines and the corresponding drop in wages as well as jobs offered for washing. Meanwhile, the numbers of girls working in outing had more than doubled from the time of Woodruff's arrival, from some forty girls employed in 1916 to over one hundred in 1928. With many employers expecting their housemaids to handle the now lighter laundry work, the unmarried girls working in white homes were supplanting their older married sisters, cousins, aunts, and mothers.[74]

The girls' contribution also greatly increased in importance as a result of intense economic pressures on the O'odham during the 1920s. As an agricultural community, the Tohono O'odham economy was based upon farming rather than wage labor, but poor rains beginning in 1918 meant poor returns on the crops, and then a very serious drought between the years of 1921 and 1926 brought dire poverty and the specter of starvation out in the country. The hundred or so young outing workers in Tucson became the backbone of support for their relatives on the reservation.[75] As Woodruff noted, the girls' families would come in to town to collect money from the young women for groceries; those who did not have any money on them would arrange for their relatives to get what they needed from the Chinese-run store just outside the village, on credit, and pay back the bill from their earnings over the following weeks. If a girl from the reservation acted "mean," her parents were likely to ask Woodruff to have her sent home.[76]

Nevertheless, there were signs of opposition to Woodruff from the O'odham families during this period, a time of political unrest and upheaval in the face of repressive and interventionist government policies. In 1925, Woodruff reported that, because the Indian girls' families were now preventing them from staying overnight at their employers' homes, a "great many of the ladies that used to keep Indian help, now take Mexican girls." The domestic workers had always faced competition from Mexican as well as African American women, although Woodruff was convinced early on that the white women preferred Indian help if they could get it. As she continued to insist on the provision of accommodation by employers, her comment indicates some resistance from the O'odham families over Woodruff's placement of their girls or, at the very least, their desire to have them less tightly controlled by employers or by the Indian Service. It may be that the families' concern over the lack of adequate protection of their girls in town and particularly over the incidences of illegitimate pregnancies even in the places Woodruff arranged (and which, Woodruff noted, the elder Indians blamed "squarely on the white man's system of civilization") underpinned Indian parents' disapproval of their girls "living in," even if they were not inclined to stop them working out altogether. Alternatively, and not incompatibly, an O'odham community desire to ensure the young women, by returning home every night, maintained their cultural connections and sense of obligations to their own people might well have been heightened not only by the draconian, communally destructive policies of the time but also by the increasing dependence upon the girls' income itself.[77] Perhaps, too, there was an increasing dislike and disdain among the O'odham for live-in domestic service, part of a broader national trend amongst younger women of color working in service of preference for "day-work."[78]

The long and savage drought finally ended with the winter rains of January 1926. Edward Stewart replaced McCormick as superintendent in the summer of that year, just as Woodruff reported that the "land upon which some of my Indians have lived for so many years, has been sold to a company of real estate dealers." Thirteen Tohono O'odham had purchased lots, most paying $100, on reasonable terms—"$5.00 down and after that one dollar a week, no taxes or interest, and when out of employment, allowance will be made for that."[79] A year later there were five more Tohono O'odham landholders in the village, and the following year no less than four of Woodruff's outing girls had bought lots in the village. One had bought two. Some of the young women were actually doing quite well now—one girl had bought a new Victrola herself, "costing nearly one hundred dollars," to host a party for the returned students from Riverside. But many other O'odham did not or could not buy lots, but instead rented rooms from the Chinese storekeeper, who was building apartment houses to rent out.[80]

By now the outing matron was nearly seventy. She had fallen and broken her arm toward the end of 1926, soon after moving to a new address on South Stone Avenue, and a nurse moved in to assist her for a time.[81] Any influence Woodruff had had over the lively young women was waning. The girls were still holding their dances in the village Sunday nights, and occasionally on weeknights as well, "out doors," with "only the moon-light when there chance to be that to light up the dance place," Woodruff complained in 1927. "It seems all I can do is to talk to them and plead with them to keep away from the dances." The police told her that they were unable to catch anyone actually drinking, and "Indians have as good a right to dance as the white people." But, claimed the distressed Woodruff, "I can realize how the Indians feel to have their children come to town and be led away by the evil that is carried on in the village . . . [I] just feel as if my hands were tied."[82]

She had also begun to go with employers to the Indian village to find girls, suggesting, perhaps, that the girls were not coming to her house for work as they once did, though she claimed she continued to answer in excess of two thousand calls a year from girls for work. Outing girls still met at her place on Thursday afternoons. They no longer wanted to sew, particularly, and they might have been coming out of kindness and respect to the old woman, as much as for the opportunity to meet with the other girls.[83]

For those younger women, the outing matron would have been a familiar figure seen around since their early childhood; many others first met her as children being sent away to the boarding schools at Phoenix and Riverside, and again at the railway, when they returned home for the summer vacations, some of them to go into outing positions.[84] Woodruff's parties had become a kind of institution also, particularly the Christmas parties she had started up back in 1916 for the working girls without family in Tucson over Christmas. With an O'odham Santa Claus handing out candy, nuts, and apples to the children and, to their amazement, speaking to them in their language, Woodruff had turned her Christmas party into a regular event for anyone from the village who wanted to come. "We always hold that [Christmas party] in my home," she wrote with satisfaction in 1927. But while the aging matron continued to invite the outing girls to hold their socials at her house, and hosted some herself even after breaking her arm, by 1928 she understood that they preferred to have their own parties in the village. They "most always ask me to come, and I go quite often," she wrote appreciatively. "I tell them the only trouble they keep their parties to[o] late, I cannot sit up night and day."[85]

Seventy was the age of retirement in the Indian Service. When the official retirement notice arrived in February 1929, informing her that her service would terminate the day before her birthday in April, Woodruff was bereft. As she read it, "life suddenly felt empty."[86]

Woodruff's request to be allowed to continue in the position for another year was considered. Advice was hastily sought as to whether she was able to drive, which was somewhat ironic—after ten years of asking for a government car, Woodruff had finally received one in November 1927 and had only just taught herself to drive. But she was deemed too old, anyway, and her application was refused.[87]

According to Woodruff, some of the O'odham, incredulous that she was being forced to leave when she worked "all the time," suggested that lies had been told to have her "put out." There were echoes of Estabrook's controversy some twelve years ago, and indeed two Indian women immediately offered to circulate a petition to send to the commissioner. Woodruff declared that she dissuaded such protest. The secretary of the interior did, however, receive three telegrams urging Woodruff's retention, including one from three leading Indian men (a chief, a judge, and an interpreter), although none from any women or domestic workers. The petitioners were advised that Woodruff's retention was "impracticable."[88]

The people of the Indian village held a farewell party for Woodruff when she left. They seated the elderly outing matron on a "queen's throne" decorated with pink and white streamers and crepe papers, and feasted her with ice cream and cake. One of the women, Mrs. Chico Romon, formally presented her with a wristwatch, thanking Woodruff "for the hundred ways you have helped the Papagos in these long years. We need somebody, and you always come. . . . We hope you will always live in Tucson, and not be far away from us."[89]

For Woodruff, who, despite Mrs. Romon's kind speech would, in the end, pack up and depart Tucson on an eastbound train, the outing work in Tucson represented "my last field of labor among the red men."[90] She evidently experienced a loss of sense of purpose with the loss of her job, and her memoirs, published a decade later, reflect the centrality of her employment in the Indian Service to her identity. The significance of her impact upon the Tohono O'odham women and their employers is considerably less apparent, but there is no doubt that the work she had been carrying out had had its effects on the relationships that existed between Indian and white women in Tucson.

Over the years the Tohono O'odham had known Woodruff, they and those who employed them had seen the work of the young women in white households become institutionalized, even professionalized. With their cooperation, Woodruff had transformed the outing program in Tucson from a means of monitoring those young working women who had triggered such anxieties to a busy employment bureau that recruited young Indian women and invited white employers to avail themselves of what was essentially a specialized racial placement service. In the process, the O'odham had seen their young women become the economic mainstay of their community, even the occasional landowner in Tucson under Anglo-American property laws, while the white Tucsonans had, it seems, come to a certain complacency about their presence in the town. As the old lady sat on her pink and white bedecked throne, on the very eve of the Depression, the question on at least some people's minds must have been—what next?

6

"A worthy, industrious people"

Libbie Light, 1929–1932

TO SAY LIBBIE LIGHT WAS GRATIFIED when she got the news of her transfer to Tucson would be an understatement. Light had been waiting for years for such a position, well before her husband, a former superintendent at the Truxton Canon agency in northern Arizona, even began to contemplate retirement from the Indian Service. When the long-awaited letter arrived, she was on unofficial furlough, impatiently biding her time at Phoenix and fending off transfers elsewhere, until either Amanda Chingren or Janette Woodruff retired. Mrs. Light was not so much happy as hugely relieved and, no doubt, very pleased with herself to find that all her complicated strategies with the Indian Office had finally paid off. The Tucson position was especially ideal, because the couple's cherished youngest daughter was enrolled at the university in town. At sixty-two years of age, Light still had enough time, too, she calculated, to get Bettie through to graduation *and* clock up enough years to retire on the top pension level. All around, it was most satisfying.[1]

The middle child of a large Irish-American family from the foothills of the Ohio Appalachians, and a devoted wife and mother, Light had more in common with Lydia Gibbs than with either of the previous outing matrons. But she was cannier than Gibbs, whom Light happened to know personally. By 1929, Gibbs was a poor widow, having been forced to retire without a pension entitlement—by none other than Light's husband—when her own husband retired, and pathetically and futilely begging the Indian Office for any kind of work to support herself.[2] Libbie Light, who in 1895 had started work in the Indian Service earlier than any of the others, Gibbs included, was a survivor.

Light took up her appointment at Tucson just as the administration of the Office of Indian Affairs entered a new, reformist era. A commission into Indian affairs led by Lewis Meriam had submitted its very critical report to the secretary of the interior in February 1928, published the same year as *The Problem of Indian Administration*. Commissioner of Indian Affairs Charles H. Burke resigned, and he was replaced by Charles J. Rhoads in April 1929, on the promise from President Herbert Hoover that the president would back the reform program outlined in the Meriam report.[3] Light's appointment to the Tucson position had been one of the last acts of the outgoing administration.

Rhoads and his new assistant commissioner, J. Henry Scattergood, would work together to implement many of the reforms recommended in the Meriam report. While Rhoads backed away from land reforms, he did follow through on other recommendations on education, health, and welfare, and his new director of education, Dr. W. Carson Ryan Jr., was one of the Meriam report's authors.[4]

The Meriam report had been ambivalent on the outing policy for girls. As it presently operated, outing was "mainly a plan for hiring out boys for odd jobs and girls for domestic service, seldom a plan for providing real vocational training." Nevertheless, a modified outing system might be useful, if administered by technically trained "guidance and employment" professionals, as part of an integrated program of training, placement, and supervision in the workforce. Domestic service was a "dead end" if a "not necessarily degrading" occupation for women, but the report conceded that it was likely to continue to feature in girls' education and employment. The government, then, should provide outing girls with opportunities for marriage, providing housing in "a comfortable building with a house mother," where they could entertain and get to know young men "in wholesome ways." These facilities could then be made available to other unmarried Indian servants working in the city.

On the subject of the outing matrons, the Meriam report was noncommittal. The authors supported the current policy of "eliminating" the field matron position by filling vacancies with trained nurses and recommended that the school matrons should be replaced altogether, doing away with the lack of qualifications and low salaries associated with these positions. The authors allowed that some "good work" was being done by the outing matrons: the Indian girls in service "have a friend to whom they can turn, in the supervising matron, with whom their relations seem in most cases to be cordial." None of the outing matrons had sufficient time to give the girls the oversight they needed, however. Though no explicit recommendations had been made, in 1929 the foreseeable direction for the outing matron program was their replacement by designated and college-trained "guidance and placement officers," assisted, perhaps, by kindly "housemothers."[5]

The maternalist ideologies that had underpinned the entry of women into the Indian Service were well on the wane, and indeed had been since the start of Commissioner Burke's administration back in the early 1920s, when an effort began to upgrade the field matron program. In 1922, a college-trained nurse, Elinor Gregg, had replaced Elsie Newton to oversee the steady replacement of the field matrons on the reservations, as they retired, by trained and professional nurses. Increasingly, it was believed by the central administration that educational and vocational training, not innate female virtue, would equip Indian Service female employees to work most effectively among Indian populations.[6] It is clear that Light's long-awaited new position was a precarious one.

In Tucson, Light was preoccupied with more immediate matters. She had her first day at work on May 1, 1929, when Woodruff drove her out to visit the Indian village. The people looked somewhat askance at the sight of their recently retired matron "piloting a strange woman" around. They may well have thought Light at least as old as Woodruff, with her stooped shoulders and her wispy hair pinned in a grandmotherly bun.[7] It would soon become evident that their new matron was quite a different person from Woodruff.

The Lights had taken up residence at 230 East Sixteenth Street, near the railway station, and farther south than any of the other residences of the matrons had been. Woodruff had been living there since the end of 1928, but within her first fortnight, the new matron requested permission to find "more suitable quarters."

The house on East Sixteenth was dilapidated, dingy, tumbledown, and generally wrecked, Light wrote to Superintendent Edward Stewart. It was "a bad example" to the Indians who visited her. But her main grievance was that those Indians who came to visit her came too close. In fact, she had to receive them in her living and dining room, which was "most unpleasant." She needed another large room that could be used as an office to meet with Indian callers. Having to speak with them in her private family area was surely not, Light argued, required by Office regulations.

She also wanted a separate bathroom for her visitors, manifestly uncomfortable to discover that her day-to-day relations were to be so intimate. "There is but a single toilet room in the house," she pointed out to Stewart in a follow-up letter. "Indian applicants waiting for work are often required to use it. As it is required for the use of myself and husband, I am compelled to clean and sterilize it after it has been used by Indians, as I consider it to be unsanitary after use by them. This is a most objectionable condition to me, and I am sure that you will consider it to be so. A house with a second toilet for use of Indians should be provided."[8] Light's racism might seem not overly remarkable for her time, but as an outing matron, it requires comment. Considering that Light's responsibility was to place the same applicants in "good" white homes, her aversion to having them in her own seems contradictory.

The contradiction, however, highlights the paradox of domestic service. It located the disruptive, profoundly troubling outsider in the heart of the white family, creating a tension only imperfectly resolved by the peculiar invisibility of the domestic servant. As whiteness scholar Ruth Frankenberg has suggested, the invisibility of non-white household live-in workers was both partial and complex. The white employer family, by performing constant and regular demonstrations of their ability "to summon and dismiss the racially different other at will," asserted that the white home was indeed "all-white" (as well as the employer's neighborhood generally).[9] For Light, the problem was that she was not in fact summoning and dismissing Indians at her pleasure, but rather, required to service them herself as they turned up on her doorstep: that simple distinction made their presence in her home a distinctly visible and discomfiting intrusion.

Throughout their long years of work on Indian reservations, the Lights had always kept themselves aloof from and above Indian people. William adamantly believed in the superiority of whites in general over Indians, and unsurprisingly, he had clashed with emerging Indian political leaders at Truxton Canon during the 1920s.[10] A melancholy, disappointed man, William's repeatedly expressed desire was to provide his wife, "too good" to be stuck on an isolated reservation, the chance she desperately wanted to live in more congenial surroundings.[11] Though Libbie herself was more concerned about the state of the family income when she sought an outing matron position, we may be sure that she had not been dreaming about living in a Tucson barrio, with Indians traipsing in and out of her bathroom.

But given the go-ahead by Superintendent Stewart to make enquiries among real estate brokers, Light found that an outing matron was no more welcome in Tucson than were the O'odham in her home. Landlords tended to balk at "possible Indian girls coming and going," as a local broker warned Woodruff back in 1922.[12] Light reported to a sardonic Stewart in June that she had found the greatest difficulty getting a real estate agent to even talk to her. In the end, she had managed to find a suitable home through the one brokerage that would deal with her, one block east of her present place. It had only the one small and "inconveniently located" bathroom, but it did have enough space to set up a separate office, allowing her to "hold the remainder of the house private as a dwelling for myself and family." It stood alone, too, so "our Indian friends would not disturb a neighbor in calling upon me."[13]

Light's regard for social niceties failed to impress the Indian Office. The matron should be informed that one of the rooms in the house had to be set up as an office, as a legal requirement, the Office directed Stewart. If she wanted to contribute out of her personal funds as she had suggested, she might consider adjusting her existing quarters to suit her family's needs. She should "appreciate that all other field matrons are furnished quarters for one person."[14]

Light took a week's annual leave then, despite the superintendent having already told her she was expected to supervise the summer outing students home from Phoenix. She wrote to Stewart from California saying that the doctor had advised her that she should take a "short rest in a cooler climate," and she asked for further leave from late July to the end of August. To Stewart's dismay, the Office approved Light's 25 days' unpaid leave.[15]

Light was evidently unprepared, also, for the heavy workload demands of her new position. For the first year or so of her appointment, she worked at a seemingly frenetic pace, all the while her attention focused on pleasing and satisfying the ladies of Tucson. When it came to the Tohono O'odham, however, she maintained a stiff and defensive distance. Lacking Woodruff's maternal affection for the girls, she also showed none of Estabrook's interest in devising uplifting extracurricular activities for them.

"I am at my post of duty day and night," Light wrote to the commissioner, a month after returning from her leave in 1929. "My work does not cease with the business day of eight hours, but . . . I receive calls from Indians and Whites until eight to nine o'clock at night, and on Sundays—for assistance in finding employment, or help for the white employers. I go in the car at any time throughout the day, or evening to secure work for the Indians, or to assist those who need aid."[16] Mornings were taken up with receiving phone calls for Indian workers—Monday mornings, in particular, were "very heavy"—and in the afternoons she went to the Indian village, often in the company of prospective employers, to find them, as Woodruff had started to do in the latter years of her tenure.[17]

In some ways Light was even busier than Woodruff had been. Tucson's white employers would call her to ask her to go and retrieve girls who had not returned to work from the weekend, or to collect girls they specifically wanted to engage. At least once, Light made a special trip to the village to inform a worker that her mistress had telephoned to say she was not needed that day. She also collected and delivered occasional gifts from employers to their workers. The ferrying of workers from the village to their employers' homes in the city became her responsibility (or rather, William's—Light could not drive, and relied on William to chauffeur). The car was the means of this increased activity, but the cause was largely Light's eagerness to accommodate her white patrons.[18]

Such willingness to serve was demonstrated in one of Light's very first ventures. Mrs. Cowper—one of Woodruff's regulars—told Light that the mother of the girl she had working for her, Agnes, had taken the girl's clothing in an attempt, believed Cowper, to force Agnes to return home. Perhaps this protest was a continuation of the resistance of O'odham parents to live-in work, perhaps it was a way of getting more, or better, clothing from Agnes's employer, or money to buy them with, but Light saw no need to consult with the girl or her mother. She went to the village with the employer and through an interpreter made the mother promise to take the clothes back "at once." When the mother then "failed to do this," Light "assisted the girl to go and get her clothing. She is still at work in Mrs. Cowper's home." The mother's and her daughter's wishes in the matter were irrelevant to Light. The employer's demands, however, deserved Light's greatest exertions.[19]

It took Light a little while to work out quite how she might relate to the Tucson employers, whose conviviality she sought as much as their custom. In the beginning, she compiled a list of select employers and began calling them on the telephone directly to see if they wanted an Indian worker. We cannot know if the patricians' wives appreciated or resented such a forward approach, but it doesn't seem that Light continued the practice.[20]

Instead, she began inviting her chosen employers to visit her office in person to talk about the girls they employed and any issues they might have. Light had noticed that some "do not understand Indians, and lack patience and understanding." She hoped to "interest them more" in the girls' welfare, she reported in August. Over the next fortnight she asked various women, "all of whom are among the best families of Tucson and who use Indian help . . . to assist me in protecting the Indians who worked for them," and by March the following year she was writing happily of the cooperation between certain employers and herself that now existed "to secure most satisfactory service from Indian help, and to safeguard their welfare."[21] Mexican employers, ignored altogether by both Woodruff and Estabrook, were pointedly excluded from such solicitations. Reporting how she forced one Mexican employer to pay a girl she owed, Light's tone was rude and abrupt. "The Indian was satisfied, but the Mexican was not," she wrote. "I made it plain that I would protect the Indian's rights."[22]

Having persuaded some of the white ladies to come across the railway tracks to see her, a not inconsiderable achievement, Light was to discover this too had its drawbacks. Soon she was complaining that the work in her office was consuming all her time. Many hours of each week were now taken up by white employers asking for advice and assistance in managing the Indian girls. Not only did she not have much time left to go to the village, she had no time left to visit the girls in homes where they worked. And sometimes it could be downright unworkable to have the ladies there. "Mrs. Mills is reporting some private information about her help, and asking my advice," she recorded irritably at one point in 1930. "I cannot talk to her as the room is full of Indians, who should not hear the conversation. I should have an entirely different house for my work, where I may have privacy in which to conduct my business when necessary."[23] Harking back to her original grievance, the discomfort Light expressed probably had more to do with the presence of the Indian guests than the employer's obtuseness. It is not clear how she thought a separate office could resolve the problem of having employers and Indian people together in the same room. It seems most likely that she meant, but was too agitated to articulate, that she would conduct discussions with white employers in her own home, while keeping Indians relegated to the official and public work space.

For Light clearly saw her involvement with Indian women domestic workers as her job, pure and simple, and quite distinct from her personal life, even if her involvement with their employers was not. Light felt there should have been a clear detachment between her work and her home life, and she resented the expectation from the Indian Office that there should be none. And after years of Woodruff's apparent willingness to devote her every waking moment to her job, we can only imagine what the Tohono O'odham girls and women made of Light's attitude.

Predictably, Light had shown no sign of keeping up Woodruff's Thursday afternoon gatherings. Several weeks into her tenure she was taken aback to be greeted by a group of Indian girls who had come to her house to "receive mail, and visit." It was, in fact, the first Thursday afternoon that Light had stayed at home herself. There was at least one more such friendly "visit" by a group of girls (two months later), but Light's reports suggest more often than not she was out on Thursday afternoons.[24] It is unlikely that the young women would have felt welcome even when she was there, and it would seem that they soon understood that any relationship with their new outing matron would be strictly business. For some, no doubt, this new arrangement suited them perfectly well.

Nevertheless, Light was still obliged to control the young women's moral behavior. Concerned by the "disgraceful" drinking in the village on the weekends, Light seemed just as frustrated as Woodruff had been by her inability to do much about it at all. She was similarly preoccupied with the marriage issue, too. But Light did not contemplate hosting soirees to guide the young women toward marriage. Symbolically, Light's first recorded intervention concerned none other than Lilly, whom Light successfully "persuaded" to marry the new man with whom she was living. Light had no compunction whatsoever about using the threat of arrest and jail to compel reluctant couples into marriage, and her pride in this stratagem and the "fear" it caused among the young women revealed her to have more in common with Estabrook than Woodruff.[25]

Unlike both of her predecessors, however, Light encouraged, rather than opposed, Indian-Mexican marriages. In one instance, she acted when the mother of an Indian girl in service asked Light to get her daughter married to the young man who stayed with her at her employer's residence. In another, she went to some lengths to have a "marriage consummated" between an Indian woman and a Mexican man that the authorities would not permit. Light's rather radical openness to such interracial marriage might reflect relaxing attitudes in Tucson about Indian and Mexican associations, or it might simply reflect her own individual conviction that both groups were on a socially and racially equal level. On the subject of Anglo and Indian sexual relationships, Light's records are silent.[26]

Light did not, it would seem, have girls stay overnight in her own home. Not until early December 1929 did she mention the possibility. Three girls had been "picked up" by police for trespass against a Mrs. Moule. They were, presumably, visiting or staying in her outdoor room with a fourth young woman who worked for Moule. Light took one of them back to her own employer, but the other two had nowhere to stay, their families being at San Xavier. The police had probably expected Light to put them up for the night, but the girls "were very saucy and insolent," apparently, and left Light's premises when she scolded them.[27] There is no other evidence to suggest that Light even contemplated allowing girls to stay overnight with her during the first year of her term.

Toward the close of 1929, Light had to deal with a tragic case involving a twenty-two-year-old domestic worker, who died in the hospital of septicemia. The girl, Nellie H——, had arrived from Sacaton a few months earlier, and Light had placed her in a doctor's household; she had gone to another employer since. The doctor who had formerly employed the deceased girl wrote to Light at the urging of his wife, to tell Light that the dying girl had named a young Pima man at Sacaton as the father of her unborn child, and to express his shock and regret that Nellie "did not confide in me sooner so that there would have been a chance of saving her life for when I first reached her I found her in serious condition due principally to the delay in calling a physician."[28] His letter might be read as an anxious assurance that he had not been involved in any way in the girl's deadly abortion, which he implied was self-inflicted. Septicemia, or "childbed fever," widely understood to be spread by untrained midwives and unhygienic doctors performing illegal terminations, was a frequent complication of instrumental abortion, and the doctor might well have worried that he would come under suspicion.[29]

Perhaps the doctor was concerned that Light might think them remiss in their supervision of the girl when she was there, and take him off her books. He went on to declare how very appreciative they were that Light had provided them a replacement worker when Nellie left their service: "They are quiet and good workers and show such good training. In fact I tease Mrs. D—— quite a bit about the superiority of their sewing. I trust the girl we now have will remain satisfactory and stay with us indefinitely for she gives entire satisfaction in all her work and ways."[30] Light's chill summation when she contacted the Sacaton superintendent—"The death of this young woman is a very sad affair. She was giving very satisfactory service to her employer"—suggests she did not see the young Indian women as anything other than disposable, if occasionally useful. Indeed, within a couple of weeks Light had written again to Sacaton, asking the superintendent to supply the names and addresses of "good girls" for work in Tucson, as she could not fill the "many calls for Indian girls" she was receiving.[31]

Light saw no need for any investigation into the girl's death, despite the circumstances. She was considerably more exercised by the case of another young woman, a local girl whom she reported on suspicion of doing away with her baby at around the same time. Light had believed Belle L—— to be pregnant when Belle first came to see her for work. She had told the girl sternly that she was "in no condition to be given a place in a home" and that she should instead go to her people, and make the father of her baby marry her. Instead, Belle went to one of Light's regular employers "to substitute" for another girl. This employer rang Light after Belle finished, wanting to know whether Light realized that Belle was pregnant. Directly afterward, another white woman contacted Light, reporting that Belle had asked her for work, but that the girl's eyes were in such bad condition—trachoma was prevalent in Tucson—that she could not consider having her in the house. This woman was startled to hear from Light that Belle, being pregnant, had been forbidden by her to seek work, saying that she had seen no evidence that Belle was pregnant at all. The following day, Belle herself rang up Light and told her that "her baby had been born, and that it was dead; that she had been to Dr. Smythe, and that her eyes were all right." Smythe was the Indian Service physician, who attended to the girls in service and others in the village from his residence in the now-disused Tucson Day School building. But as Smythe denied seeing Belle at all, and Belle had avoided Light since, Light thought the superintendent should "investigate" to see if "a crime has been committed in disposing of the child." Nothing came of this, however, although Light did pursue the young couple until they agreed to marry.[32]

Light's first Christmas, several weeks later, was a dismal affair. She had set out to arrange what she understood to be the "usual Christmas treat" of a party, before realizing that Stewart had no intention of providing supplies. Light went to her favored employers and merchants and gathered "a good supply of candy, nuts, fruits, some toys and clothing" to distribute. When Christmas morning rolled around, however, not one of the girls then working in Tucson appeared. Light had just the one visitor, an Indian man who, much to her bemusement, was looking for work. "He tried to say Merry Christmas to me," Light recorded, "but his English was not good, and he expressed it in smiles." Was he Woodruff's Indian Santa? At any rate, he helped Light make up packages for distribution among the Indian people in the village, and she went to the village to give them out: "They were happy and had a fine Christmas. Some were away from home. I have presents for them when they return. This has been a happy and busy day, well spent," she reported bravely.[33]

At the start of her first summer in Tucson in 1929, Light had discovered that the local Indian parents expected her to write to the various boarding schools requesting their children be sent home for the vacation, a practice very likely established under Woodruff.[34] Light made representations to the Phoenix superintendent on behalf of Ida B——, "a reliable woman, who will keep faith with both you and myself." The mother had already asked the Phoenix superintendent that her daughter be allowed home, but he had refused. Light was uncharacteristically touched by the mother's plight—"She lost her baby & feels very lonely and wants to see her girl"—but Superintendent John B. Brown would not relent. He told the mother that Beatrice had already gone out to work, and the people who hired outing girls did not like to "give them up before the summer is over."[35] Mrs. B—— was the only parent on record that Light tried to help at that time, although there could have been others. Soon afterward, Light went on her extended leave, and nothing more was heard of Beatrice.

In the lead-up to the next summer vacation period in 1930, Light made more strenuous efforts on behalf of O'odham parents. She was, in fact, unexpectedly emphatic in her praise of some, describing one mother as "one of the best of our Indian woman [*sic*] . . . worthy of the consideration you may give her request," while another father was "an excellent man . . . will take the best of care of his daughter." An aunt and grandmother had "a good home" and would "take excellent care" of the girl they had reared since childhood. For a mother who wanted her daughter home from Phoenix to help with a newborn baby, Light argued, "the daughter is of proper age, and . . . has acquired the necessary training to fit her to assist the family."[36] She managed to coax the reluctant superintendent of the Fort Mojave Indian School to let a girl, Susanna, come home to her people. Although Susanna's five-year term at the school had expired, the superintendent planned to send her to Los Angeles to work in the summer, as was done for "all the girls . . . that are old enough in accordance with the instructions from the Indian Office." He did not want to "unsettle" the other girls by allowing anyone to go home, but gave in to Light, grudgingly, "if her people need her."

Light had apparently enquired about Susanna's return (and her brother's) the year before as well. As her interchange with this superintendent makes clear, outing from the schools was systematically preventing many young Indian women from returning to their families and communities, even after their schooling was complete. Light's close attachment to her youngest daughter may have made her more sympathetic to the Indian parents—she had told the Fort Mojave superintendent that she herself was glad to have her own daughter near her, in Tucson.[37] But this is not to say that she contested the removal of the girls to boarding school in the first instance, and Light also continued to try, not always successfully, to have troublesome girls sent away from Tucson to Phoenix and elsewhere.[38]

Remarkably, Light would undergo a major change of heart after the summer of 1930. Her unexpected defense of a young O'odham worker on trial for murdering her baby marked a distinct shift in Light's attitudes. From that point acting as an advocate for several young women who were in very serious trouble, Light would go quite a bit further in that regard than either Estabrook or Woodruff ever had. She went on to embrace her responsibilities toward the Tohono O'odham girls and their community with enthusiasm, declaring, on the eve of her retirement, that of all the positions she had held in the Indian Service, she had made her most important contribution as an outing matron. But the dramatic turnaround in Light's attitude remains inexplicable in her records, and requires some exercise of the imagination to understand.

We might begin with a curious letter Light received in May 1930 from a young woman named Juana J——. Two months earlier, Juana had come to see Light in Tucson, in company with an Indian man, either a friend or a relative, to tell Light that she was "in trouble." Juana had been working for Mrs. Cowper (of the confiscated clothing incident). Cowper, a widow with two children, had allowed Juana to keep her own one-and-a-half-year-old daughter with her.[39] Now at the hospital at Sells, Juana had just given birth to her second illegitimate baby. Juana's letter, however, concerned her older sister Marisa. Light had first learned of Marisa's pregnancy when she was called to the home where Marisa worked by Marisa's employer, who wanted the outing matron to give the girl a lecture about having a man stay with her in her room. Marisa told Light that her Indian boyfriend refused to marry her, and Light had sent her to stay with the girls' father, at one of the reservation villages.[40] Juana asked Light to have her sister sent to join her at Sells. "She might kill the baby I know," wrote Juana anxiously. "She had a flossie about two month after I had a flossie so please sent her down to Sells before there had baby [*sic*]," Juana went on. "I am not suppose to tell you about this flossie but I just have to say that word I know you dont like to hear about this flossie."[41]

"Flossie" was a contemporary slang expression meaning a sexually promiscuous woman: an older, experienced girlfriend, perhaps a prostitute.[42] Juana's usage, however, obviously diverges. She was, I suspect, referring to the taking of an abortifacient, a reference to any of the variety of purges, purgatives, and douches that women used at that time to induce miscarriage. Her reluctant yet emphatic use of the taboo word in her correspondence with Light might be read in the same way that historian Cornelia Dayton has approached the use of the expression "taking the trade" in eighteenth-century New England: as a sign that young women living in dread of illegitimate pregnancy were familiar with the clandestine use of abortifacients.[43] Juana's fears that her sister would "kill the baby" may have been overstated, perhaps even calculated to urge the matron to bring her sister to her, but might also suggest that the resort of neonaticide was, also, not unfamiliar.

At the time of writing, Juana was being held in custody at Sells. She was almost certainly facing court on the reservation under the laws against cohabitation. Years upon years of draconian laws targeting Indian couples, and impacting most punitively upon young Indian women who bore children out of Anglo-American wedlock, years of repression that began with the first outing matron's campaign against "Red Slavery" and continued under the regimes of Woodruff and now Light had placed the Tohono O'odham domestic workers who proceeded with their pregnancies in an invidious position. It is not hard to see that a dangerous underground pattern of illicit abortion and infanticide might have become entrenched in Tucson by the time Light took up her position.

If this was so, careful Woodruff never breathed a mention of it in any of the hundreds of weekly, quarterly, and annual reports she filled out over the years. In her published memoirs, however, she recounted, in dramatic detail, an episode where she was convinced that one of the Indian girls had killed her newborn baby. Woodruff had suspected the girl, Lyda, of being pregnant, despite the girl's impassive denials, and then, sure enough, a tiny corpse wrapped in a bath towel was found hidden in an obscure nook of the girl's employer's house. Confronted by the young woman's stolid refusal to admit knowing anything at all about the infant, the usually compassionate Woodruff was vindictive. She was most disappointed that the girl was not charged with murder, as "there was no way of telling whether she or someone else had been guilty of the act, or whether the child had been born dead or alive," and pleased that Lyda was punished anyway, by being forced to "work a sentence" at the Sells hospital. For Woodruff, this story was an illustration of the inveterate and inexplicable "immorality" of many Indian girls.[44] In the same way that Woodruff had failed to make the connection between mother-of-twins Felicita's predicament and the laws that enmeshed and oppressed the O'odham community, Woodruff could not see that young mothers like Lyda had very few options. Certainly they were more likely to be punished for proceeding with the birth of an illegitimate child than they were for not doing so. Altogether, the outing matron records show a profound imbalance between the numbers of women hauled before court having given birth to an illegitimate baby and the almost complete absence of any record of penalties for abortion or infanticide—with one, single, critical exception.

When the hot Tucson summer came on again in July 1930, Light—much to Stewart's intense annoyance—again took leave, six weeks this time, including fifteen days of sick leave on the grounds of "impaired health."[45] She returned to work in early September and, in her first week back, escorted three girls from Tucson to the Phoenix Indian School. While in Phoenix, Light discovered that Lena N—— had been arrested and put in jail there over the summer, charged with infanticide of her newborn baby. Light immediately went to visit Lena in the jail.[46]

Light knew Lena from her days at Truxton Canon. Lena, of a Tohono O'odham family at Sells, started at the boarding school there when Light was the school matron. When Lena's term expired in 1929, the superintendent (William's successor), wanting to send her home, asked Light to arrange Lena's transportation from Tucson to her family's home on the reservation. Whether or not Lena got all the way home is not clear, but four months later, in September 1929, Light placed her to work for the wife of an editor in Tucson. Later, Lena was with an architect's family, before being reported to be sick by the wife and admitted to the Indian hospital at Sells. There was no mention of Lena after that for some time, until early June 1930, when Light recorded that her employer since March, Mrs. Fawsdon, was planning to go away to Oracle, in the Catalina foothills north of Tucson, for the summer. Light intended to place Lena with the family of a Jewish farrier until the Fawsdons' return, although apparently she did not.[47]

Reverend Fawsdon and his wife were regular patrons, and Light had not had any qualms giving the minister special permission to take Lena with him when he was assigned to Phoenix. "It was a fine place for a girl," Light insisted, recording her visit to Lena in jail in her weekly report. "Unknown to him or to me, Lena had gotten in trouble by a Mexican cab driver in Tucson."[48] She immediately wrote to the superintendent of the Phoenix Indian School about Lena. Phoenix's outing matron Amanda Chingren had retired in the middle of the year, and as no appointment had been made in her position yet, the responsibility for overseeing the girls working in Phoenix fell to him. Light said that the girl had told her that this taxi driver, known only by the name of "Rum," had twice come to her room and forced himself upon her, while she was still living in Tucson, and that Rum had left for Los Angeles some months before she went to Phoenix with the minister. Lena had then given birth at the Fawsdon residence in Phoenix, Light explained to the superintendent. Lena had fallen unconscious while she was in labor, and when she came to discovered the baby's dead body. "I have known this girl for many years," Light wrote, "and I have considered her an outstanding Indian girl, for morality and truthfulness. I cannot believe that she destroyed the baby, nor that she is guilty of the crime of murder. I wish to render all the assistance possible." Light asked to be allowed to testify at the trial. "I do not mean that I would try to prevent her punishment if she were found guilty," Light assured the superintendent. "I cannot believe that she is a wilful murderer, and I would do what I can to assist her in her time of trouble and need."[49]

Lena's worried mother had written to Light by that time. She had not heard from her daughter for over two months, the last time being when Lena was at Oracle, when she had promised her mother that she would be home on the 15th of September to accompany the family on an important trip. This would have been to Magdalena, Sonora, Mexico, for the Festival of San Francisco Xavier, and Lena's mother would have expected Light to realize the significance of her daughter's non-appearance.[50]

Light's support for Lena stands in sharp contrast to her indifference toward the Sacaton girl who had died, and to her hostility toward Belle. Her attitude also constrasts with Woodruff's distrust of Lyda. It is remarkable that in Lena's case Light was so much more sympathetic than Woodruff, and also that Light was so prepared to believe and defend Lena. So remarkable, in fact, that the question of the reason for Light's shift in attitude demands some kind of hypothesis.

Light's trust in Lena may have been due to her having known her before, and perhaps the same fact explains why Lena could have confided in her former school matron. Nevertheless, elements in the story alert us to the possibility that it was fabricated, in part or in whole. The mysterious taxi driver might dispose too conveniently of the question of who the baby's father might have been, and whether he may have indeed been an accomplice. The claim that Lena was unconscious when the baby was born meant that it would not be possible for a court to adjudicate on whether the baby was born dead or alive (the same reason, of course, that Lyda was not charged). Actually, the story is so suspiciously watertight, that the question is rather why Light believed it.

Perhaps Light really did think Lena the most truthful Indian girl she had ever known. There is, however, one major complication. Buried among Light's day-to-day records, there is a significant detail that was omitted altogether from Light's recount.

In early July 1930, just before Light went on leave, Reverend Fawsdon had brought Lena in to town from his wife's summer residence at Oracle, telling Light that Lena was "seriously sick." Light was familiar with employers complaining that their workers were sick, which was often code for "pregnant" (or suspected to be so). In fact, when the Fawsdons brought their previous worker Carmel in the year before saying that she was sick and should go home, Light did not bother getting a doctor's opinion: Carmel simply told her that she did not need to see a doctor, and Light found her another place instead.[51] In response to the reverend's concern about Lena, however, this time Light *did* take the girl to see the Indian Service doctor in Tucson.

But the mystery deepens unexpectedly on reading Light's notation that Dr. Smythe had given Lena a "thorough examination" and that he had assured Light that the minister was "mistaken," that "the girl was all right, and able to return to work."[52]

Lena's baby was apparently born that same month, either alive or stillborn. Lena, therefore, had to have either just given birth or miscarried or, more likely, to have been still pregnant when Smythe examined her. In either case, it seems very odd indeed that a "thorough examination" by a medical practitioner would not have detected anything at all, even if Lena was brought in for some other suspected illness.

Was Smythe then completely incompetent? Had he lied, and to what end? In any case, why would Light protect him? Perhaps she had not taken Lena to the doctor at all. Or had the matron lied when making her first record of Lena's examination, and the doctor now chose to remain silent? Lena's employers, the minister and his wife, also, must have decided not to say anything about it—or surely Light would have had to. Did they all forget? Were they all implicated, somehow?

Myriad scenarios, every one of them perplexing, might be hypothesized. But recall Belle's explanation to Light—her baby was born dead, she had been to see Dr. Smythe, she was all right—and Smythe's strenuous denial he had seen the girl at all. Could Light have discovered that the Indian Service doctor had been acting illegally as an abortionist for the Indian girls, even at their employers' requests?

It is not beyond possibility that the doctor was acting as an abortionist or, at the very least, supplying abortifacients. Despite the well-known involvement of the medical profession in criminalizing abortion in the nineteenth century, and the self-protective zeal with which doctors often sought to identify abortionists, doctors were regularly approached by women seeking abortions, and doctors were at times indeed providers of illegal abortions, albeit secretively, during this period.[53] Some Indian Service doctors undoubtedly abused their position, such as the resident physician on St. George Island

(Alaska) who confessed in 1911 to having seduced two Aleut girls who came to his office for treatment, with one becoming pregnant as a result and dying in childbirth in unclear circumstances.[54] In the Indian Service's medical program at the time, as the authors of a history of the Indian health service have explained, salaries were low, turnover was high, and "many of the professionals who joined the service were marginally qualified."[55] With the ever-high demand for the Indian women's domestic services, coupled with the harsh penalties on Indian women who gave birth to children outside Anglo-American wedlock, the temptation for Tucson's Indian doctor to supplement his income by exploiting the market for Indian abortion might have been very strong.

There is only circumstantial evidence for such a hypothesis, but it would certainly explain the circumstances. Let us imagine that Smythe assured Light that Lena was not pregnant, even as Smythe either provides Lena with the means to induce a miscarriage or gives her some treatment at his surgery that will result in a stillbirth later. Perhaps this was provided on the understanding that it was the employer's request. Shortly afterwards, Light having gone away, Lena miscarries at the Fawsdons' home in Phoenix, but fails to do away with the body herself for some reason—perhaps she did fall unconscious. The minister is then faced with the choice of reporting the birth to the police or becoming an accomplice by disposing of the body himself. Professing his surprise, disbelief, and horror, he stands by as the girl is arrested and taken away for murder.

Light then returns from her pleasant sojourn on the Californian coast to learn that Lena has been charged with infanticide. Knowing full well that the girl had a medical examination under her direction showing she was neither pregnant nor postpartum, Light goes to see her and to demand an explanation. Light is keenly aware that Lena's public trial will not reflect well upon her at all. Recalling Belle's telephone call, she insists that Lena tell her exactly what happened.

So Lena tells her. Perhaps she tells Light who the real father of her baby is, and it was not some Mexican taxi driver. Maybe she tells Light that she could not bring herself to get rid of her baby's body. A truly sinister, but still plausible, possibility: she had refused to take Smythe's treatment, and on giving birth to her live baby, her enraged employer forced her to smother the infant, or did the job himself, before calling the police to arrest her. Maybe Lena offers Light a much longer, deeply woven explanation, about her "illness" at the beginning of the year, when she ended up at the hospital at Sells; about Belle, about Lyda, about even Nellie; about an abortion racket that might have been going on under the very nose of the outing matrons. We will never know what Lena really told Light in the prison cell, but whatever it was, it was absolutely convincing.

Libbie Light was no Estabrook, but she was shaken enough to want to protect Lena. It is possible that Light concocted, with Lena, what she knew to be a story not just legally watertight, but one that the minister would be unable and unwilling to challenge. Perhaps, cunning Light knew very well that by not making mention of the doctor's examination, neither the minister nor the doctor would be willing to contest the girl's character Light gave her, and the case would collapse. And perhaps it was a quiet visit from Light, and a few dropped hints, that convinced Dr. Smythe that now was probably a good time to retire, and get out of Tucson.[56]

Or, maybe, it was just as Light reported. Lena told her she came to with a dead baby alongside her, the rapist father had long vanished, and Light believed her without hesitation, dismissing the doddery old doctor's failure to notice anything back in July. A cynic might suggest Light was in on the original abortion and, along with Smythe and Fawsdon, wanted to ensure that Lena did not spill the beans in court—but the same cynic would have to believe that the Indian girl's word might count for anything against that of the government matron, the government doctor, and a reverend minister. But whatever the reason that Light decided to champion Lena, it appears that her visit to Lena in Phoenix marked a definite change in her attitude toward the Indians of Tucson.

In early October, Light wrote back to Lena's mother, telling her that Lena was in jail and that she hoped to testify for Lena, but still had heard nothing further about a trial.[57] Visited by another clergyman on the subject of Lena soon afterwards, Light noticed that he had assumed she would not be interested in helping the girl. She soon put him right. "Missionaries are strange creatures," Light remarked airily. "They assume that no one does anything for the Indian, but themselves. Answered Supt. Elliott's letter about Juana J——, promptly."[58]

The new superintendent at Sells, Jasper Elliott, who had replaced Stewart that month, had asked Light for a character statement for Juana J——, facing trial on the reservation. Light stated that she had known Juana since first taking up her appointment and had assigned her to various homes in Tucson during 1929: "I have observed her conduct and action during this period, and I am glad to say that she has been a good girl. I have not seen her out late at night, or associating with women of doubtful character. I have never known her to drink intoxicating liquor, or to act in a manner other than decent and honorable. I have never seen her associating with men, but on the contrary, she seemed to be inclined to be alone, or with her sisters when away from her home."[59]

One has to wonder how Juana got pregnant if she never went out nor associated with men, and perhaps Light intended the implication that sexual relations had been forced upon Juana, perhaps while she was at work. It was a very positive testimonial of character, especially considering that the letter from Juana that Light had in her files might be considered a little incriminating. Perhaps Light now understood what Juana had been so urgently trying to tell her.

Next, Light took Marisa and her four-month-old baby into her own home until she could prevail upon Marisa's boyfriend to marry her. With the help of the Presbyterian missionary Eleanor Struthers, the Indian policeman (Woodruff's old ally, Tohono O'odham Hugh Norris), and Marisa herself, Light managed to get him before the county attorney's office in mid-October and threatened with prosecution for child support. Light decided that she would keep Marisa and her baby "until her case is settled." The young man then came to talk with Light and asked the matron to speak with his father. Paternal opposition, not Marisa's reputation, was the reason her boyfriend was reluctant to marry Marisa. Apparently, Light was able to talk the boy's father around, and the young couple married the next week, the new husband taking Marisa and the baby home to his father's house. "They seemed to be happy," Light commented, somewhat uncertainly.[60]

A week later Lena was released from jail. There is no evidence that in the end Lena's case went to trial, and maybe Light's intervention had something to do with it. She arrived by train from Phoenix late one night, and Light collected her and took her to her place to stay.

The next day Light took Lena to see the new Indian Service doctor at Tucson, Smythe's replacement, who advised sending Lena out to the Sells hospital for recuperation.[61] (One can't help wondering if, like Lyda, she was forced to work there too in "penance.")

This series of tragic events highlights graphically the ensnared position of the Tohono O'odham girls. Caught between the punitive state and the expectations and needs of their own community, vulnerable in domestic service to both predation and prosecution, there was little chance the young women could assert any kind of real control of their own sexuality and reproduction. Yet while Light had evidently come to a more sympathetic position toward the O'odham girls, she never really comprehended the structures that constrained their lives and choices so harshly. Instead, she fell back on stereotypes of native promiscuity. Some six or seven months later, as she helped an unhappy young working girl return to her mother in the country after her employer caught her with a man, Light remarked, ruefully, that despite showing promise in domestic service, "the primitive instincts of the savage controlled her." Light might describe one girl as "an excellent young woman" and another as "an exceptionally good mother" in situations where she saw them as behaving "like Whites," but Light retained her fundamental sense of racial superiority and distance when confronted with issues surrounding Indian sexuality.[62]

As the Depression took deeper hold, times were getting very tough for the Indians in Tucson. In December 1931, Light had Elliott send out a circular to local businesses advising them that the Indian people were seriously affected by the worsening economic conditions and asking for them to make contributions to Light, to make "the coming Christmas a more cheerful one for the Papagos." The Indian men were forced to compete with unemployed whites and others for a rapidly shrinking pool of jobs, while the once relatively good wages for the outing girls were plummeting. Light found a place for Lena in January 1932, for instance, that paid only $5 a week, or 35¢ an hour, as compared to the $7 to $14 weekly wages girls were getting in 1929. Lena would "remain only until I can secure a more desirable place for her," promised Light, but by the end of the next month another girl was working for this employer, at an even lower wage, and there was no mention of Lena. Light calculated in April 1932 that the combined earnings of the Indians in Tucson had virtually halved since the time of her arrival, from about $35,000 a year in 1929 to $18,000 in 1932.[63] Although the O'odham continued to cultivate their own crops and many returned to their homes in the country, they were more dependent on the cash economy than ever before, and hampered by drought throughout the early 1930s.[64]

A handful of correspondences between Light and Indian women looking for work from farther afield indicates how dire the situation was getting. Maryanna Romero wrote from Florence in January 1932 asking Light for a job in Tucson. Her father had died, and she was supporting her mother and her four siblings. "I sure want a work [*sic*] on account of my living. . . . I don't care where you can find it but that will be alright because I sure need one anyway." A pencilled letter, undated and desperate, literally begged Light to help the writer find work: "Nothing is left for my eats. I feel ashame [*sic*] to ask you to help me but I just can't starve to death." Light's reply to another enquiry in April 1932 was very discouraging. "Work in Tucson is very scarce," Light wrote. Not only had wages been drastically reduced, but there were "many Indians" in Tucson "ready to step into any vacant position." She advised the woman to ask among her "white friends" for any possible work.[65]

Domestic work for the Tohono O'odham women had long been important for the economic survival of their families and communities and therefore a source of pride, but in the maelstrom of the Depression the need for work took on a more poignant, desperate aspect. Light's correspondence indicates that within the town, Indian girls and women could no longer take and leave positions just as they chose, that they were themselves becoming dependent upon "white friends" who might employ them or recommend them to those who could. This situation would have meant that the outing matron's position increased in power with regard to the Indian community, even as it became less significant for individual white employers who could, apparently, now easily find any number of people, of any race, willing to work for them. It appears that both matron and maids became mutually dependent in a way that had not been seen before.

It was around this time that Mary Stewart, Rhoads's assistant director of education in Washington, DC, asked Light to send her thorough "information relative to the position of Field Matron" at Tucson. Suspecting, correctly, that the Indian Office was considering abolishing the position, Light argued vigorously against doing so. "This office is known to hundreds of White employers of Indian Labor, and calls are made upon it when labor is available," Light stated. "Were the Office abolished, the Indians would lose thousands of dollars because [of the] lack of contact with the Public. There is no other agency through which the White employer, and the Indian laborer may be brought in contact."

"The position was established many years ago, for the benefit of the Indian men and women, who have lived in proximity to Tucson, Ariz., since the city was founded," wrote Light. "The principle [*sic*] duties of the place are to seek employment among the citizens of the City, for Indian workers of every class." Disclaiming any personal motive, she declared that she was motivated solely by her interest in the welfare of the Papagos. "They are a worthy, industrious people, and I think every effort should be made to assist them in securing employment, and thus supporting themselves, as they have done so faithfully in the past." More than ever before, they needed this assistance, she continued. It would be a false economy to withdraw it, because the destitution that would result would require greater expenditure than maintaining the position. Inspired to further heights by her own rhetoric, Light avowed the singular importance of her work: "It is my belief that at no other place and in no other position have I rendered more valuable service to the Indian, than I have been able to accomplish here. I shall separate from the Indians and from the work reluctantly, but with a conviction that I have accomplished much for the welfare and advancement of the Indian."[66]

The date of Light's retirement was fast approaching. One of the reforms implemented out of the Meriam report was the lowering of the compulsory retirement age to sixty-five years, and Light was turning sixty-five that August. At Phoenix, Chingren had been forced to retire in the middle of 1930, as Light well knew.[67] Light herself had been under threat since the same time, when Superintendent Stewart, exasperated by her second long summer vacation, tried to force her to take an early retirement. The wily Light had outsmarted him, and the Office, at the time, by fudging her age.[68] Now, however, she knew that she would have to fight openly if she wanted to keep her employment.

As Light realized, the white employers now had little if any need for her assistance, but it was the Indian people for whom she worked, and whose support she relied upon. In March 1931, Light had written to Stewart's successor Elliott, reporting a rumor among the O'odham in Tucson—she might well have started it herself—that the outing matron position was to be abolished. Light claimed that the Indian people had asked her to seek Elliott's help to prevent its abolishment because without this position white people would not employ Indian labor. She argued that it was only the outing matron's role as moral and social guardian of Indians, and protecting them particularly from the supposedly undesirable influences of their Mexican and Chinese neighbors, that made the "White citizens of the community" open to employing Indians when so many other workers were available. The position might be given any title, but "a high class, female industrial employee" should be located among the Indians "for many years, or until employment conditions improve."[69]

Light did secure Elliott's support at that time, and in April 1931, the Office had noted that the need for an "employment agent" should be investigated in Tucson. Now, as Mary Stewart investigated that need a year on, Light began to lay plans for her own retention. As well as Elliott's support, she had also, apparently, gained the support of a new and rising Indian Service official, Richard M. Tisinger. Tisinger, the superintendent of the Pima and Papago schools, had been recently placed in charge of developing an educational program for the Southwest jurisdiction. Tisinger and Elliott sent a joint telegram to Ryan, requesting that Light be kept on into 1933, to assist in the establishment of a planned new school program. This was a new development, and Mary Stewart contacted Elliott asking for his "frank opinion" about the kind of woman needed for the "new place" to be established at Tucson. "Would you like a woman more or less of Mrs. Light's type?"[70]

Tisinger replied on Elliott's behalf. "The position as it now exists is largely concerned with placement," Tisinger began. "The time is ripe for a slight change in accent or purpose of this worker." By this time, a loan fund for higher education aspirants had been established, and Tisinger's plans included setting up a scholarship for young Native American men to attend the university in Tucson (the University of Arizona). He had already secured funding to remodel the old Tucson Day School for their hostel. If Indian parents could also enroll their children in local schools instead of sending them away, and if homes in the Indian village were accredited to billet children from the country, Tisinger envisaged the village would become an "educational center" instead of a "slum." The new appointment should be chosen with a view to these aims.[71]

By Light's calculations, just one and a half more years in the Indian Service would give her the full thirty years' service required to claim the government pension at the highest rate.[72] When her official notice of retirement arrived in June, she applied for a continuance. She had the Indians' confidence and cooperation in full, she claimed. Both the Indians and the white employers had urged her to stay on, stated Light, even offering to petition the Indian Office, although she had discouraged such action.[73]

Perhaps they had. Light knew, however, that petitions were not enough. Elliott and Tisinger had both requested her retention, she went on. They wanted her assistance with their planned special projects for Indian education to secure "the cooperation of the Indians whose confidence and acquaintance I have to a favorable degree." The superintendent forwarded her letter to the Indian Office along with his strong expression of admiration for her capabilities. The Office had previously notified Elliott that the field matron positions held by Light and, on the San Xavier reservation, by the aging Mary Doyle were to be abolished and replaced by a single field nurse position servicing both areas. Suggesting Light be retained "as Placement Agent or any other designation" to continue the work she was doing and to assist the new field nurse, Superintendent Elliott argued that too often, experienced and effective workers had been replaced by those whose training was useless because of their inability to handle "often exasperating health and moral conditions."[74]

However, the Indian Office had already struck upon a different solution. Not a field nurse, but the current outing matron at Phoenix, Chingren's replacement Gracie Taylor, had already been told she was to be transferred to take over the very important placement work at Tucson. Despite her best efforts, Light was forced to retire, on an annuity based on her service of "about 27½ years."[75]

Although it would seem that Light had at least succeeded in persuading the central Office to maintain the outing work in Tucson, her successor would consider the position an undeserved demotion, and most bitterly resent being sent to Tucson. Perhaps Taylor was right, as the Office might well have decided the easiest way of reforming the system at Phoenix—their evident determination here—was to shift her to Tucson. But to whatever extent Light had persuaded the Office of the importance of the outing work in Tucson, Gracie Taylor would, to just that same extent, convince them of its worthlessness and irrelevance.

7

"Mrs. Taylor calls it 'messenger work'"

Gracie Taylor, 1932–1934

WHEN GRACIE'S MOTHER DIED and her preacher father went away, her brother and sister were only little children, and she was not much older. Taken in by their Quaker grandparents in northern Michigan, the children stayed there until young Gracie married Aaron Taylor, a widowed poultry merchant, thirty years her senior, who was prepared to take on his new bride's teenage siblings, too, alongside his own son. For that kindness and care, Gracie was perpetually grateful. When Aaron became too old to work in 1915, she took a position as a teacher in the Indian Service, hoping she might eventually secure a field matron position where Aaron might be permitted to join her. Despite the policy against appointing field matrons "with home ties," she eventually wound up as the field matron at a village on the San Carlos reservation in southeastern Arizona, her elderly husband in tow. Widowed in her mid-40s, and restless at isolated Bylas, in 1929 Taylor tried for various outing matron jobs, including the one at Tucson, just as it was promised to Light, before finally landing the new position replacing Amanda Chingren at Phoenix in October 1930.[1]

The Phoenix outing matron position had been vacant for a month. The Rhoads administration may have been unsure about continuing it, but with the help of Taylor's niece in Pennsylvania, who was a member of the same congregation of Friends as the new assistant commissioner, J. Henry Scattergood, Taylor had secured the position and a new title. At a time when skeptical glances were being cast at the outing system, and retiring matrons were being replaced either by field nurses or college graduates with employment qualifications, Taylor was designated a "senior placement matron." Taylor was flummoxed on her arrival at Phoenix—ladies "clamoring" for girls, summer students returning to school, other girls "scattered about over the city," and Taylor without a clue how to find them—but she valiantly set about to make a success of it, and by the time she learned that she was to go to Tucson in June 1932, she had settled in comfortably enough and did not want to leave.[2]

But all the time Taylor had been at Phoenix, significant changes were taking shape at the Indian Office headquarters in Washington, DC. Legislation and funding to establish a new national Indian "employment agency" were secured at the end of 1931. Commissioner Charles J. Rhoads then appointed a full-time director of Indian employment in 1932, Ernest R. Burton, with the responsibility to organize the "more effective coordination" of adult placement services with the educational program, and to coordinate Indian Service employment activities with public employment offices around the country. At Burton's request, the youth and student employment was delegated to Assistant Director of Education Mary Stewart, in effect leaving her in charge of the employment of girls and women, and of the outing matrons. Stewart immediately established a system of appointed assistant guidance and placement officers to take the place of the outing matrons, both to develop educational and training opportunities for Indian girls and boys, and to manage their employment.[3]

In April 1932, at the same time as she investigated the Tucson situation, Stewart had asked Taylor, who was then working out of her residence as Chingren had always done, for her thoughts on setting up a formal employment office for women in Phoenix. Taylor's labored response revealed her to be out of step with the reformist inclinations of the administration. "Very few" of the Indians she dealt with in Phoenix were capable of work other than housework or positions in the boarding schools, according to Taylor, and even those who were could earn better money in domestic service. With employment opportunities disappearing all around, private domestic service was the only viable option for girls that Taylor could see. "The protection, influence and training that the girls get in the home is what most of them need," she asserted, and the supervision of the

Indian Service would be needed "for a long time to come. If turned loose, so large a percent of them would become prostitutes that people would be afraid to take any of them into their homes."[4]

It was possibly at this juncture that it occurred to Stewart, having just informed the Sells agency superintendent Jasper Elliott that Light's position would be abolished, to send Taylor to Tucson. An old acquaintance of Taylor from the San Carlos reservation was in fact being relocated to Phoenix to set up a new Indian employment bureau under Burton's direction. Ted Shipley's experience had been in overseeing the employment of Navajo and Apache workers in the cotton industry. It might be most expedient, Stewart considered, to have Shipley's wife take over the female placement work from Taylor, either formally or informally, at least until another arrangement presented itself.[5]

In the first week of June, Burton called on Taylor at her home in Phoenix, with a telegram from the central Indian Office telling him that she was being transferred to Tucson. Taylor, who had been expecting instead to hear that she was to get new and upgraded working quarters in Phoenix, was shocked and upset. She immediately wrote to Scattergood, demanding to know whether this transfer meant "promotion or demotion" and declaring it was "unfair" to make her move aside for somebody else. She declared that she would trade her experience for "half a dozen degrees," and that whoever replaced her at Phoenix would need at least a year to reestablish all the networks she had made. Burton meanwhile sent off his own letter warning that Taylor had not reacted well, but advising against taking seriously any claims she might make regarding the complexity of her work. Stewart did not even bother to read Taylor's missive, directing her staff that no matter what it said, she believed the transfer desirable, and asking only that if anyone had any doubts upon reading Taylor's letter, that they forward her a copy.[6]

Protest from Taylor's superintendent, Carl Skinner, the principal of the Phoenix Indian School, on the grounds that the work of the placement matron consisted "of a great deal more than placement" and required a woman in whom the girls could confide—he was unaware of the suggestion that Mrs. Shipley might take up the role—was no more successful. He was briskly told that the placement position henceforth came under the jurisdiction of employment and his only responsibility was for the schoolgirls, for whose supervision he was expected to use his own staff.[7] Even Taylor's Quaker niece got nowhere when she appealed to Scattergood. In a personal postscript, Scattergood noted that funds were curtailed "& we have to use what we have to the best advantage." He enclosed a copy of the soothing letter he had written to Taylor, which explained that there was a need at Tucson for "considerable help along the lines of placement and home assistance" and that this work was of "more immediate importance" than the work in Phoenix. Scattergood had assured Taylor that they had no plans to replace her at Phoenix, and that her move had been decided upon "purely from the standpoint of meeting the most important job first and stretching our resources as far as possible." He hoped that she would "understand the spirit back of this change because we know that you can contribute what is needed at Tucson." Taylor did not reply, although her niece wrote back thanking Scattergood for the "very great compliment" the department had made in selecting her aunt for such an important task: "I am sure she ought to feel very happy in the new position."[8]

Taylor most certainly did not. Although Stewart and the Indian Office might have been given pause by Light's insistence on the importance of her position, Taylor arrived suspecting she had been downgraded, and it did not take her long to feel that she was fully confirmed in that belief. Alienated from the Tohono O'odham and resentful of the expectations that the white employers had of her, Taylor was not the kind of woman to keep her grievances to herself. She made her low opinion of the work she been assigned clear to the Office. She would find no favor with Richard M. Tisinger, the Indian Office's superintendent of the Pima and Papago schools, and when the new Collier administration came in, determined to push through major reforms in a way that the Rhoads and Scattergood administration never had, Taylor's protests would rebound upon her.

The irony was not just that Light would have liked to keep her position, but that somebody else at least as committed as Light, and arguably better suited than both Light and Taylor, had earnestly hoped for it. In November 1931, Mrs. Mary A. Jones, a Chippewa teacher at the Phoenix Indian School, sought Tisinger's support for her application when Light retired. In April 1932, Jones wrote to Dr. W. Carson Ryan Jr., the director of Indian education, putting herself forward. The Phoenix school was discontinuing the lower grades that she taught, and Jones knew she would likely be transferred. With her daughter just finishing her first year of high school, Jones was worried about where she might be sent next. Residence in Tucson as the placement matron would allow her to keep her daughter with her through high school and college, she had told Ryan. It was not just pragmatism that motivated her, though. In comparison with teaching, Jones told Ryan, the "possibilities of the position of placement matron are unlimited and I feel that in such a position I can serve my people more effectively."[9]

While numerous Indian women held positions as teachers and matrons in the schools, much fewer Indian women ever held outing, or field, matron appointments under the Indian Service.[10] Jones cast her motives for the outing position in a way typical of those who aimed for the field matron positions, emphasizing their desire to help their people (from a pan-Indian rather than tribal outlook) and their need to look after their children,[11] although there are also clear parallels with Light, who had similarly asked for outing matron work to enable her to be near her daughter.

Had Jones been appointed at Tucson, her career might have followed the trajectory of one of the most influential Native American women to be employed in the Indian Service, and one of the very few to ever work as an outing matron. Cherokee Ruth Muskrat Bronson started as a teacher at Haskell Institute in 1925 and was the outing matron for that school during the late 1920s. Given one of Stewart's new assistant guidance and placement officer appointments in August 1930, overseeing domestic placements at Kansas City, Bronson's career advanced steadily, and two years later she was in charge of administering an educational loans fund and scholarships scheme that she had helped develop. In 1935, she was promoted to associate guidance and placement officer and relocated to Washington, DC.[12] But Jones, quite a bit older than Bronson and lacking her impressive college qualifications,[13] did not seem to appeal. That the unhappy Taylor did, although neither younger nor better qualified than Jones, seems the height of irony.

Taylor arrived in Tucson from Phoenix on July 8, 1932, a month to the day from when she had learned she was being transferred and a week after she officially took up the appointment, as she had to wait until the Lights, reluctantly, moved out of the premises on East Sixteenth Street.[14] Unlike her predecessors, Taylor made no reports of her work in this early period, at least none that have survived. Her glumness, however, can be gleaned from her correspondences. "Hope you found everything all right," Taylor wrote to her former landlord, sorting out her arrears. "I hated to leave my pretty flowers, but that is always my luck." Indian women writing to her, as they had to Light, asking her about jobs in Tucson, met with a consistently despondent response. Taylor told one woman that "there is so little work down here that I cannot place all the Papago girls," and another, "This town is so much smaller than Phoenix that there is not so much demand for help." While Light had also been discouraging, Taylor's replies, verging on outright complaint, reveal her deep sense of grievance about her transfer.[15] To one of her former Phoenix "patrons" (Taylor had wanted to find a girl the woman had employed), the new outing matron was candid: "I think a lot about my girls up there and wonder what they are doing. I am not at all happy over my transfer but will have to make the best of it. Have a better house, climate better but my heart is in Phoenix."[16]

Taylor also continued to make efforts to find places for Phoenix women in preference to Tucson's Indian women, including more skilled positions in hospital work (a new sanatorium having opened up in Tucson) and as maids on the "guest ranches" that catered to tourists during the fall season. Partly this was because she could not actually find the Tucson women. Writing to a Mrs. Mannie Easchief in Phoenix, who had evidently played a similar role in Taylor's career as Mrs. Tiger had for Janette Woodruff, Taylor asked her about any Phoenix girls who might be looking for work. There had "not been many girls from around here asking for work," and Taylor confessed, "I do not know where the Papago girls all are."[17]

She was getting no help in that direction from Light, aggrieved herself and satisfied to watch her replacement flounder. Light gave Taylor a list of twelve employers' names and left her to her own devices, although Light was still in Tucson at least a month after Taylor's arrival and made continual promises to help her.[18]

Taylor's mood would only have darkened when she learned that her own replacement had arrived in Phoenix in the middle of November. Irene Jane Coonan was the new assistant guidance and placement officer at Phoenix, and she came to see Taylor in Tucson in December, wanting her records from Phoenix.[19] A bright and adventuresome woman in her early thirties, Coonan looked to be more than capable of handling the Phoenix work.

Coonan's career began in July 1930, when she was appointed assistant guidance and placement officer at Minneapolis, Minnesota, for a new Indian employment service there. Originally responsible for overseeing girls' and women's employment in the city, Coonan was soon put in charge of the whole office after her male colleague—who accused her of being "frivolous"—resigned in a jealous huff. Next she was transferred to the Kansas City placement office to take over from Bronson, who had gone to Oklahoma in early 1931 to start up the educational scholarships scheme. From Phoenix, Coonan retained her responsibility for the Kansas City center, but left her assistant clerk, a Mrs. Frances Adams (probably an Indian woman) to manage in her absence.[20]

Coonan had the new downtown office that Taylor had coveted and a reformer's zeal to "do a good deal of constructive work." Although supplied with a local assistant by Shipley—Mrs. Easchief's twenty-year-old daughter Viola—Coonan arranged to bring over Peggy (Belva) Coats in the new year to be her clerical assistant in Phoenix. Coats was a Haskell graduate and Coonan's former junior clerk at Kansas City. In February, Coonan started up a girls' afternoon tea on Thursdays in the YWCA. "Miss Eachief had assured me that not ten girls would appear," Coonan smugly reported to Stewart on her first venture, "but we had forty-two and she had to rush out in the midst of the entertainment to lay in an extra supply of refreshments." Using Taylor's list of some three hundred Phoenix employers and information she had gleaned from Easchief, Coonan had Coats draw up a list "of all the girls and their employers regardless of whether or not they were placed by us," and she set about making contacts with them all. One of them was Josephine Roberts, a young Indian woman in Phoenix of whom Taylor was very fond. Roberts wrote to Taylor in January 1933 and mentioned in passing that she had recently "had the pleasure" of meeting Coonan. "She was very nice," Roberts reported. "I hope you are well and like Tucson better."[21]

But Taylor's own activities as far as can be discerned seemed to have ground to a halt altogether. Her efforts at the end of the previous summer to place girls on the tourist ranches, a pet scheme of hers for which she had held high hopes (they "would add a bit of color that would appeal to eastern people," she suggested), had been wholly unsuccessful. As one proprietor explained to Taylor, she had had to "let go" the Indian girl working for her back in August and would not be needing "any girls for a while yet . . . unless the dude season is a roaring success which I very much doubt as most Easterners, more so than Westerners, are so much poorer than before." The others Taylor wrote to just ignored her.[22] The Depression and her alienation from the O'odham community were making it extremely difficult for Taylor to make any headway, and her unfamiliarity with the white employers was a major obstacle.

She was not going to get any closer to the employers, either. Over the winter of 1932–1933, Taylor moved out of Light's old house by the railyards and into the old Tucson Day School quarters. Since the Indian Service doctor (Smythe's successor) had been relocated to Sells, Tisinger and his wife lived there, looking after the four young men attending the University of Arizona as scholarship students. On their departure in December, Taylor moved in. She had been unhappy at East Sixteenth Street, being frightened by the number of "tramps" coming past from the railway every day, but whether she moved to the old school on the outskirts of the Indian village at her own request (as Tisinger would claim) or whether she was moved there at Tisinger's imperious command (as Taylor saw it) is uncertain. Tisinger wanted her there to housekeep for the students when he and his wife left, and it seems likely that as soon as she made one of her incautious complaints about her residence, he swiftly arranged her move.[23] For the first time since Lydia Gibbs's time, the outing matron was living back on the very outskirts of Tucson's southern limits on the border of the Indian village.

Taylor pointedly failed to visit Coonan when she went to Phoenix herself in March. Coonan had asked her if a girl working there from Tucson wanted to transfer to another employer in Phoenix: Taylor claimed the girl did not, but she called upon the Phoenix employer herself, without Coonan, and informed her thus. "I did not know where to locate you," Taylor told Coonan rather mulishly, after the event. Tactfully understanding, Coonan contacted Taylor a little later, to ask whether Taylor could find places for any of the girls from Phoenix Indian School in Tucson. Taylor did not appreciate being patronized, and did not reply.[24]

Taylor was evidently strained and depressed. Losing her parents at a vulnerable age, and spending most of her adulthood under the wing of an elderly husband, Taylor was inclined to be pessimistic. A faded photograph taken of her at the time she entered the Indian Service shows a round-faced, dark-haired woman with a pensive, worried expression. A bookish woman, probably only circumstances had prevented her from having gone on to higher education herself. Alone among the Tucson matrons, Taylor read avidly and broadly, while her results in the Civil Service field matron examinations easily surpassed both Estabrook and Woodruff (Light never sat the exams). Some of her letters, especially those written from Bylas, evidence Taylor's skills as a writer. They also show she had a sharp wit that she did not hesitate to use in her correspondence with the Indian Office. She had no compunction in writing to the Republican politician Warren Harding in 1920, on the eve of his ascension to the US presidency, to express her opinion on the Indian boarding schools. Taylor commented acerbically that the only thing the schools did for the Indians was to send their children back to spread tuberculosis on the reservations. Furthermore, she protested to Harding the injustice of an administration that refused to consult with the people it supposedly served, and stated that most of "the original owners of this glorious country" had "no voice, whatever, in the making of any laws under which they live."[25] But if Taylor was remarkably intelligent and "well-informed," as numerous superintendents and inspectors had observed, she did not possess that "happy facility of cheering up sullen discouraged people."[26] Brooding in Tucson, Taylor was immune to Coonan's solicitude and sunny charm.

In April 1933, Ruth Bronson visited Coonan in Phoenix and together they went to Tucson, so Bronson could see how Tisinger's scholarship scheme was working out. While they were there they called in at Taylor's residence. Coonan reported that Taylor had said she would be "glad to help" her find places in Tucson for the Phoenix student girls over the summer, but that she doubted there would be any work for them, with jobs so scarce; she was really finding it hard to place any girls or women at all, and more of her time was taking up distributing rations and charity flour among the Indians in the village.[27] There is no doubt that Taylor actually said quite a bit more to her two visitors at the time. As Taylor would reveal in the long letter she wrote to Mary Stewart detailing her unhappiness at the Tucson Day School location, Bronson—an Indian woman, no less—had agreed with her that her situation was appalling and told her that "she wouldn't stay in such a place," and Taylor had apparently asked her to speak to the Office on her behalf.[28]

Taylor might have been clever, but she was not wise. If she was aware that Stewart was making enquiries of Coonan about the placement work she, Coonan, was doing in Phoenix—as Stewart had enquired of her the year before—Taylor remained oblivious to the implications. The Office was now very seriously considering disbanding the outing work in Arizona. Stewart probed Coonan, asking her if more of her work really would be classified as "welfare," and whether perhaps the Indian women of Phoenix were not quite ready to avail themselves of a fully equipped employment service. Coonan's considered and politic response was that she intended to threaten the communities on the reservations with the withdrawal of her services, unless the girls and women working complied with the expectations on them (namely, to stop leaving their places to go back and forth to the reservations).[29] It was not an ideal time for Taylor to declaim how she could not find work for girls or women, and how she spent all her time instead distributing food to the needy.

And further changes were imminent. At the end of that month, April 1933, a new commissioner of Indian affairs, John Collier, was sworn in. Collier, long an outspoken critic of Indian Affairs administration and particularly of the cultural assimilation policies, had been profoundly disappointed with the Rhoads and Scattergood administration. Now, appointed by the new president, Franklin D. Roosevelt, on the advice of his powerful secretary of the interior, Harold Ickes, Collier and his new assistant commissioner, William Zimmerman, would work "at a frenzied pace" to try to push through the reforms that Rhoads had not achieved.[30]

The new commissioner took an immediate and close interest in what was happening with the outing matron in Tucson. Only four days after taking office, Collier wrote to Coonan expressing his concern that Taylor had not been making regular reports: "As far as we are able to judge, a goodly portion of her work does not deal directly with placement. . . . We should like to know how much of her time is given to placement, the character of the work done, what is accomplished, and the need for that type of work in Tucson."[31] Then, without waiting for Coonan's reply, he wrote to Taylor, advising her that Coonan would be visiting her shortly in Tucson as the Office was "gathering some data . . . regarding the employment situation." When Coonan did reply, simply to say that she could not comment much on Taylor's work, the commissioner directed her to make another trip to Tucson to provide "in as much detail as possible, the information asked for." Coonan had only just taken possession of a car provided by the Indian Office—"I celebrated . . . by hauling girls all Saturday morning"—and she set off for Tucson the next day. Coonan spent the next two and half days in Tucson with Taylor, accompanying her about her business.[32]

Coonan's official report on Taylor was sent in a few weeks later. Coonan provided a detailed description of Taylor's "placement work," which Taylor estimated took up about a quarter of her time. "A large part of the placement work is of a nature peculiar to the Indian Service," Coonan began:

> Mrs. Taylor calls it "messenger" work. The Indians live in a village several miles in area on the outskirts of town. None of them has a telephone. A large number of the calls which come in are not from employers who wish some applicant on file at the bureau referred, but from employers who for some time have employed a certain Indian man or woman and again wish his services. They do not want the bother of going to the village themselves so they call the Indian office to have the message delivered. As Mrs. Taylor has no assistant she has herself to take the message to the village. If the Indian desired is not at home and she finds on telephoning that the employer is willing to try someone else she must again return to the village to look up some other worker to refer.

Evidently the pattern established under Light had persisted with Taylor, although being now located in close proximity to the Indian village, Taylor no longer had to make the two-mile drive back and forth. Coonan put the situation bluntly: Taylor was a "go-between for the Indians who have no telephone and employers who would not engage Indians if they had to bother to locate them."

Coonan was concerned nevertheless that the central administration understood there was a distinct need for the placement service. There were "approximately 500 Papagoes" in Tucson, and in addition to those already working, the Sells superintendent had remarked there were about a hundred more girls on the reservation who would take the work if it could be found for them. Taylor had also reported there were about fifty more girls in the Indian village wanting work.

With the closure of the mainstream federal employment office in Tucson that month, the YWCA was the only other agency providing no-charge placement services in Tucson. Coonan's enquiries of the director, Mrs. Buchanan, however, disclosed that employers after Indian girls were being referred from there to Taylor, and that the YWCA was disinclined to assist Indian women. "Very few Indian girls apply to us for work and not many Indian women," Buchanan apparently told Coonan. "We are not very successful in placing them. Most of our calls are from Easterners who do not wish to employ Indians. I do not understand Indians and am not very successful in dealing with them."

Coonan pointed out that there was, in fact, a demand for their labor in Tucson, considering that Taylor was managing to place from 4 to 5 girls and women a week, or about 200 to 250 a year, which could be compared to the 620 non-Indian women placed out in the past twelve months by the YWCA. Assisting Indian women to find this work, Coonan argued, was a method of ensuring that more Indians were "self-supporting" and less were on the "ration rolls." Coonan's case was that the government was obliged to continue to furnish a placement service—at least, if they still wanted Indian girls and women to be employed.[33]

It was a question she might well ask. Collier supported the preservation of "traditional"—that is, non-urban—Indian cultures and would in time appoint a new director of education, Willard W. Beatty, to develop a "progressive education" curriculum, teaching skills connected with rural life.[34] The 1928 Meriam report on Indian affairs had not been enthusiastic when it came to women's paid work. Where

Indian people lived off the reservations in towns, the report's authors regarded the ideal to be "a permanent home for every Indian family, supported, in the main, by the earnings of the husband." They had further called for a government policy that deliberately targeted Indian gender relations, arguing that the traditional balance of labor had been "destroyed" in many Indian communities: "The men's work as hunters, trappers, and warriors has disappeared, but the work of women continues much the same as ever. Government offices should use every effort to make the men realize that new tasks should replace the old, and that every man should assume the same responsibility for the protection and care of his own family as his ancestors did for theirs."[35] We might imagine that the Collier administration shared a similar outlook. However, the vision of urban women as housewives supported by the wage labor of men conflicted with the everyday realities of Indian life in the Southwest, not to mention the long-standing importance and significance of women's economic role in Tohono O'odham society. When the Depression took hold, it was simply untenable. At the same time, across the United States the economic crisis resulted in a renewed enthusiasm for the patriarchal family structure generally, a focus on social policies that sought to find ways of bolstering the position of men, and severe public pressures against the employment of women, especially married women.[36] The impact of the Collier administration on Indian women's roles has been characterized as mostly negative, at least in terms of the political status of Indian women, but there has been no study of its impact on Indian women trying to earn a living in towns and cities at the time.[37] It might be presumed, however, that Collier did not admire the economic contribution of Indian girls and women as domestic servants in the urban households of white women, and that his support for Tucson's outing program could not be taken for granted.

Now Coonan argued that the placement work should be enhanced and strengthened at Tucson, and to that end Taylor should be supported as much as possible. Coonan recommended that, for a period of time, at least a few months, Taylor be permitted to employ an Indian girl from the village, who could take phone calls in her absence and handle routine and menial work, including carrying messages to the village. But most importantly, such an assistant could provide the lonely and frightened Taylor with much-needed companionship.

Being the "only white woman in the village" apart from a missionary's wife, Taylor felt her isolation. She was "in an extremely nervous state," and to have an assistant living with her would relieve her "mental anguish" and thereby improve her efficiency.[38]

Coonan also enclosed a personal note to Stewart, giving her additional details, which she "did not care to include" in her report to the commissioner. Coonan told Stewart that a menopausal Taylor had been ill over the past winter, enduring several operations: "A Mormon woman who came to the house on business found her in such a condition that she returned to her home for some clothes and came in and stayed with her." Now, Taylor was "much better" and "inclined to take a more cheerful view of her situation. You know she felt that the transfer was a reflection on the work she had been doing, and she has brooded quite a good deal over it. . . . The work is woefully in need of organization as are the chores of a social service nature for which she is responsible. Had it not been for her illness and attitude of chagrin because of her transfer she could probably have done more towards systematizing both." Taylor had told Coonan she was unclear whether she was working under the supervision of Burton or of Stewart. "[A] friendly note from you would be good for her morale," Coonan suggested.[39]

No "friendly note" was forthcoming. In the interim, Stewart had requested a report from Taylor directly on her activities, and had received Taylor's long and anguished letter in response. She could have a proper report to Stewart "out in a day or two," Taylor had begun: "The work here is such that a very accurate report would be impossible without I had help [*sic*]. It is entirely different from the work in Phoenix and so much of it does not make a very fancy report. Work is very scarce and of course the Indians are poor." Launching then into her litany of misery—"Some nights it sounds like all the demons of hell were turned loose"—Taylor referred to the discussion she had recently had with Coonan, but without showing a great deal of enthusiasm for a project of building up her placement work. "I think Miss Coonan's idea was that I had better stay with it and ask for help so that I could get out and make the job really worth while," she wrote:

> The big house makes a lot of housekeeping. The Indians come at all hours and employers remind me occasionally that they

> have tried to get me and failed as though I should never leave the house.
>
> I might be able to get some one through the Y.W.C.A. to come out and stay with me, if I could find anyone that could stand the bedlum [*sic*]. So far Tisingers things have been stored in my spare room but suppose they will soon be getting them out.
>
> If you can withhold any decision for a few days I will see what I can do.[40]

The effort Coonan made to convince the Office that the placement work might be developed usefully with Taylor in charge was undone by Taylor's ill-chosen response, and it would not have helped that Taylor did not, it appears, send in the promised report.

Two weeks later, Collier replied to Taylor, agreeing that her "living conditions, as you describe them . . . , are more than unsatisfactory, and you cannot be expected to continue with the situation unchanged," but any decision would be postponed until they heard further from her. That same day, Collier contacted Superintendent Elliott and asked for his recommendation as to "the wisdom" of Taylor continuing at the Tucson Day School location. Collier asked whether it was necessary in fact to keep a government employee at this site at all and, if so, whether an arrangement other than "a woman alone" might be better.[41]

Tisinger wrote to the commissioner himself a couple of weeks later. "Personally, I see no reason for alarm," he told Collier. Taylor was just disgruntled about her transfer from Phoenix in the first place. Her real complaint was "that she could not see the need for abandoning the fine project in Phoenix and transferring her to Tucson where there was very little need for such work. . . . Within a year she finds need for an assistant. Frankly, I do not believe she needs additional help. In fact, I doubt seriously if we can justify the position unless the employee has as her major activities the development of public school relations, and the care of the Hostel for the University boys. I doubt if Mrs. Taylor has the initiative, interest and personality to do this part of the job."[42] Five days later Elliott also replied. While the conditions around the old Tucson Day School were "unfavorable," he stressed that it was important that an Indian Service employee be stationed there, especially if the hostel was to continue another year as planned. He suggested a "trained social worker" be appointed, preferably one with a husband "as it is very difficult to find a lone woman who feels safe to reside here." This employee could "care for such employment work as arises."[43]

The original idea of having a capable and maternalist woman installed to manage Indian domestic workers' relationships with their employers was altogether eroded now, and in its place was the notion of having an educated professional, whose responsibility was more broadly toward managing and monitoring the Indian community, and no longer directed in any way toward the non-Indian community. It is interesting to note that the assumption continued that such an employee should be female. Nevertheless, a shift in attitudes toward gender and women's position as workers can be clearly discerned in the qualification that she should now be best accompanied by a protective male guardian.

Taylor managed to forward her official annual report to the commissioner in July. Her results, in terms of numbers of placements, compared unfavorably with the report filed for the Los Angeles outing center by the outing matron then, Frances Hall, and with that sent in by Coonan for Phoenix, although it did not look quite so poor alongside Etta Long's report for the Sherman Institute. The dramatic difference lay, however, in the numbers of "follow-up visits" made, that is, visits by the outing matron to see the girls working in service. Taylor carried out only 24 such visits in contrast to Hall's 987, Coonan's 331, and even Long's very respectable 209 visits.[44] More than anything, this discrepancy highlights that Taylor was not coping with the role expected of her.

Collier had already decided against Taylor by this point. Stating his conviction that Taylor was completely unsuited to the work in Tucson, Collier asked Elliott and Tisinger to provide a further, detailed recommendation of the sort of person they wanted there, including the qualifications required and the duties that would be performed.[45]

Tisinger's reply outlined four duties of the person to be employed in her stead. These were first, "Cultivation of public school relations," involving "many problems which a trained social worker or visiting teacher should study and analyze"; second, overseeing the students in the hostel, requiring the on-site "presence of an interested, sympathetic" employee; third, "Relief work," that is, taking care of those on the ration list and checking on the sick; and finally, rather grudgingly, "Employment"—"No doubt there is need for this form of activity. Miss Coonan's report of recent date should show the need in this direction." Evidently, from Tisinger's perspective, placement work was an insignificant, if inescapable, part of the position he envisaged. The new appointment "should be a well trained and rather highly cultured type of individual in order to accomplish the desired results," the education superintendent went on, and he recommended that because the cottage was "located in a more or less undesirable section of the city," only a "married couple" should be considered for the position, "or else select an employee who could find a friend to share the cottage with her."[46]

Assistant Commissioner William Zimmerman contacted Taylor in early July. The "whole situation" at Tucson had been under consideration, he told her. Though he hinted at an impending "drastic budget retrenchment," she was told that definite plans had not yet been made, but they would write again. To Elliott, Zimmerman wrote that while there was general agreement that someone was needed at Tucson, and that Taylor could not handle the work alone, appointing a social worker would entail setting up an entirely new position, "which is out of the question at present." As he had told Taylor, there was need for a major budget cut, but he promised the Sells superintendent that the Office was trying to find a way of giving him "more competent assistance."[47]

Indeed, cuts made to the Indian Service appropriations at the start of the new fiscal year in 1933 meant employment services for Indian girls and women were coming under the administration's critical eye. With regard to the two major California outing centers, Los Angeles under Hall, and Berkeley under Bonnie Royce, it was stated that the expenditure entailed of almost $14,000 a year "in one State only for women and girls" was hard to justify. The abolishment of the Berkeley outing center and the appointment there of a guidance and placement officer who would oversee the transfer of Indian services to local social agencies was recommended, while at Los Angeles, where the placement work had been more impressive, the reduction in the budget nevertheless required "a very considerable retrenchment in the work there."[48] There was no mention of the outing centers elsewhere in the Southwest, and the expenditure was likely to be considerably less in Arizona, but we can be sure that the Office would not have wanted to increase their spending here in any way at all. Unsurprisingly, in August, the commissioner told Tisinger that it was "practically certain" that they would be unable to appoint a couple to work from his hostel with their current budget, as the number of Indian people "served did not justify the expense": "We can, however, probably find a more able person than Mrs. Taylor."[49] Such words would have surely galled Taylor.

At the heart of Taylor's disappointment about being moved to Tucson was a deeper unhappiness about the marginality of her position. Entrapped in the old cottage on the edge of the Indian village, Taylor could see that the intermediary nature of the outing matron position in Tucson was a distinct disadvantage for the person in that role. The outing matron position had deteriorated from a position of authority, even some status, to being a virtual dogsbody. All of the outing matrons—and Gibbs before them—had indicated that the work involved was onerous, unrelenting, and often frustrating. Yet up until Taylor's appointment, the position had some kind of meaning and significance that compensated for the workload. It was a meaning that had accrued largely from the symbolic power of maternalism. With the ideal rapidly crumbling, the work of the outing matrons increasingly seemed as menial, tedious, and pointless as the work of the Indian women in white homes itself.

Nevertheless, Taylor wanted—and no doubt needed—to keep her job. In September 1933, she would get a reprieve. The Office's plans to remove her stalled unexpectedly when Tisinger angered Collier by misunderstanding his suggestion, wilfully or otherwise, that he might arrange for one of the boys accommodated in the hostel to assist the person appointed in place of Taylor in the housekeeping. Tisinger had not envisaged his prized scholarship students acting as a matron's unpaid janitors and message boys. He brightly replied that he could easily find someone if there were "funds for such additional labor," whereupon Collier answered, rather sharply, that it was expected that students receiving housing from the government might "give some return to the Government for what they are getting." Perhaps, said Collier, the Office had been mistaken about the nature of the problem at Tucson "for it is not easy to understand the details of local situations from this distance." Collier suggested Tisinger and Elliott talk things over with Taylor instead and work out some alternative plan, then, of providing her with assistance. "When we wrote you we hoped to make some change in the situation. Thus far it has not been possible to make any practical arrangements which would be better than the present one." All machinations for Taylor's replacement promptly stopped at that point.[50]

Perhaps Tisinger, who had been away from Tucson for some time by then, was quickly preoccupied by other matters in his demanding position as state supervisor of Indian education for Arizona. Taylor might have found someone to stay with her around that time, also, though the details are sketchy.[51] Over the next few months, there are signs, too, that her relationship with Coonan improved. Taylor had written to Coonan in September 1933 asking rather stiffly whether Coonan might find out, "at your convenience," whether an Indian woman living in Phoenix, but whose children were in school in Tucson, might be interested in taking a position at Tucson's new Desert Sanatorium. Coonan apparently wrote straight back with little questions and some local gossip, and Taylor, thawing a little, responded with some gossipy details of her own. The assistant cook's position at the sanitorium was becoming vacant because the worker currently there was "not very satisfactory." She was "glad" to hear from Coonan that Edith A—— was returning to her employer, as she had been there three years "and it is really a hard place to fill." She told Coonan that she had provided Mrs. G—— (an employer that Light had known to be detested by the girls) with a girl from Phoenix—"I think Mrs. G——'s place might be a little difficult at least her daughter-in-law says it is harder than hers." And Taylor was surprised to hear from Coonan that another girl she knew had been charged for forging a check in Phoenix—"She worked for Mrs. H—— a summer or two and she thought Francine about perfect." Taylor actually made a social visit to Coonan when she next visited Phoenix, Coonan having invited her in her letter, and Coonan wrote her again very warmly, telling her, "It was nice to see you again even for a short time: I hope the next time you come down I'll get a chance to see more of you."[52]

It seems not many people at all saw much of Taylor. Living where she now did, it is certainly very unlikely that Taylor would have been troubled by the visits of Tucson ladies seeking her advice, even had she known them better, although Taylor was presumably inevitably drawn in to village life much more closely than any of the previous outing matrons had been. But Taylor's unwillingness or inability to keep regular records of her day-to-day work persisted (or, if she did make them, they have not yet been located in the bottomless repositories of the federal archives), and so we are left with barely any insights into what she was doing from mid-1933 onward, and no idea at all about her relationships with either the Tohono O'odham girls or their white employers, as the outing program in Tucson drew quietly but inexorably to its close.

After a gap of some eight months since his last correspondence with Tisinger about Taylor, Commissioner Collier wrote to Elliott recalling "our correspondence last spring in regard to Mrs. Gracie S. Taylor, Senior Placement Matron at Tucson": "The type of work she does there is doubtless useful and keeps her very busy, but it is rather in the nature of a field matron's duties than a placement officer's. It is no longer possible to carry the expense of that office with the greatly reduced appropriation for employment—the fund from which the expenses of this office are now paid." Collier reminded Elliott that Taylor had been assigned to Tucson mainly to carry out Tisinger's hostel project. Copying Tisinger into the letter, Collier asked that if Elliott and Tisinger still wanted a "contact person" at Tucson, they make their specific recommendations as soon as possible.[53]

Tisinger replied a few weeks later with his suggestions both for Taylor's replacement and for a paid assistant who could take over the placement work altogether. As the number of hostel students had fallen to one, the position located at Tucson did not justify spending a lot of money, but it would be a setback to the attempt to train Indian leadership in Arizona, he argued, were the hostel to be discontinued.

Tisinger suggested the transfer of one Miss Doris Weston to Tucson; she could supervise an Indian assistant who could "handle the detail work." Tisinger proposed that Mrs. Jose Pablo, the wife of one of the reservation stockmen and "one of the outstanding Papago women," be given the job.[54]

Doris Weston was a New Hampshire–born woman in her late thirties who had started in the Indian Service as a girls' school matron in 1928, the year the Meriam report was published. In March 1934,

Weston had been reassigned from the Santa Rosa school on the Sells reservation to help Elliott with a "comprehensive" educational program. At the start of that year, a number of northern O'odham villages had been added to the Sells agency, and Elliott persuaded the Indian Office to allow him to employ Weston to conduct a "careful survey" of these newly acquired villages, taking a census of the people and establishing contact with them, with a view to setting up schooling for them.[55]

Somewhat younger than her predecessors, Weston remained a product of the older system, not holding the professional qualifications that were now considered ideal for such educational work. Instead, conflict between the head teacher at Santa Rosa and Weston might account for her reassignment. In the course of an investigation of corporal punishment in the schools that would be carried out by the Collier administration in August 1934, the principal of Santa Rosa accused Weston of having cruelly punished eight children when she was employed there, by making them kneel in the hot midday sun. (The charge was investigated, but as none of her other associates could recall the alleged incident, except one who could not recall any details, and she herself did not admit anything, it was decided that no action needed to be taken.) If Elliott was aware in early 1934 of the head teacher's complaints about Weston, perhaps her special assignment had been an expedient way of dealing with this employee.[56]

That investigation was still to come in May 1934, when Tisinger forwarded Elliott a copy of his letter recommending Weston to replace Taylor. Tisinger explained that he saw no reason why Weston could not supervise the educational work in the Tucson Indian village, along with her duties out on the reservation. But he did not expect her to have anything to do with the placement work and, clearly resenting having to allot any part of his budget whatsoever to it, continued, "I would prefer seeing this work under a woman like Mrs. Joe Pablo." Elliott endorsed all Tisinger's recommendations to the Office, declaring that the placement work at Tucson "hardly justifies the present cost, and it is believed that an Indian woman of Mrs. Pablo's ability could carry it on satisfactorily," as well as the housekeeping at the hostel.[57]

Clearly, neither Tisinger, nor Elliott now, saw any value or purpose in the outing program. Not only was it no longer seen as necessary to control and supervise the behavior of Indian women working in town, they did not see even the need to assist Indian women in finding work, the argument that Light had made successfully only a few years previously. Taylor herself had been unwittingly instrumental in that change in outlook by her vocal complaints. Tisinger manipulated the question of Taylor's replacement to install a person to administer his educational reform program and in the process secured the assistance of an Indian woman, presumably at a lower wage, to keep up the housekeeping at the hostel. It seems ironic that as domestic service fell out of favor as an occupation for Indian women in the authorities' eyes, Indian women were put forward as being perfectly suited to carry on whatever placement work might be still expected.

Following a special meeting convened in Kansas City in May 1934, Mary Stewart made the formal recommendation that the position of senior placement matron at Tucson be abolished and "Mrs. Taylor should be dropped." Things moved quickly after that. Elliott and Taylor were both notified in June that Taylor's position was effectively abolished from the end of that month, and that as there was no other vacancy for Taylor, she was to be "separated" from the Indian Service. Elliott was asked to supply a statement of costs for repairs to the Tucson Day School buildings necessary to fit them for Weston's and Pablo's accommodation.[58]

How might we imagine Taylor felt when she received the assistant commissioner's letter? "I want you to know that I sincerely regret whatever inconvenience may be caused you in the abolishment of this position," Zimmerman wrote, "and that we appreciate very much the good work you have done for the Indians while in the Service." As Taylor left no recorded response, we can only speculate. Taylor could apply for a small Indian Service pension when she reached the age of fifty-five, in 1938, but she faced an uncertain future. No doubt she felt she had been duped and discarded, as she had suspected all along.[59]

This time there was no protest from the Tohono O'odham. Taylor did apparently enlist the support of her political contacts. The outspoken and argumentative Arizona Democratic senator Henry Ashurst wrote to Collier about the abolishment of her position, but the senator was smoothly told that the changes being made by the administration in "the policy of handling placement work for girls and women" over the past two years were made in the interests of "efficiency and economy."[60] Ashurst, a former chairman of the Senate Committee on Indian Affairs, who had intervened on Superintendent McQuigg's account many years earlier and urged Woodruff's retention in 1929, then forwarded a letter from a Reverend Beal of Tucson claiming that Taylor had been most "unfairly dealt with."[61]

John Collier, insulted, responded at length to Ashurst, declaring that this was not so. His letter highlights the way in which the new administration saw what was being done in terms of reform to the outing system and the outing matrons themselves. The kind of position held by Taylor, "requiring no very definite training or qualifications," Collier told Ashurst, had been gradually abolished, and Taylor's was one of the last to go. The reason for the abolishment of these positions was the cut in appropriations for Indian employment. No new position had been set up in lieu of Taylor's former position, and the work that would be undertaken by Weston, from the house in which Taylor formerly resided, would "cover a broader range" than Taylor's work. "We regret very much the loss and disappointment which this change has meant to Mrs. Taylor," the commissioner concluded, "but under the circumstances no other action was possible."[62]

Isabella Greenway, a popular Arizona congresswoman, then wrote to Collier, as a fellow Democrat, asking him to consider finding another position for Taylor in the Indian Service. But Zimmerman told Greenway firmly that the only position of matron remaining was in the boarding schools, requiring "a specific type of training and experience" that Taylor did not have. The kind of position she had held was abolished altogether, and there was no vacancy in any position in the Indian Service for which she would possibly be eligible. It was an ignominious end to Taylor's career, and indeed to the outing matron program in Tucson as a whole.[63] outing was over in Tucson, and would quickly be forgotten.

8

"—*For a time, at least*"

History and the Outing Matrons

ON THE EVE OF DORIS WESTON'S appointment at Tucson in July 1934, the state supervisor of Indian education, Richard Tisinger, expressed the hope that the planned arrangement for Mrs. Pablo to assist Weston would go ahead: "They should make a good pair." But if Jose X. Pablo's wife, a senior woman who had helped Janette Woodruff in the 1920s, did in the end take over the responsibility for supervising Indian domestic employment, Weston does not appear to have been anxious to give her the credit. Instead, Weston soon became enthusiastic about developing a career in Indian domestic placement work herself, envisioning "unlimited possibilities ahead for a permanent business of increasing growth and value."[1]

Weston quickly observed that Indian women were "fast becoming the main support for both children and husband," apparently unaware that this had been the case since at least the start of the Depression.[2] A report she made on employment in 1935 revealed that other patterns continued unchanged. Most of the Indian women earned their livelihood through paid housework; married women with homes in the village preferred day work, while "single girls" usually lived on their employers' premises. Tucson's Jewish families liked to employ Indian girls, Weston noted with interest, and even had their own representative who contacted her with their requests, but there were also "many white women who prefer the Indian over all others. . . . The better class of women is of course interested in her social and economic advancement, aiding and advising her whenever she can. . . . any race prejudice is reduced to the minimum. Working girls should recognize their opportunities and realize that all about them are helpful individuals and city organizations ready to boost them when they themselves are ready to be boosted." Weston had in mind introducing a system of "training" for the young women, enabling them to demand higher wages. "As a committee of one, I am personally going to see what can be done to further the training of these girls who go so unprepared into the homes of their employers. Some opportunity will present itself this year," she wrote hopefully.[3]

Weston's faint tone of admonition toward the Indian women suggests her ongoing struggle to control them. Her card files revealed another pattern that continued—the girls' determination to suit themselves. Eliciana G——, for instance, who "walked out" of a job Weston had found her after only three days, telling Weston that from now on "she would find work in town by herself," was not untypical.[4] Where once Woodruff had railed against those young women who refused to "mind" her, Weston had no option but to accept their assertiveness and independence without complaint. With no record of how and what Mrs. Pablo was doing in regard to helping the young women find employment, we can only assume that many of the girls saw offers of assistance, from Weston at least, as unnecessary and irrelevant.

Nevertheless, Weston evidently found the work of placing the Indian girls and women stimulating and rewarding. So much so, in fact, that after only one month at Tucson she approached the Indian Office's regional employment supervisor in Los Angeles, E. L. Compton, about the possibility of taking the newly established position of social worker in Los Angeles in place of the outing matron there. Refused partly on the grounds of her lack of university qualifications, Weston then drew up an ambitious "Indian Employment Expansion Plan" for Tucson.

Weston's plan could be seen as an assertion of the importance of women's work, both her own and that of the Indian domestic workers. It entailed setting herself up in a downtown business office, from which she could arrange and organize positions for Indian women with white employers as a professional, modern agency. It would have meant a strong endorsement and recognition of the economic contribution made by O'odham women workers, as well as establishing a key authoritative role for herself as an employment agent.[5]

But neither Tisinger nor the new superintendent at Sells, Theodore Hall (he had replaced Jasper Elliott in September 1934), were at all impressed, and both were distinctly opposed to Weston relocating downtown. Forwarding her plan to Commissioner of Indian Affairs John Collier's new director of education, Willard W. Beatty, Hall remarked offhandedly that undoubtedly much good could be done by broadening Weston's field, but as it was she "devoted practically her full time to employment matters," and were her field broadened any further, she would not be able to attend to any of her community work duties. Hall proposed instead that Weston be reassigned to the Office's Indian employment division, under Compton's direction, while he was provided a replacement community worker, stationed on the Sells reservation.[6]

Any suggestion that funding might go into placement work for women was unlikely to meet with approval. All around Weston at that very moment, the Indian employment services that catered to girls and women were being scaled back or closed altogether—not just the old outing matron positions that had been targeted at the start of the 1930s, but even the various guidance and placement offices that had been set up in their stead. At Phoenix, young Viola Easchief was now left in charge of women's employment, under Ted Shipley's direction, as first Irene Coonan and then Belva Coats departed. Coonan, who returned to Kansas City, was replaced there in 1935 when she got married, but the Kansas center itself was shut down altogether in July 1936, just as Weston sent through her plan.[7] By that time, the outing centers at Los Angeles and Oakland in San Francisco, under threat since 1933, were each in the charge of a social worker. Weston was mistaken in thinking the position at Los Angeles might provide opportunities for expanding a placement business. The role of the social worker here, as at the Berkeley outing center at Oakland, was to oversee the transfer of all the placement functions to other agencies.

A statement concerning the Oakland center prepared by the assistant director of education, Mary Stewart, the following year gives a clear depiction of the official attitude to women's employment. Explaining that the present office was based on an "entirely different policy" from the original, Stewart elaborated that the center should serve as a link, not between employers and Indian women but between the Indian people and white social and welfare services in the cities. The social worker's role was to assess and refer applicants to those mainstream services that would serve them best. The emphasis then had shifted distinctly from regulating Indian women's paid work (and managing the relations within employment) to funnelling indigent Indian people into welfare services. "This service involves training not only the Indian in adjustment to his environment but the white groups in their responsibility to him," Stewart concluded. The concern about attitudes and behavior of Anglo-Americans continued, but now they were to be reconstructed not as benevolent and civilizing employers but rather as the willing providers of the social services they constructed for the poor and indigent of their own.[8]

In July 1936, Stewart's successor, Paul Fickinger, directed Hall to use his authority over Weston: "As I understand it, her chief employment activity evolves [*sic*] around the placing of Indian girls and women in household positions. Perhaps this work is not as important as some other phases of activity which could logically come within the scope of her direction. . . . She is one of your employees, classified as a community worker, and the problem seems to me to be one of administrative direction which you yourself can control."[9]

Fickinger also suggested Hall move Weston back out to the Sells agency headquarters on the reservation. Two years on, Hall did move Weston to Sells, where her main responsibility was to be handling applications by Indians for social security benefits—"A most logical use of Miss Weston's time," Fickinger commented. Although Weston tried to continue arranging domestic placements for women in Tucson, from April 1939, she ceased any such work altogether.[10]

As the anonymous writer of that newspaper piece advertising Indian servants in 1902 had predicted, the outing program was not going to last forever. In Tucson, it had lasted twenty-five years—twenty if we acknowledge it concluded when Taylor's position was abolished. The outing program had undergone some significant shifts in purpose and practice since the appointment of Tucson's first outing matron, Minnie Estabrook. It began with the impulse by a beleaguered superintendent to control Indian women's troublesome presence in a race-conscious town, and the need to ensure that relations between the races were orderly and contained and the authority of the Indian

Service upheld. Institutionalized and expanded under Janette Woodruff's direction during the 1920s, outing had become a kind of combined employment bureau and reassurance to white employers by Libbie Light's time. And then, it became mere "messenger work," the matron's position a wasted allocation of jealously eyed resources. If a pressing urgency to control the behavior of Indian girls and women was the underlying reason for the outing system in Tucson in the beginning, that originating impulse had long been forgotten. The role of the outing matron, similarly mystified and obscured, would fade soon from memory and history.

An assumption had grown up over the years that outing and the outing matrons had been provided by the state as an act of benevolence toward an improvident and vulnerable people. This was clearly the way the history of outing was viewed by Light when she defended her position in 1931 and 1932. Doris Weston, similarly concerned to stress the importance of her work, prepared her own "Brief History of Tucson Indian Employment Bureau" not long after she started at Tucson, tracing the beginnings of the institution to Lydia Gibbs's move out of the Tucson Day School and into town. But Weston seemed to know nothing of the outing matrons who followed Gibbs, with the exception of her immediate predecessor Gracie Taylor.[11]

Janette Woodruff attempted to capture the history of outing in Tucson in her retirement. With the help of a college history teacher in Cheney, Washington, Woodruff prepared an autobiography based on her personal memoirs, records, and reminiscences. In the book, published in 1939, Woodruff, her plain-speaking voice replaced with the dulcet tones of a lady philanthropist, was vague about both her predecessor Minnie Estabrook and her successor Libbie Light. She represented her own work, however, as helping unfortunate and grateful Indians. Nostalgic and heavily romanticized, and imbued with a strong defense of her "civilizing" mission, Woodruff's history became unfashionable, while its unreliability made it less than useful for historians, other than as a document of such attitudes.

The complacency and self-satisfaction evinced by Woodruff, Light, and Weston in their understanding of outing was a product of the outing system itself: it produced its own effects on Anglo attitudes toward Indian people by officially attempting to fix young Indian women in a position of subservience and deference to white women.

Notwithstanding the young women's own active engagement with the system on their own terms and the development of a distinctive urban female culture that their work in town gave rise to and intersected with, the outing system generated a belief that Indian women actually needed the assistance of the outing matrons in finding and keeping work. Outing obscured the fact that Indian girls and women had worked on their own terms prior to the introduction of the system, that they had continued to do so throughout the various regimes of the outing matrons, and that they would continue to work to support their families and larger communities when government intervention ended, right up into the late twentieth century.[12] Intended to control and contain the turbulent presence of young Indian women in white households and suburbs, outing had successfully concealed the agency of Indian women in their own past. Jarring with the lived experience of the O'odham women who fought hard for their own and their families' survival, it is not surprising that it would seem to have been dismissed entirely from the Indian women's recollections, along with the outing matrons themselves.

My hope in this book has been to offer an alternative history, one that underlines the profound anxieties and tensions that gave rise to the outing program in the Southwest and in Tucson, particularly, explains how these ran throughout the duration of the program, and illuminates the paradoxes and conflicts they generated for the women instructed to carry out the program. With regard to those Indian girls and women who worked as servants in Tucson's households, my main concern has been to respect their role as active agents in their own histories, not as symbols of Indian despair but rather as flesh and blood working women whose lives and experiences were critical to the historical development of cross-cultural relations as well as to the survival and strength of their own families and communities. But their fuller histories, histories that centralize and articulate their perspectives and interpretations, remain histories yet to be told. The outing matrons whose sources inspired me to begin to delve further in the first place have been the central focus of this study.

The matrons, too, were real working women, who played their own active and pivotal roles in a shared history of women's experience. As white women living in the midst of colonization, the outing matrons were not ciphers of colonization nor were they—especially they—by any means innocent bystanders.[13] As the outing matrons carried out the project and policy of controlling O'odham women's domestic labor, their role and posture prescribed by maternalist ideals, they were among the most active agents of colonization. Officially excluded from making policy, the outing matrons nevertheless had a major influence on the nature and development of the outing program on the ground.

In addressing the complicity and accountability of the Tucson outing matrons, we can examine their location in the structures of colonization in terms of their relationship with Indian people, particularly with Indian girls and women, and more broadly within cross-cultural history. It is clear that as white women, they were "always already" in situations of power in their relations with the O'odham, inheriting agency and empowerment from the processes of colonization that preceded them.[14] Furthermore, they were invested with the authority, if not always the legal power, of the state—Estabrook of course had set out to acquire such extra power—and all, even Woodruff, were prepared to use that to their fullest extent to shore up their own position in relation to the O'odham. At the same time, the policies of regulating Indian labor and managing relationships between white and Indian women in the home were carried out by women who were themselves, despite their whiteness, positioned at the less-powerful end of the dominant society, both in terms of the administration of Indian affairs and in terms of their interstitial class status as lower-middle-class rural women (with the notable exception of Estabrook). Their position was unusually complex and their power unusually nuanced, in that they were positioned as intermediaries between Indian and white women in Tucson, and between both those groups and the state.

It would be simplistic to see the outing matrons as the representatives and agents of the white women who employed the O'odham girls and women in their homes. Although they may have been inclined, to varying degrees, to make alliances with the white employer community and to curry the favor of leading white women, the outing matrons were no more the instrument of the white mistress than they were of the Indian maid. At times when they pressed their own power over Indian women, it was as much to impress the white employers with their authority as the Indian community—and vice versa. There is no doubt that some white employers, perhaps most, believed that the outing matrons *should* be acting on their behalf and in their interests, and much of the time, the employers' interests did align with those of the state. But not always, and particularly when it came to the crucial issue of controlling Indian women's sexuality and their mobility, not for all employers, and not for all matrons.

The outing matrons were, of course, the agents of the state. But even in this regard their mediatory position—as well as their individual motives and plans—complicated and refracted their role. At the outset, during Estabrook's time, it might seem that from the state's perspective it would have been preferable if the O'odham women were not working in town at all. The fact that they did so was the problem that demanded a solution. It goes without saying that the outing matrons would have a vested interest in Indian domestic service, as this was the rationale for their own employment. Heavy-handed, eagle-eyed Estabrook, however, ended up stirring up even more problems for the authorities. Under Woodruff's solicitous and smoothing regime, in contrast, the domestic employment of O'odham women in Tucson was accepted and endorsed by the state—despite the Indian Office's early qualms about the wages the young women were receiving and the temptations they were being exposed to. This change was brought about largely by Woodruff's adroit capacity to represent the issues and needs of Indian workers and white employers back and forth to each other, while ensuring both groups were aware of her primary directive to control the Indian women's sexuality, and her ability to then represent both back to the federal administration. Woodruff seems to have been a skilled cultural broker and diplomat, even allowing for the care she took in maintaining that image.

Light was different. She came into the role evidently expecting to act as the employers' friend and ally, and for the first year and a half of her appointment, that was how she acted. Yet it was Light who might have uncovered a pattern of illicit and traumatic sex abuse and abortion that revealed the outing's tranquil surface in Tucson in the 1920s to be an illusion, masking very deep running waters indeed. Light's shift in perspective at this point, symbolized in her protective defense of Lena and Juana, was clumsy and undeniably self-interested, but in couching her defense of the outing matron position in terms of its importance to the O'odham women and their community, she succeeded in persuading a reluctant central administration it was worth continuing. For Taylor, however, smarting over her transfer from Phoenix, the role of the outing matron in Tucson was all but redundant, as indeed it was for the reformist Collier administration.

The outing matrons' intermediary role meant that their day-to-day lives were intimately connected with those of the white employers and, even more so, with those of the O'odham workers. Because of this enmeshment, personal connections with individual Indian girls and women could have a profoundly formative influence on the way the outing matrons carried out their responsibilities. The impact of Woodruff's initial relationship with Mrs. Tiger, for instance, undoubtedly set the tone for Woodruff's tenure over the coming years, and we cannot underestimate the importance of Tiger and the other women who worked in Tucson in directing the way that Woodruff approached her work. Recall too, the petitioners who wrote of Estabrook, "We were just beginning to get acquainted with her," when she was sent away: had she tried to work more closely with them from the outset, she may have lasted longer. Light's determination to maintain her social distance from the O'odham girls and women was challenged to some extent by the girls' and their families' expectations of her, and apparently undone altogether by whatever transpired between her and Lena in a prison cell in Phoenix, which in turn had a transformative effect on her activities. Even the despondent and lonely Taylor, alienated as she was from both the employers and the O'odham in Tucson, demonstrated in her unwillingness to separate from the Indian women she knew in Phoenix the significance of such personal connections forged between matrons and maids.

The outing matrons trod the line between those Indian and white women who came together in the arena of household domestic work. Intervening on behalf of the colonizing state, they were the human conduit between the Indian and the Milgahn communities, regulating and invigilating this potentially destabilizing point of cross-cultural relations—the "go-betweens." In the process, they also became the link between those households and the central administration of the state, the Office of Indian Affairs in Washington, DC. It was a position that was both liminal and ambiguous. The outing matrons, required to delineate the categories and boundaries of rule, might find themselves on the one hand making representations to the Office on behalf of the needs of the Indian women, as they perceived them to be, and on the other hand carrying out policies and practices that overrode Indian interests and indeed were designed to constrain indigenous power and autonomy. They had to ensure that within white homes white employers were adequately supervising and controlling Indian women, and yet to carry out that duty effectively, they had to win the trust and support of both employers and workers, as well as the larger communities of both. All the paradoxes, anxieties, and tensions that eddied and swirled around the young Indian women working in white women's homes fell to the outing matrons to negotiate and manage.

For Gracie Taylor, trapped in the decaying quarters of the old Tucson Day School by the expectations of white employers during the day, and by her own fears at night, literally alone on the border between white and Indian Tucson, it was all too much. Outmoded and unwanted, Taylor had not yet lived even half her life when she was retrenched. Incredibly, Taylor would live to be 102 years old. When she died in 1985, the last outing matron of Tucson was buried next to her husband in an Arizona cemetery some 60 miles from the San Carlos reservation where she had been field matron, and 125 miles on Interstate 10 heading east out of Tucson.[15] But her fretful, restless voice still rises from the archives of an interventionist state and demands that this history, in all its painful complexity, not be forgotten.

Acknowledgments

THIS BOOK WOULD NEVER have come to be, had not the wonderful, and extremely knowledgeable, Gwen Granados first drawn my attention to some little-known records of these women who worked for the Indian Service in Arizona, when I was visiting the National Archives and Records Administration repository at Laguna Niguel in 2007. I am also indebted to archivist George Briscoe, especially, for his crucial help in locating the material at the central repository in Washington, DC. At the National Personnel Records Center in St. Louis, Missouri, archivist Theresa Fitzgerald has been incredibly supportive. Jill McCleary at the Arizona Historical Society has been a great help as well. I'd also like to acknowledge the small and hard-working armies of retrievers at the places I've been, who untiringly brought me carts upon carts laden with boxes and boxes, and in some instances advised me directly.

This book started out as a conference paper, and I'd like to thank the panel organizer, Susan Gray, for her ongoing collegial interest in my work. Two members of the audience from Tucson, Margie Youngo and Roger Nichols, were especially encouraging and generous in their responses, and I greatly appreciated their assistance when I later visited Tucson and their ongoing encouragement to develop this book. A very big thank-you to Christine Szuter, who put me in touch with Patti Hartmann, the acquiring editor of the University of Arizona Press (UAP). Patti saw the value in the project, and her enthusiasm has been carried over by Kristen Buckles. It has been a real pleasure to work with Kristen and the rest of the staff at the UAP, as well as my copyeditor Sharon Hunt. The anonymous readers of the original proposal and manuscript offered cogent and useful advice.

The University of Newcastle, in New South Wales, Australia, provided the funds to carry out the original research back in 2007.

Further research, and the writing of the book, were carried out with the generous support of an Australian Research Council Future Fellowship. My fellow academics and support staff at the Research Institute for Social Inclusion and Wellbeing and in the School of Humanities and Social Sciences at Newcastle University have given me a warm and collegial environment to work in. I've appreciated the help and advice I've received from various colleagues and friends, including Mary Romero, Cathleen Cahill, Lisa Featherstone, and Karen Vered.

And of course there is my beautiful family, whose support is constant and unwavering. My husband, John Maynard, a fellow historian and soul mate, has not only been my sounding board and advisor but has also held the home front and looked after our three boys while I've been away researching, most dramatically during a freak storm in 2007. To John I am deeply grateful, for his love and his belief in me, and for his steadying reminder of the most important things in life.

Notes

Abbreviations

AHST	Arizona Historical Society, Tucson
ARCIA	*Annual Report of the Commissioner of Indian Affairs*
CCF	Central Classified Files, Bureau of Indian Affairs
CIA	Commissioner of Indian Affairs
IRA	Indian Rights Association Papers, Series I, Correspondence, 1864–1968
LR	Letters Received, Bureau of Indian Affairs, 1881–1907
LSE	Letters Sent, Education, Bureau of Indian Affairs
PIS	Phoenix Indian School
PISEO	Phoenix Indian School Employment Office
RG 75 NAB	Records of the Bureau of Indian Affairs, Record Group 75, US National Archives and Records Administration, National Archives Building, Washington, DC.
RG 75 NAFW	Records of the Bureau of Indian Affairs, Record Group 75, US National Archives and Records Administration, National Archives Southwest Region, Fort Worth, TX
RG 75 NAR	Records of the Bureau of Indian Affairs, Record Group 75, US National Archives and Records Administration, National Archives Pacific Region, Riverside, CA (formerly Laguna Niguel, CA)
RG 146 NPRC	Records of the US Civil Service Commission, Record Group 146, National Personnel Records Center, St. Louis, MO
RSSE	Records of the State Supervisor of Education (Arizona)
SIA	Sells Indian Agency (Papago)
SIEFCW	Sells Indian Agency (Papago) Indian Employment Files of the Community Worker Doris L. Weston
SRFM	Sells Indian Agency (Papago) Reports of the Field Matrons 1910–1932

Chapter 1. Introduction: The Outing Matrons of Tucson

1. G. Taylor to M. Stewart, May 18, 1933, Box 3 (T–Z), RSSE, PIS, Boxes 1–3, RG 75 NAR.

2. Joseph, Spicer, and Chesky, *The Desert People*, 72.

3. Report of the Superintendent of Schools, Indian School Sites, *ARCIA* 1906, 445.

4. For a narrative overview of Tohono O'odham history, see Erickson, *Sharing the Desert*.

5. Trennert, "From Carlisle to Phoenix," 267–291; "Victorian Morality," 113–128; and *The Phoenix Indian School*. Outing gets a mention in virtually all general histories of Native American boarding schools (as well as at least a passing reference in histories of specific schools), but for the most significant examples (in order of appearance), see Adams, *Education for Extinction*, 159–163; Archuleta, Child, and Lomawaima, *Away from Home*, 35–37; Reyner and Eder, *American Indian Education*, 139; Lomawaima and McCarty, *To Remain an Indian*, 50–51; Adams, "Beyond Bleakness," 47. For outing programs in the San Francisco Bay area, see Willard, "Indian Newspapers"; Willard, "Outing, Relocation and Employment Assistance"; Markwyn, "'It Was a Place for the Girls to Meet'"; Jacobs, "Working on the Domestic Frontier"; Jacobs, *White Mother to a Dark Race*, 352–369. For the Haskell Institute, see Child, *Boarding School Seasons*, 81–85; Vuckovic, *Voices from Haskell*. For the Sherman Institute, see Paxton, "Learning Gender"; Gilbert, *Education beyond the Mesas*. Ward Churchill has been the most well-known exponent of outing as genocide, arguing that the arduous forced labor of children contributed to their physical destruction, the aim of the boarding school policies: Churchill, *Kill the Indian, Save the Man*, 48–51. The outing program in Tucson, almost entirely overlooked, has been explained as an effort by government authorities to "accelerate assimilation by teaching Indian women to adopt Anglo gender roles": Meeks, "The Tohono O'odham, Wage Labor, and Resistant Adaptation, 1900–1930," 477. Eric Meeks has also referred to outing in Tucson in passing, particularly the "alternatives to dependence" it offered Indian women, in his seminal study of Arizona's racial history: Meeks, *Border Citizens*, 60–62.

6. Ludlow, *Ten Years' Work for Indians at the Hampton Normal and Agricultural Institute*, 36–37; Walker-McNeil, "The Carlisle Indian School," 164; Pratt, *Battlefield and Classroom*, 194–195, 214–215. See also Pratt, "The Way Out," 1177–1180; Lindsey, *Indians at Hampton Institute*, 37–38.

7. Adams, *Education for Extinction*, 157.

8. See, especially, Jaimes, "American Indian Woman," 331–335.

9. The literature on white women and colonialism is extensive. The collection *Western Women and Imperialism* edited by Chaudhuri and Strobel is well known. Other collections and monographs include Ware, *Beyond the Pale*; McClintock, *Imperial Leather*; Najmi and Srikanth, *White Women in Racialized Spaces*; Cole, Haskins, and Paisley, *Uncommon Ground*; Pickles and Rutherdale,

Contact Zones. For white feminism and colonization, see Burton, *Burdens of History*; Newman, *White Women's Rights*; Paisley, *Loving Protection?*; Midgley, *Feminism and Empire*.

10. Trennert, "Victorian Morality," 126. For "true womanhood" and the women employed by the Office of Indian Affairs, see Bannan, *"True Womanhood" on the Reservation*; Herring, "The Creation of Indian Farm Women; Emmerich, "'To Respect and Love and Seek the Ways of White Women,'" 42–93, and passim; Mathes, "Nineteenth-Century Women"; Emmerich, "'Civilization' and Transculturation"; Osburn, "And As the Squaws Are a Secondary Consideration," chap. 5; Wall, "Gender and the 'Citizen Indian'"; Jacobs, "Clara True and Female Moral Authority." Somewhat differently, Jane Simonsen notes that this ideology blended seamlessly with the contemporary movement that brought middle-class women into the professions: Simonsen, *Making Home Work*, 97–109. For the notion of "true womanhood" generally, see Welter's article, "The Cult of True Womanhood."

11. Emmerich, "'To Respect and Love and Seek the Ways of White Women,'" 71–73; see also Bannan, *"True Womanhood" on the Reservation*, 8–9. For mission women in the context of North American colonization particularly, see Pascoe, *Relations of Rescue*; Deutsch, *No Separate Refuge*.

12. Trennert, "Victorian Morality," 122.

13. Carter, "'Completely Discouraged,'" 79–80.

14. See Moore, "'That Critical Juncture'"; Paisley, *Loving Protection?*; Haskins, *One Bright Spot*.

15. Jacobs, *White Mother to a Dark Race*, 88–93, 354, 359–362. See also Jacobs, "Maternal Colonialism."

16. Cahill, *Federal Fathers & Mothers*, 7, 63–81, 259. See also Cahill, "Only the Home Can Found a State," 247, 260–263, 266. Similar conflicts were embodied in the transgressive career of one of the most powerful white women in the Indian Service, Superintendent of Indian Schools Estelle Reel. See Lomawaima, "Estelle Reel, Superintendent of Indian Schools."

17. For intermarriage, see Woodworth-Ney, "The Diaries of a Day-School Teacher"; Cahill, "'You Think It Strange That I Can Love an Indian'"; Ellinghaus, *Taking Assimilation to Heart*, 82–104; Jacobs, "The Eastmans and the Luhans." For Native American women teachers and matrons, see Cahill, *Federal Fathers & Mothers*, 104–135; Emmerich, "'Right in the Midst of My Own People'"; Rose, "Susan Bordeaux Bettelyoun"; Ahern, "An Experiment Aborted"; Collins, "A Future with a Past"; Gere, "Indian Heart/White Man's Head"; Simonsen, *Making Home Work*, chap. 5; Tetzloff, "Elizabeth Bender Cloud."

18. Emmerich, "'To Respect and Love and Seek the Ways of White Women,'" 91, 95–98, 105–106.

19. Personal record of Amanda Chingren, May 25, 1911, Amanda Chingren Personnel File, RG 146 NPRC. For Woodruff, US Bureau of the Census, *United States Federal Census*, 1870, 1880, and 1900.

20. Comaroff, "Images of Empire, Contests of Conscience," 165–168.

21. Hoxie, *A Final Promise*, 242.

22. See Lomawaima, "Domesticity in the Federal Indian Schools," 230–231; see also Lomawaima, *They Called It Prairie Light*, 86.

23. For discussion of this concept, derived from Michel Foucault's work, see Dean, *Critical and Effective Histories.*

24. See Szasz, *Between Indian and White Worlds.*

25. See Stoler, *Haunted by Empire*, especially Stoler's chaps. 1 and 2; for the American West as a colonized country, see also Belich, *Replenishing the Earth.*

26. McClintock, *Imperial Leather*, 161–164. For domestic service and race/class status, see Palmer, *Domesticity and Dirt*; Rollins, *Between Women*; Tonkinson, "Sisterhood or Aboriginal Servitude?"; Romero, *Maid in the U.S.A.* For domestic service and colonialism, see Hansen, *Distant Companions*; Banerjee, *Men, Women and Domestics*; Chaudhuri, "Memsahibs and Their Servants in Nineteenth-Century India"; Cock, *Maids and Madams*; Locher-Scholten, "So Close and Yet So Far"; Stoler and Strassler, "Memory-Work in Java." Virtually no work has been done on the history of Native American domestic servants, specifically, but there is enough evidence to show that Indian women certainly did work as household servants in the periods of Spanish and both English and Anglo-American colonization. See various references in Salmon, *Domestic Service*, 49–51; Hurtado, "'Hardly a Farm House,'" and *Indian Survival on the California Frontier*; Knack, "Newspaper Accounts of Indian Women in Southern Nevada Mining Towns," and "Nineteenth-Century Great Basin Indian Wage Labor"; Smith, *The View from Officers' Row*; Riley, *Confronting Race*; Silliman, *Lost Laborers in Colonial California.*

27. Rollins, *Between Women*, 155–203; see also Romero, *Maid in the U.S.A.*, 136–141, 153–156.

28. Stoler, "Tense and Tender Ties," 47, 48.

29. Joseph, Spicer, and Chesky, *The Desert People*, 94.

30. Blaine, *Papagos and Politics*, 32.

31. McCarthy, *A Papago Traveler*, 2, see also 72, 82–83, 92.

32. Underhill, *Papago Woman*, x, 16, 32. Underhill did seek Taylor's assistance in locating a male Indian guide at one point: R. Underhill to Mrs. Taylor, n.d., c. March 1933, Correspondence of Senior Placement Matron Gracie S. Taylor 1929–1934, SIEFCW, Box 147, RG 75 NAR. Underhill's ethnological studies of the O'odham, often undertaken in collaboration with Chona, continued into 1934 and 1935 when the community worker Doris Weston was in Tucson, Underhill getting along very well with Taylor's successor later in the 1930s: see various correspondences in Arts & Crafts, SIA Health & Social Welfare Correspondence of the Community Worker Doris L. Weston, Box 214, RG 75 NAR.

33. Underhill, "The Autobiography of Chona, a Papago Woman," 79. As has been noted, "White influence is minimal in [Chona's] story," either by her choice, or Underhill's. Bataille and Sands, *American Indian Women*, 55.

34. Manuel and Neff, *Desert Indian Woman*, 54.

35. Stoler, *Along the Archival Grain*, 23–25, 46–51.

Chapter 2. "Herein may lie the solution to the servant-girl question—": Gender, Race, and Outing

1. "Poor Lo as House Servant," *Castle Rock Journal* (Castle Rock, Douglas County, Colorado), August 29, 1902, 7, from *Chicago Chronicle*, The Colorado Historic Newspapers Collection, http://www.coloradohistoricnewspapers.org (accessed January 4, 2008).

2. R. H. Pratt, Report of the School at Carlisle, August 21, 1886, *ARCIA* 1886, 19; Report of the School at Carlisle, September 12, 1884, *ARCIA* 1884, 186; Report of the School at Carlisle, September 7, 1887, *ARCIA* 1887, 258; Thompson, "John D. C. Atkins," 182–186; Report of the Commissioner of Indian Affairs, September 21, 1887, *ARCIA* 1887, 15–16; Prucha, "Thomas Jefferson Morgan," 193, 197–198.

3. Daniel Dorchester, Report of the Superintendent of Indian Schools, September 5, 1889, *ARCIA* 1889, 316–317.

4. For Haskell's first outing, see Gilcreast, "Richard Henry Pratt and American Indian Policy," 325; Trennert, "From Carlisle to Phoenix," 276; Vuckovic, *Voices from Haskell*, 26. Vuckovic gives the date of summer 1888. For Chemawa, see Trennert, "From Carlisle to Phoenix," 276; Reddick, "The Evolution of Chemawa Indian School," 463, 456. According to Reddick, this experiment (boys were sent to work for a local hops farmer) took place in 1885, but unfortunately she does not provide a source for this date.

5. Pratt correspondence to General Howard, 1895, quoted in Gilcreast, "Richard Henry Pratt and American Indian Policy," 326. See also Pratt, *Battlefield and Classroom*, 314–315; Walker-McNeil, "The Carlisle Indian School," 170–171; Bell, "Telling Stories out of School," 172–176; Gilcreast, "Richard Henry Pratt and American Indian Policy," citing Pratt to Commissioner T. J. Morgan, August 9, 1899 (Pratt papers), 325.

6. T. J. Morgan to W. B. Backus, June 9, 1891, *ARCIA* 1891, 154–55. See also other Backus-Morgan correspondence, *ARCIA* 1891, 151–55. "Let Indians Work," *The McCook Tribune* (McCook, Nebraska), June 19, 1891, Library of Congress, Chronicling America: Historic American Newspapers, http://chroniclingamerica.loc.gov (accessed October 21, 2010). "No Chance for Lo," *The Omaha Daily Bee* (Omaha, Nebraska), June 11, 1891, 8, Library of Congress, Chronicling America: Historic American Newspapers, http://chroniclingamerica.loc.gov (accessed October 21, 2010). Trennert, "From Carlisle to Phoenix," 277.

7. Daniel Dorchester, Report of the Superintendent of Indian Schools, August 16, 1892, *ARCIA* 1892, 586, 588.

8. W. N. Hailman, Report of the Superintendent of Indian Schools, October 1, 1895, *ARCIA* 1895, 340–341.

9. There is extensive literature on this subject. See Castro, "After the Slavers"; Brooks, *Captives and Cousins*; Guiterrez, *When Jesus Came, the Corn Mothers Went Away*; Silliman, *Lost Laborers in Colonial California*; Knack, *Boundaries*

Between; Malouf and Malouf, "The Effects of Spanish Slavery on the Indians of the Intermountain West"; Rawls, *Indians of California*, 81–133; Lack, "Slavery and the Texas Revolution," 181–202, 184.

10. See Hurtado, *Indian Survival on the California Frontier*, 5, 130, 198; Bringhurst, "The Mormons and Slavery"; Ricks, "A Peculiar Place for the Peculiar Institution," 127–130; Castro, "After the Slavers," 374–375, 381; Johnston-Dodds, *Early California Laws and Policies Related to California Indians*, 8–9, 14; Lamar, *The Far Southwest*, 89.

11. "Indian Slavery in New-Mexico," *The New York Times*, February 27, 1863, The New York Times Archives, 1851–1890, http://www.nytimes.com (accessed October 20, 2010).

12. Goff, "William T. Howell and the Howell Code of Arizona," 231. Sections 14–17, Chapter 56, Territory of Arizona Statutes, in Hoyt, *The Compiled Laws of the Territory of Arizona, 1864–1877*, 544–545. Farish, *History of Arizona*, vol. III, 97–101.

13. See Szasz, *Indian Education in the American Colonies, 1607–1783*, 64–66, 219–226; also Hailman, "Education of the Indian," 5.

14. R. H. Pratt, Report of School at Carlisle, August 18, 1885, *ARCIA* 1885, 215; Pratt correspondence, 1900, quoted in Gilcreast, "Richard Henry Pratt and American Indian Policy," 320. Similarly, over in Oregon, the Chemawa superintendent told an interested local settler in 1882 it was "quite out of the question" to allow girls to go out as servants: M. C. Wilkinson to Jay Francis, June 10, 188[2], quoted in Collins, "The Broken Crucible of Assimilation," 498–499.

15. R. H. Pratt, Report of School at Carlisle, September 30, 1882, *ARCIA* 1882, 177–178; Almeida, "The Role of Western Massachusetts," 70, citing Teacher's Meeting Minutes, March 12, 1883; Anne H. Whorten, Report of the Lincoln Institution, Indian Department, November 29, 1886, *ARCIA* 1886, 262–263; Patterson, Emma C. "Your Town and My Town: The Spread Eagle Inn," *Suburban and Wayne Times* (Wayne, Pennsylvania), June 2, 1950, n.p. transcript by Radnor Historical Society, http://radnorhistory.org/archive/articles/ytmt/?tag=native-americans (accessed January 13, 2011).

16. W. Rich, Report of School at Phoenix, September 10, 1892, *ARCIA* 1892, 654; W. Rich, Report of School at Phoenix, July 1893, *ARCIA* 1893, 403; Trennert, "From Carlisle to Phoenix," 281.

17. H. Hall, Report of School at Perris, August 1, 1899, *ARCIA* 1899, Part 1, 389; Harwood Hall, Report of School at Perris, August 7, 1900, *ARCIA* 1900, pt. 1, 482; Estelle Reel, Report of Superintendent of Indian Schools, October 1, 1903, *ARCIA* 1903, pt. 1, 369; Paxton, "Learning Gender," 181.

18. W. Rich, Report of School at Phoenix, July 1893, *ARCIA* 1893, 403; J. E. Ross, Report of School at Genoa, October 13, 1896, *ARCIA* 1896, 379.

19. H. B. Peairs, Report of Haskell Institute, August 8, 1900, *ARCIA* 1900, 487–488. See Trennert, "From Carlisle to Phoenix," 281, for discussion

of Superintendent Harwood Hall's scheme by which Phoenix girls were sent to work in southern California.

20. D. Dorchester, Report of the Superintendent of Indian Schools, September 5, 1889, *ARCIA* 1889, 316–317.

21. E. Reel, Report of the Superintendent of Indian schools, October 20, 1899, *ARCIA* 1899, 442–443; and November 12, 1902, *ARCIA* 1902, 395.

22. E. Reel, Report of the Superintendent of Indian Schools, November 12, 1902, *ARCIA* 1902, 395.

23. W. A. Jones, Report of the Commissioner of Indian Affairs, October 15, 1903, *ARCIA* 1903, 14–15.

24. See Trennert, "From Carlisle to Phoenix," 281–282. E. Reel to Commissioner, May 6, 1900, 31806-1900, LR, RG 75 NAB. Trennert, *The Phoenix Indian School*, 88–89, citing Goodman to CIA, April 11, 1902, 22877-1902, LR, RG 75 NAB. This file is now missing from the records held at NAB. Emma McCowan, head matron at the school under McCowan's superintendency, had received a pay rise, and there is no record of any new appointment being made: *ARCIA* 1899, pt. 1, 642; *ARCIA* 1900, pt. 1, 724; *ARCIA* 1901, pt. 1, 749. When Goodman arrived, the former superintendent's wife had left, of course, and the most senior of the assistant matrons, apparently filling in for her, sent through her application for the position of head matron at the same time, stressing her capacity to superintend the outing girls: K. Orr to Commissioner, April 9, 1902, 22876-1902, LR, RG 75 NAB.

25. W. Jones to Supt. Indian School, Phoenix, Oct. 9, 1902, 58918-1902, LSE, RG 75 NAB (referring to previous communication dated April 22, 1902, probably the letter seen by Trennert, Goodman to CIA, April 11, 1902, 22877-1902, LR, RG 75 NAB).

26. List of Persons Employed in the Indian School Service on June 30, 1902, *ARCIA* 1902, 691. M. Schach to Commissioner, September 25, 1902, 58693-1902, LR, RG 75 NAB. W. Jones to Supt. Indian School, Phoenix, Oct. 9, 1902, 58918-1902, LSE, RG 75 NAB. Trennert, *The Phoenix Indian School*, 88–89, citing Goodman to CIA, October 24, 1902, 64577-1902, LR, RG 75 NAB. Schach was transferred to Albuquerque and a Charlotte Snyder, possibly the wife of the clerk, took over as head matron: List of Persons Employed in the Indian School Service on June 30, 1903, *ARCIA* 1903, 553, 574.

27. L. McPhee to J. B. Alexander, November 18, 1902, 1360-1903, LR, RG 75 NAB.

28. C. W. Goodman to Commissioner, Jan. 2, 1903, 1360-1903, LR, RG 75 NAB.

29. C. W. Goodman to Commissioner, Jan. 2, 1903, 1360-1903, LR, RG 75 NAB.

30. W. A. Jones, Report of the Commissioner of Indian Affairs, October 17, 1904, *ARCIA* 1904, 32. C. W. Goodman, Report of School at Phoenix, September 8, 1904, *ARCIA* 1904, 435.

31. F. E. Leupp, Report of the Commissioner of Indian Affairs, September 30, 1905, *ARCIA* 1905, 5, 12.

32. Knack and Littlefield, "Native American Labor." See also O'Neill, "Rethinking Modernity," 2–3, 7; O'Neill, *Working the Navajo Way*, esp. 2–4; Berman, *Circle of Goods.* Ruth Underhill asserted that an "aboriginal form of wage work" was an "old custom" with the Tohono O'odham and it was "impossible" to say whether or not it predated the Spanish era and the development of a cattle and wheat economy: Underhill, "Acculturation at the Papago Village of Santa Rosa," 313.

33. F. E. Leupp, Report of the Commissioner of Indian Affairs, September 30, 1906, *ARCIA* 1906, 8; F. E. Leupp, Report of the Commissioner of Indian Affairs, September 30, 1907, *ARCIA* 1907, 26.

34. Parman, "Francis Ellington Leupp, 1905–1909," 230; Leupp, *The Indian and His Problem*, 122.

35. See *ARCIA* 1889–1906; see also Witmer, *The Indian Industrial School*, 35, 52.

36. Reports Concerning Indians in Arizona, 115–138, *ARCIA* 1903, 134; Report of School Superintendent in Charge of Pima Agency, *ARCIA* 1903, 130–131; J. B. Alexander, Report of School Supt. in Charge of Pima, Pima Training School, Sacaton, July 22, 1904, *ARCIA* 1904, 148; List of Persons Employed in the Indian School Service on June 30, 1903, *ARCIA* 1903, 574; List of Persons Employed in the Indian School Service on June 30, 1904, *ARCIA* 1904, 677; List of Persons Employed in the Indian School Service on June 30, 1905, *ARCIA* 1905, 559. H. Marten to Commissioner, January 11, 1911, IRA. Personal record of Amanda Chingren, May 25, 1911; Amanda Chingren, retirement record card; A. Chingren to F. Leupp, September 30, 1908, Amanda Chingren Personnel File, RG 146 NPRC.

37. J. B. Alexander to Commissioner, September 7, 1908; J. H. Dortch to James Alexander, May 13, 1909, Amanda Chingren Personnel File, RG 146 NPRC.

38. O. Lipps to E. King, undated, c. August 12, 1918, Correspondence of Oscar H. Lipps, 1918, K–R, Records of the Superintendent, Records of the Chilocco Indian School, RG 75 NAFW. Meriam et al., *The Problem of Indian Administration*, 593–598.

39. E. E. Newton to Commissioner, June 3, 1909, Amanda Chingren Personnel File, RG 146 NPRC.

40. E.E.N. to Miss Cook, June 6, 1909, Amanda Chingren Personnel File, RG 146 NPRC.

41. Pratt correspondence, 1900, quoted in Gilcreast, "Richard Henry Pratt and American Indian Policy," 320, see also 373–382.

42. E. E. Newton to Commissioner, June 3, 1909, Amanda Chingren Personnel File, RG 146 NPRC.

43. J. H. Dortch to A. Chingren, June 29, 1909; F. H. Abbott (Acting Commissioner) to A. Chingren, August 6, 1909, Amanda Chingren Personnel File, RG 146 NPRC.

44. Various correspondences and efficiency reports, 1909–1911, Amanda Chingren Personnel File, RG 146 NPRC.

45. R. Valentine, Report of the Commissioner of Indian Affairs, November 1, 1910, *ARCIA* 1910, 8. For Johnson, see Thoburn, *A Standard History of Oklahoma*, 1742–1744, entry on Mrs. Emma D. Goulette (nee Johnson).

46. See documentation in General Services 31975-10 824, CCF 1907 1939, RG 75 NAB.

Chapter 3. "The good an outing matron can do": The Start of Outing in Tucson, 1913–1914

1. H. McQuigg to E. E. Newton, May 15, 1913, Field Matron Lydia A. Gibbs 1911–1919, SRFM, Box 190, RG 75 NAR.

2. H. McQuigg to Commissioner, May 16, 1913; H. McQuigg to the Commissioner, July 19, 1913, Field Matron Lydia A. Gibbs 1911–1919, SRFM, Box 190, RG 75 NAR.

3. Reports of Farmer in Charge of San Xavier Papago (J. M. Berger), August 27, 1901, *ARCIA* 1901, 189–190; August 28, 1902, *ARCIA* 1902, 168; and November 25, 1903, *ARCIA* 1903, 441–442. For details on the traditional movement of the Tohono O'odham, see Hackenberg, "Pima and Papago Ecological Adaptations," 164–167; Fontana, *Of Earth and Little Rain*, 38–47.

4. Reports of Farmer in Charge of San Xavier Papago (J. M. Berger), August 27, 1901, *ARCIA* 1901, 189–190; August 28, 1902, *ARCIA* 1902, 168; and November 25, 1903, *ARCIA* 1903, 441–442. For the establishment of the Presbyterian Tucson Indian Training School, see H. Brown, *Historical Circular of Indian Training School, Tucson, Arizona*, 3, 13–16. The superintendent of the Phoenix Indian School had controversially recruited thirteen older "Pima" (Akimel O'odham) students from the Tucson school in 1892: Trennert, *The Phoenix Indian School*, 36–38. Peter Booth notes the influence in 1900 of an African American female preacher, Julia Schaeffer, in Tucson's Indian village, as well as Presbyterian evangelizing in 1903: Booth, "Creation of a Nation," 92, 94–95.

5. Blaine, *Papagos and Politics*, 32. For the employment of the O'odham, see Reports of Farmer in Charge of San Xavier Papago (J. M. Berger), August 27, 1901, *ARCIA* 1901, 189–190; August 28, 1902, *ARCIA* 1902, 168; and November 25, 1903, *ARCIA* 1903, 441–442.

6. See A.P.K. Safford, Report of the Governor's Office, Arizona Territory, August 5, 1870, *ARCIA* 1870, 138; H. Bendell, Report of the Arizona Superintendency, August 22, 1871, *ARCIA* 1871, 351; E. A. Howard, Report of Pima Agency, 1887, *ARCIA* 1887, 6; C. M. Johnson, Report of Pima Agency, August 1888, *ARCIA* 1888, 4; C. M. Johnson, Report of Pima Agency, July 1, 1889, *ARCIA* 1889, 120; C. W. Crouse, Report of Pima Agency, August 18, 1890, *ARCIA* 1890, 5; J. R. Young, Report of Pima Agency, September 1, 1894, *ARCIA* 1894, 104.

7. Underhill, "Acculturation at the Papago Village of Santa Rosa," 313. See also Joseph, Spicer, and Chesky, *The Desert People*, 28–30.

8. H. Bendell, Report of the Arizona Superintendency, August 22, 1871, *ARCIA* 1871, 351; R. A. Wilbur, Report of the Agency Papago Indians, August 26, 1871, *ARCIA* 1871, 365–366, and September 15, 1874, *ARCIA* 1874, 290; J. W. Cornyn, Report of Agency Papago Indians, September 14, 1875, *ARCIA* 1875, 212; Eppinga, *Tucson, Arizona*, 44; transcript, Harry Drachman radio interview broadcasts, February 3, 1949–January 16, 1951, 95, AV0003, AHST.

9. R. G. Wheeler, Report of the Pima Agency, August 29, 1885, *ARCIA* 1885, 4; E. A. Howard, Report of the Pima Agency, 1887, *ARCIA* 1887, 6; J. M. Berger, Report of Farmer, Papago Reservation, August 4, 1893, *ARCIA* 1893, 117.

10. Meeks, *Border Citizens*, 17.

11. See Meeks, *Border Citizens*, 17, 21, 22–23, 25; Sonnichsen, *Tucson*, 91; Luckingham, *The Urban Southwest*, 51; Otero, *La Calle*, 41–52; Sheridan, *Los Tucsonenses*, 121–130.

12. McCarthy, *A Papago Traveler*, 6, 24; Blaine, *Papagos and Politics*, 135, fn. 9. See also Meeks, *Border Citizens*, 60, 84–85. For Chukham, see Joseph, Spicer, and Chesky, *The Desert People*, 95.

13. H. Brown to J. Prall, May 22, 1905, Letterbook III, 1903–1906, Tucson Indian Training School Records, 1888–1953, MS 0809, AHST. Circular, Frazier Herdon, August 27, 1897, in Miscellaneous Indian Training School, Series III, F. 42, Elsie Prugh Herndon papers, 1895–1934, MS 1038, AHST. H. Brown to W. Murray, October 13, 1904; H. Brown to E. Pomeroy, October 24, 1904; H. Brown to E. Matthews, October 26, 1904; H. Brown to the CE Society, September 20, 1905; H. Brown to C. Shipman, January 29, 1906; H. Brown to E. Meeker, February 8, 1906; H. Brown to E. Philips, June 7, 1907; H. Brown to A. [illeg.], May 1, 1908, Letterbook III, 1903–1906, Tucson Indian Training School Records, 1888–1953, MS 0809, AHST.

14. "Mama" to "Papa," dated Wednesday 1910, Drachman family correspondence, personal, f. 555, Mose Drachman Papers, MS 0226, AHST. For the Drachmans, see Drachman, *This Is Not a Book*, 18; also Rochlin and Rochlin, *Pioneer Jews*, 89–90.

15. H. McQuigg to E. E. Newton, May 15, 1913, Field Matron Lydia A. Gibbs 1911–1919, SRFM, Box 190, RG 75 NAR.

16. Emmerich, "'To Respect and Love and Seek the Ways of White Women,'" 91, 95–98, 105–106.

17. C. Hauke to Civil Service Commission, December 29, 1910; J. Doyle to Commissioner, January 4, 1911; H. McQuigg, Efficiency Record Lydia Gibbs, April 1, 1911, October 1, 1912; L. Gibbs, Request for Transfer, July 19, 1913; Record of Mrs. Lydia A. Gibbs, February 25, 1920, Lydia Gibbs Personnel File, RG 146 NPRC. H. McQuigg to the Commissioner, July 19, 1913, Field Matron Lydia A. Gibbs 1911–1919, SRFM, Box 190, RG 75 NAR.

18. Mary Doyle Personnel File, RG 146 NPRC. See also Emmerich, "'To Respect and Love and Seek the Ways of White Women,'" 112–113.

19. H. McQuigg, Report on Education Division, Employment Section, June 30, 1910, US Bureau of Indian Affairs, *Superintendents' Annual Narrative*. J. Robe to D. Boyd, March 10, 1911; J. Robe to D. Boyd, April 7, 1911; M. Allaben to Robe, April 29, 1911; J. Robe to D. Boyd, May 22, 1911; J. Robe to D. Boyd, June 7, 1911; J. Robe to D. Boyd, November 13, 1911, Correspondence 1910, Tucson Indian Training School Records, MS 0809, AHST.

20. C. Hauke to H. McQuigg, June 21, 1913 (quoting undated letter report from Supervisor Newton), Field Matron Lydia A. Gibbs 1911–1919, SRFM, Box 190, RG 75 NAR. See also Lydia Gibbs Personnel File, RG 146 NPRC.

21. H. McQuigg to E. E. Newton, May 15, 1913; H. McQuigg to Commissioner, May 16, 1913, Field Matron Lydia A. Gibbs 1911–1919, SRFM, Box 190, RG 75 NAR.

22. C. Hauke to H. McQuigg, 21 June 1913 (quoting undated letter report from Supervisor Newton), Field Matron Lydia A. Gibbs 1911–1919, SRFM, Box 190, RG 75 NAR.

23. H. McQuigg to Commissioner, July 19, 1913, Field Matron Lydia A. Gibbs 1911–1919, SRFM, Box 190, RG 75 NAR.

24. See, for instance, Fahmi, "'Ruffled' Mistresses and 'Discontented' Maids"; Urban, "Irish Domestic Servants"; Horn, *The Rise and Fall of the Victorian Servant*, 135–136; McBride, *The Domestic Revolution*, 73–78; Sutherland, *Americans and Their Servants*, 127–132; Hansen, *Distant Companions*, 252.

25. Meeks, *Border Citizens*, 17, 37, 37–43; Sonnichsen, *Tucson*, 135–136, 180.

26. Browne, *Adventures in Apache Country*, 22, 138.

27. Farish, *History of Arizona*, vol. III, 347–348. Sonnichsen suggests that the Indian name was an area designation rather than the name of a group, and Stjukson may have been a permanent village where the O'odham spent fall and winter before moving out to their fields: Sonnichsen, *Tucson*, 7–8.

28. Jose Alvarez, Minutes of Council with Papago Indians at Indian Oasis, September 21, 1916, O–W, Phoenix Area Office Subject Files 1916–1942, Box 57, RG 75 NAR.

29. Bancroft, *History of Arizona and New Mexico*, 551. Reports of Farmer in Charge of San Xavier Papago (J. M Berger), August 27, 1901, *ARCIA* 1901, 189–190; August 28, 1902, *ARCIA* 1902, 168; and November 25, 1903, *ARCIA* 1903, 441–442. Blaine, *Papagos and Politics*, 12, 13; Meeks, *Border Citizens*, 76.

30. C. Hauke to H. McQuigg, August 8, 1913; H. McQuigg to Commissioner, September 27, 1913, Field Matron Lydia A. Gibbs 1911–1919, SRFM, Box 190, RG 75 NAR.

31. H. McQuigg to Commissioner, September 13, 1913, September 27, 1913, Field Matron Lydia A. Gibbs 1911–1919, SRFM, Box 190, RG 75 NAR.

32. Enquiry by Indian Court under Instruction of Supt. Thackery into the Case of [Alice E——], September 5, 1913; F. Thackery to H. McQuigg,

September 8, 1913; G. Hilzinger (County Attorney) to H. McQuigg, September 14, 1913; H. McQuigg to F. Thackery, September 16, 1913, Field Matron Lydia A. Gibbs 1911–1919, SRFM, Box 190, RG 75 NAR. H. McQuigg to Commissioner, September 1, 1913; F. Thackery to Commissioner, n.d., stamped received September 29, 1913; M. Estabrook to Commissioner, June 29, 1914, San Xavier 108529-13-175, CCF 1907–1939, RG 75 NAB. I am using pseudonyms to protect the privacy of the families.

33. H. McQuigg to Commissioner, September 1, 1913; F. Thackery to Commissioner, n.d., stamped received September 29, 1913, San Xavier 108529-13-175, CCF 1907–1939, RG 75 NAB.

34. H. McQuigg to F. Thackery, September 26, 1913, Field Matron Lydia A. Gibbs 1911–1919, SRFM, Box 190, RG 75 NAR.

35. G. Hilzinger to H. McQuigg, September 14, 1913, Field Matron Lydia A. Gibbs 1911–1919, SRFM, Box 190, RG 75 NAR. F. Thackery to Commissioner, n.d., stamped received September 29, 1913, San Xavier 108529-13-175, CCF 1907–1939, RG 75 NAB. For the Jack Johnson trial, see Ward, *Unforgivable Blackness*, 298–346.

36. Enquiry by Indian Court under Instruction of Supt. Thackery into the Case of [Alice E——], September 5, 1913; F. Thackery to H. McQuigg, September 8, 1913; H. McQuigg to F. Thackery, September 16, 1913, Field Matron Lydia A. Gibbs 1911–1919, SRFM, Box 190, RG 75 NAR.

37. Meeks, *Border Citizens*, 81–84.

38. For the anti-cohabitation laws, see Johnson, "Sharing Bed and Board"; Garza, "Common Law Marriage," 541–553. Garza argues that despite the existence of anti-miscegenation laws, interracial marriage could be technically recognized under common-law marriage doctrines: Garza, "Common Law Marriage," 544. For the extended laws against intermarriage, see Meeks, *Border Citizens*, 81; also Franco, "Unlawful Love," 377–390; Pascoe, "Miscegenation Law, Court Cases, and Ideologies of 'Race' in Twentieth-Century America," 469, 475; Pascoe, *What Comes Naturally*, esp. chap. 3.

39. H. McQuigg to Commissioner, September 1, 1913, San Xavier 108529-13-175, CCF 1907–1939, RG 75 NAB. F. Thackery to H. McQuigg, September 8, 1913, Field Matron Lydia A. Gibbs 1911–1919, SRFM, Box 190, RG 75 NAR. I am using a pseudonym here to protect the privacy of descendants.

40. H. McQuigg to Commissioner, September 13, 1913, September 27, 1913; H. McQuigg to A. Chingren, 25 October 1913, Field Matron Lydia A. Gibbs 1911–1919, SRFM, Box 190, RG 75 NAR. The case he was referring to was probably one involving a girl who had come from the Presbyterian Mission Indian Training School at Escuela, Arizona: Copy, H. McQuigg to Rev. J. Record, October 20, 1913, Field Matron Lydia A. Gibbs 1911–1919, SRFM, Box 190, RG 75 NAR.

41. H. McQuigg, Lydia Gibbs Efficiency Report, November 1, 1913, Lydia Gibbs Personnel File, RG 146 NPRC.

42. S. H. Chapin to Commissioner, February 2, 1914, San Xavier 18376-14-410, CCF 1907–1939, RG 75, NAB. In 1905, Chapin was a field matron in Nebraska: S. H. Chapin, Report of the Field Matron among Winnebago, *ARCIA* 1905, 253. She would return to the field matron service later, and in 1934, she held one of the six remaining field matron appointments, at the Colorado River Agency: Emmerich, "'To Respect and Love and Seek the Ways of White Women,'" 307.

43. Petition from the Citizens of Tucson to Commissioner, n.d., c. February 2, 1914; Petition from the Clergymen of Tucson to Commissioner, n.d., c. February 2, 1914, San Xavier 18376-14-410, CCF 1907–1939, RG 75 NAB.

44. Petition from the Indian Young Women Working in Tucson to Commissioner, n.d., c. February 2, 1914, San Xavier 18376-14-410, CCF 1907–1939, RG 75 NAB.

45. Various correspondences and reports, 1914–1915, Lydia Gibbs Personnel File, RG 146 NPRC.

46. E. Meritt to H. McQuigg, April 6, 1914; E. Meritt to S. H. Chapin, April 6, 1914, San Xavier 18376-14-410, CCF 1907–1939, RG 75 NAB.

47. E. Meritt to L. Gibbs, May 18, 1914, Lydia Gibbs Personnel File, RG 146 NPRC. J. Weeks to C. Sells, March 5, 1914; C. Sells to J. Weeks, March 9, 1914; Personal record of Minnie Estabrook, December 24, 1913, Minnie Williams (Estabrook) Personnel File, RG 146 NPRC. M. Estabrook to J. Rogers, January 28, 1913; E. Holden to Commissioner, March 17, 1914, Hoopa Valley 20871-14-734, CCF 1907–1939, RG 75 NAB. For the settlement movement in this period, see Davis, *Spearheads for Reform*; Trolander, *Professionalism and Social Change*, 7–29.

48. E. Meritt to Supt. Holden, April 8, 1914, Minnie Williams (Estabrook) Personnel File, RG 146 NPRC.

Chapter 4. "Naturally a trouble-maker": Minnie Estabrook, 1914–1915

1. McQuigg to Commissioner, telegram, May 8, 1914, San Xavier 18376-14-410, CCF 1907–1939, RG 75 NAB. M. Estabrook to H. McQuigg, 12 May 1914, 27 May 1914, Field Matron Correspondence Minnie M. Estabrook 1914–1916, SRFM, Box 189, RG 75 NAR.

2. Minnie M. Williams formerly Minnie M. Estabrook, resume, n.d., c. June 1934, Minnie Williams (Estabrook) Personnel File, RG 146 NPRC. "Mrs. Estabrook arrests the Red Slaver of Tecolote," undated, unsourced clipping, c. August 1915, San Xavier 126437-15-175.2, CCF 1907–1939, RG 75 NAB.

3. E. E. Newton to Commissioner, March 16, 1915, San Xavier 18376-14-410, CCF 1907–1939, RG 75 NAB.

4. Copy, E. Meritt to M. Estabrook, April 16, 1914, Minnie Williams (Estabrook) Personnel File, RG 146 NPRC. For her visit to Chingren, see *The Native American*, May 9, 1914, vol. 15, 250.

5. C. Sells to J. Rogers, November 10, 1913; C. Sells to M. Estabrook, November 10, 1913; M. Estabrook to Commissioner, November 12, 1913; Minnie M. Williams formerly Minnie M. Estabrook, resume, n.d., c. June 1934; Personal record of Minnie Estabrook, December 24, 1913, Minnie Williams (Estabrook) Personnel File, RG 146 NPRC. US Bureau of the Census, *United States Federal Census*, 1880, 1890, 1900, 1910, and 1920. Cathleen Cahill has noted the Indian Service actively discouraged applicants with child-caring responsibilities, although it was inconsistent in actually following stipulations against their employment or their being accompanied by their children, resulting in chronic problems for both the parents and the administration: Cahill, *Federal Fathers & Mothers*, 93–98.

6. E. Meritt to Supt. Holden, March 9, 1914, Minnie Williams (Estabrook) Personnel File, RG 146 NPRC.

7. [M. K. Sniffen] to H. Welch, January 25, 1911, IRA.

8. H. Marten to E. Linnen, August 17, 1914; M. Estabrook to H. Marten, August 15, 1914; C. Sells to Mr. Traylor, May 6, 1915; Deposition of Henry J. McQuigg, June 10, 1915; H. S. Traylor to Commissioner, June 30, 1915; H. McQuigg to Commissioner, September 18, 1915, San Xavier 89961-1914-154, CCF 1907–1939, RG 75 NAB. E. E. Newton to Commissioner, March 16, 1915; H. McQuigg to Commissioner, April 27, 1915; see also H. McQuigg to Commissioner, May 7, 1915; H. McQuigg to Commissioner, May 22, 1915, San Xavier 18376-14-410, CCF 1907–1939, RG 75 NAB.

9. H. McQuigg to Commissioner, May 14, 1914; M. Estabrook to H. McQuigg, June 27, 1914; M. Estabrook to C. Sells "Through Supt. H. J. McQuigg," October 13, 1914, Field Matron Correspondence Minnie M. Estabrook 1914–1916, SRFM, Box 189, RG 75 NAR. H. McQuigg to Commissioner, September 14, 1914; M. Estabrook to H. Marten, August 15, 1914, San Xavier 89961-1914-154, CCF 1907–1939, RG 75 NAB.

10. M. Estabrook to H. McQuigg, June 12, 1914; M. Estabrook "Goods delivered May 28, 1914, by Mr. Phillipson"; M. Estabrook to H. McQuigg, June 27, 1914, Field Matron Correspondence Minnie M. Estabrook 1914–1916, SRFM, Box 189, RG 75 NAR.

11. M. Estabrook to H. McQuigg, July 2, 1914, Field Matron Correspondence Minnie M. Estabrook 1914–1916, SRFM, Box 189, RG 75 NAR.

12. M. Estabrook to H. Marten, August 15, 1914; Deposition of Henry J. McQuigg, June 10, 1915; Deposition of Minnie M. Estabrook, June 10, 1915, San Xavier 89961-1914-154, CCF 1907–1939, RG 75 NAB.

13. M. Estabrook to H. Marten, August 15, 1914, San Xavier 89961-1914-154, CCF 1907–1939, RG 75 NAB.

14. M. Estabrook to C. Sells "Through Supt. H. J. McQuigg," October 13, 1914 [referring to earlier Estabrook report, August 8, 1914], Field Matron Correspondence Minnie M. Estabrook 1914–1916, SRFM, Box 189, RG 75 NAR.

15. H. McQuigg to Commissioner, September 14, 1914, San Xavier 89961-1914-154, CCF 1907–1939, RG 75 NAB.

16. C. Sells to M. Estabrook, September 24, 1914; M. Estabrook to C. Sells "Through Supt. H. J. McQuigg," October 13, 1914, San Xavier 89961-1914-154, CCF 1907–1939, RG 75 NAB. See same in Field Matron Correspondence Minnie M. Estabrook 1914–1916, SRFM, Box 189, RG 75 NAR.

17. E. Newton to Commissioner, November 8, 1910, General Services 98013-10-917.1, CCF 1907–1939, RG 75 NAB.

18. M. Estabrook to H. McQuigg, June 27, 1914; M. Estabrook to C. Sells "Through Supt. H. J. McQuigg," October 13, 1914; M. Estabrook to H. McQuigg, November 16, 1914, Field Matron Correspondence Minnie M. Estabrook 1914–1916, SRFM, Box 189, RG 75 NAR. For similar activities planned by settlement movement workers in New York at the time, see Fronc, *New York Undercover*, 130, 138–139.

19. M. Estabrook to C. Sells "Through Supt. H. J. McQuigg," October 13, 1914, Field Matron Correspondence Minnie M. Estabrook 1914–1916, SRFM, Box 189, RG 75 NAR.

20. M. Girton to M. Allaben, July 11, 1915; M. Allaben to M. Girton, July 20, 1915, Correspondence 1910, Tucson Indian Training School Records, MS 0809, AHST.

21. O. B. Goodall, Report of an Inspection of San Xavier School and Agency, Arizona, October 16, 1914, San Xavier 24877-1915-806, CCF 1907–1939, RG 75 NAB.

22. Although it's not clear who exactly "Mrs. Soloman" was, she was very likely Hattie Solomon, daughter of a Jewish German family who married Charles Solomon, a Jewish German banker in Tucson: US Bureau of the Census, *United States Federal Census*, 1910, 1920, and 1930. The O'odham were aware of the fine distinctions within Tucson society, their word for Jewish people being Tutulko, used also for any person whose nationality was unclear: see Blaine, *Papagos and Politics*, 11.

23. H. McQuigg to M. Estabrook, October 29, 1914 [quoting undated letter, which I have not been able to locate], Field Matron Correspondence Minnie M. Estabrook 1914–1916, SRFM, Box 189, RG 75 NAR.

24. E. Meritt to H. McQuigg, November 3, 1914, San Xavier 89961-1914-154, CCF 1907–1939, RG 75 NAB.

25. Deposition of Andrew G. Pollock, June 10, 1915, San Xavier 89961-1914-154, CCF 1907–1939, RG 75 NAB. E. B. Meritt to H. McQuigg, January 2, 1915, Field Matron Correspondence Minnie M. Estabrook 1914–1916, SRFM, Box 189, RG 75 NAR.

26. H. McQuigg to Commissioner, February 1, 1915, Field Matron Correspondence Minnie M. Estabrook 1914–1916, SRFM, Box 189, RG 75 NAR. H. McQuigg to Commissioner, March 30, 1915, San Xavier 18376-14-410, CCF 1907–1939, RG 75 NAB.

27. E. E. Newton to Commissioner, March 16, 1915; E. Meritt to McQuigg, April 1, 1915, San Xavier 18376-14-410, CCF 1907–1939, RG 75 NAB.

28. H. McQuigg to M. Estabrook, April 6, 1915; E. Meritt to M. Estabrook, June 4, 1915; M. Estabrook to E. Meritt, June 18, 1915, San Xavier 18376-14-410, CCF 1907–1939, RG 75 NAB.

29. E. E. Newton to Commissioner, March 16, 1915, 18376-14-410, San Xavier CCF 1907–1939, RG 75 NAB. Minnie M. Williams formerly Minnie M. Estabrook, resume, n.d., c. June 1934, Minnie Williams (Estabrook) Personnel File, RG 146 NPRC. E. Meritt to H. McQuigg, February 5, 1915; H. McQuigg to Commissioner, February 17, 1915; E. Newton to Commissioner, March 9, 1915, Records of the Inspection Division, Special Agent Files 1907–1921, E. E. Newton, RG 75 NAB.

30. C. Sells to H. McQuigg, November 20, 1915; H. Traylor to Commissioner, June 30, 1915, San Xavier 89961-1914-154, CCF 1907–1939, RG 75 NAB.

31. M. Estabrook to H. McQuigg, November 19, 1914; McQuigg to Estabrook, 21 November 1914, Field Matron Correspondence Minnie M. Estabrook 1914–1916, SRFM, Box 189, RG 75 NAR. E. E. Newton to Commissioner, March 16, 1915; M. Estabrook to C. Sells, Report for Month Ending August 8, 1914, San Xavier 89961-1914-154, CCF 1907–1939, RG 75 NAB.

32. M. Estabrook to H. McQuigg, February 6, 1915, Field Matron Correspondence Minnie M. Estabrook 1914–1916, SRFM, Box 189, RG 75 NAR. I am using a pseudonym to protect the privacy of descendants.

33. Chingren Outing Matron Report, Annual Report 1914–15, 827.1 1910–1930, Field Matron's Reports, PIS, CCF 1891–51, Box 161, RG 75 NAR.

34. Transcription, "The Revised Statutes of Arizona, 1913. Penal Code. Title C. Bastards," n.d., c. September 2, 1914, San Xavier 108529-13-175, CCF 1907–1939, RG 75 NAB.

35. See "He Took Them Both in Self Defense," undated, unsourced clipping, c. August 1915, San Xavier 126437-15-175.2, CCF 1907–1939, RG 75 NAB.

36. M. Estabrook to Commissioner, June 29, 1914, San Xavier 108529-13-175, CCF 1907–1939, RG 75 NAB. M. Estabrook to C. Sells, Report for Month Ending August 8, 1914, San Xavier 89961-1914-154, CCF 1907–1939, RG 75 NAB. E. E. Newton to Commissioner, March 16, 1915, San Xavier 18376-14-410, CCF 1907–1939, RG 75 NAB. I use pseudonyms for the women charged to protect their families' privacy.

37. E. Meritt to H. McQuigg, July 27, 1914, September 19, 1914, San Xavier 108529-13-175, CCF 1907–1939, RG 75 NAB. For the proposals in 1918, see Jensen, *Calling This Place Home*, 233–234.

38. E. E. Newton to Commissioner, March 16, 1915; H. McQuigg to O. Comstock, JP, February 24, 1915; O. Comstock to H. McQuigg, February 24, 1915; M. Estabrook to E. Newton, April 19, 1915; Superintendent [McQuigg] to E. Newton, April 21, 1915, San Xavier 18376-14-410, CCF 1907–1939, RG 75 NAB. I am using pseudonyms to protect the privacy of descendants.

39. H. McQuigg to M. Estabrook, March 2, 1915, San Xavier 18376-14-410, CCF 1907–1939, RG 75 NAB. I am using a pseudonym to protect the privacy of descendants.

40. H. McQuigg to M. Estabrook, March 2, 1915, San Xavier 18376-14-410, CCF 1907–1939, RG 75 NAB.

41. E. E. Newton to Commissioner, March 16, 1915, San Xavier 18376-14-410, CCF 1907–1939, RG 75 NAB.

42. Deposition of Minnie M. Estabrook, June 10, 1915, San Xavier 89961-1914-154, CCF 1907–1939, RG 75 NAB.

43. H. Traylor to Commissioner, June 30, 1915, San Xavier 89961-1914-154, CCF 1907–1939, RG 75 NAB.

44. Luis Valdez statement, September 13, 1915; H. McQuigg to Commissioner, September 18, 1915, San Xavier 89961-1914-154, CCF 1907–1939, RG 75 NAB.

45. M. Estabrook to Commissioner, September 3, 1915, San Xavier 96898-1915-410, CCF 1907–1939, RG 75 NAB.

46. H. McQuigg to Commissioner, September 18, 1915, San Xavier 89961-1914-154, CCF 1907–1939, RG 75 NAB. I am using a pseudonym to protect the privacy of descendants.

47. H. McQuigg to Commissioner, November 9, 1915, Minnie Williams (Estabrook) Personnel File, RG 146 NPRC.

48. H. McQuigg to Commissioner, September 18, 1915, San Xavier 89961-1914-154, CCF 1907–1939, RG 75 NAB.

49. H. Traylor, "Papago Indians in Tucson," n.d., stamped received July 6, 1915, San Xavier 89961-1914-154, CCF 1907–1939, RG 75 NAB.

50. M. Estabrook to H. McQuigg, October 11, 1915, Field Matron Correspondence Minnie M. Estabrook 1914–1916, SRFM, Box 189, RG 75 NAR. It should be noted that no Hispanic names appeared on Estabrook's list.

51. [Mrs. R. Kensey] to H. McQuigg, November 3, 1915; H. McQuigg to Commissioner, November 9, 1918, Minnie Williams (Estabrook) Personnel File, RG 146 NPRC.

52. J. Oliver, Efficiency Report, Janette Woodruff, May 1, 1915, Janette Woodruff Personnel File, RG 146 NPRC.

53. C. Sells to J. Woodruff, October 16, 1915; J. Oliver to Commissioner, October 29, 1915; C. Sells to J. Woodruff, November 8, 1915, Janette Woodruff Personnel File, RG 146 NPRC. C. Sells to M. Estabrook, November 8, 1915, Minnie Williams (Estabrook) Personnel File, RG 146 NPRC.

54. M. Estabrook to Commissioner, November 20, 1915; E. Meritt to M. Estabrook, December 7, 1915, Minnie Williams (Estabrook) Personnel File, RG 146 NPRC.

55. Ladies of Tucson to C. Sells, November 15, 1915; Outing Girls and Others to C. Sells, telegram, November 15, 1915, Minnie Williams (Estabrook) Personnel File, RG 146 NPRC.

56. H. Traylor to Commissioner, June 30, 1915, San Xavier 89961-1914-154, CCF 1907–1939, RG 75 NAB. For community attitudes, see M. Doyle to J. Martin, 16 May 1917, Field Matron's Weekly Reports Mary Doyle 1916–19, SRFM, Box 190, RG 75 NAR. Statement of Richard Lewis, August 19, 1914; J. Cachora to C. Sells, October 9, 1914, San Xavier 89961-1914-154, CCF 1907–1939, RG 75 NAB.

57. T. Pratt to Commissioner, November 15, 1915, Minnie Williams (Estabrook) Personnel File, RG 146 NPRC.

58. C. Sells to P. Marcho et al., November 18, 1915; C. Sells to F. Steward et al., November 30, 1915; C. Sells to T. Pratt, November 30, 1915, Minnie Williams (Estabrook) Personnel File, RG 146 NPRC.

59. Various reports and correspondences, 1916–1936, Minnie Williams (Estabrook) Personnel File, RG 146 NPRC.

60. Davis, *Spearheads for Reform*, xx, 135–138; Connelly, *The Response to Prostitution in the Progressive Era*.

Chapter 5. "I try to keep the girls from going to the dances": Janette Woodruff, 1915–1929

1. Blaine, *Papagos and Politics*, 32; Woodruff, *Indian Oasis*, 228.

2. Photograph of Janette Woodruff, 1900; H. McQuigg, Efficiency Report, Janette Woodruff, May 1, 1916; J. Martin, Efficiency Report, Janette Woodruff, December 11, 1916; T. McCormick, Efficiency Report, Janette Woodruff, November 1, 1917, Janette Woodruff Personnel File, RG 146 NPRC. E. Meritt to H. McQuigg, March 2, 1916, San Xavier 24014-1916-917.1, CCF 1907–1939, RG 75 NAB.

3. L. Chubbock to M. Cook, November 20, 1907; C. Larrabee to L. Chubbock, December 2, 1907; L. Chubbock to Commissioner, December 17, 1907, Nevada 93013-1907-917.1, CCF 1907–1939, RG 75 NAB. J. Woodruff to Commissioner, January 24, 1908; F. M. Conser to US Indian Agent, Crow Agency, Montana, January 25, 1908, Crow 3511-08-162, CCF 1907–1939, RG 75 NAB. Woodruff, *Indian Oasis*, 131–132, 157–169. L. Creel to Commissioner, January 20, 1908, Crow 99530-1907-917.1, CCF 1907–1939, RG 75 NAB. Various correspondences and reports, 1910–1915, Janette Woodruff Personnel File, RG 146 NPRC.

4. Woodruff, *Indian Oasis*, 18. Record and Qualifications of Janette Woodruff, Matron, May 5, 1906; J. Woodruff to H. Hall, April 25, 1911, Janette Woodruff Personnel File, RG 146 NPRC. "Wisconsin Marriages, pre-1907." US Bureau of the Census, *United States Federal Census*, 1870, 1880, and 1900.

5. Gamber, "The Female Economy," 133–139, 237–238.

6. Woodruff, *Indian Oasis*, 18–19.

7. Cahill, *Federal Fathers & Mothers*, 64–65.

8. Cowan, *More Work for Mother*, 155.

9. As Helen Bannan pointed out, the field matron's salary of $720 was well above the average national earnings in 1892 when it was instituted, and until 1908 was the most lucrative female-designated position in the Indian Service: Bannan, *"True Womanhood" on the Reservation*, 7. The salary did stay unchanged, at $720, at least for Woodruff, until 1925, when she received a pay raise to $1200 per annum, and then another in 1926, to $1380; 1927 to $1440; and by 1929, when she retired, $1560 a year: Woodruff, *Indian Oasis*, 25–30, 157–169; *ARCIA* 1901, 733; various correspondences and reports, 1906–1929, Janette Woodruff Personnel File, RG 146 NPRC.

10. Cahill, *Federal Fathers & Mothers*, 65, 89, 98–99.

11. J. Woodruff to H. Hall, April 25, 1911; copy, C. Hauke to J. Woodruff, May 13, 1911; J. Mack to J. Woodruff, July 18, 1911, Janette Woodruff Personnel File, RG 146 NPRC.

12. Woodruff, *Indian Oasis*, 206, 220–221. C. H. Asbury to Commissioner, November 28, 1916, General Services 8954-15-917.1, CCF 1907–1939, RG 75 NAB. Various correspondences, 1915–1921, Janette Woodruff Personnel File, RG 146 NPRC. Shortly after withdrawing her application for transfer, Woodruff asked the superintendent to support her application for a transfer to the Immigration Service, explaining apologetically that it was the Immigration matron's relatively generous salary—$105 a month—that made it attractive. Nothing came of this, however. J. Woodruff to Mr. McCormick, February 3, 1922, Field Matron's Weekly Reports Janette Woodruff 1921–22, SRFM, Box 191, RG 75 NAR. Her superintendent was advised that such a transfer could only be considered if an application for her transfer was received from the Immigration Service, but evidently this was not forthcoming: E. Meritt to T. McCormick, February 17, 1922, Janette Woodruff Personnel File, RG 146 NPRC.

13. Erickson, *Sharing the Desert*, 99–131. See, for a full and nuanced historical discussion of Tohono O'odham politics in the period, Booth, "Creation of a Nation."

14. US Bureau of Indian Affairs. *Annual Report, 1920.*

15. Meeks, *Border Citizens*, 92–93.

16. Woodruff, *Indian Oasis*, 242. J. Woodruff to H. McQuigg, January 24, 1916, Field Matron Janette Woodruff 1915–1918, SRFM, Box 190, RG 75 NAR.

17. J. Woodruff to Commissioner, 31 January 1917; C. Sells to J. Woodruff, 23 February 1917, Field Matron Janette Woodruff 1915–1918, SRFM, Box 190, RG 75 NAR.

18. Woodruff, *Indian Oasis*, 242. Janette Woodruff, Quarterly Report Ending June 30, 1920, Field Matron Correspondence Janette Woodruff 1919–1920, SRFM, Box 191, RG 75 NAR.

19. J. Woodruff, Field Matron Report for the Month of December 1916, Field Matron Janette Woodruff 1915–1918, SRFM, Box 190, RG 75 NAR.

20. Woodruff, *Indian Oasis*, 242–243. I am using the names Woodruff used in her memoirs, which are pseudonyms.

21. Woodruff, *Indian Oasis*, 225.

22. J. Woodruff, Field Matron's Weekly Report, Weeks Ending October 3, 1925, November 21, 1925, Field Matron Weekly Reports Janette Woodruff 1925–26, SRFM, Box 191, RG 75 NAR. Woodruff, *Indian Oasis*, 294.

23. J. Woodruff, Field Matron Report for the Month of May 1917, Field Matron Janette Woodruff 1915–1918, SRFM, Box 190, RG 75 NAR. J. Woodruff to T. McCormick, July 1, 1919, Field Matron Correspondence Janette Woodruff 1919–1920, SRFM, Box 191, RG 75 NAR. J. Woodruff to E. Stewart, June 30, 1928, Field Matron Weekly Reports Janette Woodruff 1927–1929, SRFM, Box 191, RG 75 NAR.

24. J. Woodruff to T. McCormick, July 1, 1918; see also J. Woodruff to Commissioner, July 1, 1917, Field Matron Janette Woodruff 1915–1918, SRFM, Box 190, RG 75 NAR. Woodruff, *Indian Oasis*, 243–244.

25. J. Woodruff to T. McCormick, July 1, 1918, Field Matron Janette Woodruff 1915–1918, SRFM, Box 190, RG 75 NAR. J. Woodruff to T. McCormick, Annual Report on the Outing Girls, July 1, 1919, Field Matron Correspondence Janette Woodruff 1919–1920, SRFM, Box 191, RG 75 NAR. Woodruff, *Indian Oasis*, 245.

26. J. Woodruff to T. McCormick, Annual Report on the Outing Girls, July 1, 1919, Field Matron Correspondence Janette Woodruff 1919–1920, SRFM, Box 191, RG 75 NAR. J. Woodruff to T. McCormick, July 1, 1918, Field Matron Janette Woodruff 1915–1918, SRFM, Box 190, RG 75 NAR. Woodruff, *Indian Oasis*, 245–246.

27. J. Woodruff to Commissioner, April 30, 1917, Field Matron Janette Woodruff 1915–1918, SRFM, Box 190, RG 75 NAR.

28. J. Woodruff to Commissioner, February 28, 1917; J. Woodruff to J. Martin, July 15, 1917, Field Matron Janette Woodruff 1915–1918, SRFM, Box 190, RG 75 NAR. J. Woodruff to T. McCormick, Annual Report on the Outing Girls, July 1, 1919; J. Woodruff to T. McCormick, January 21, 1920, Field Matron Correspondence Janette Woodruff 1919–1920, SRFM, Box 191, RG 75 NAR. The sale of liquor in Arizona had been outlawed since the start of 1915: Sonnichsen, *Tucson*, 182.

29. Kelly, "Charles Henry Burke, 1921–29," 259; Murphy, *The People Have Never Stopped Dancing*, 86–87, 95, 107, 116.

30. Murphy, *The People Have Never Stopped Dancing*, 93–94, 97–98; Booth, "Creation of a Nation," 240–241, 244, 247–253; Blaine, *Papagos and Politics*, 44. For the rain ceremonies themselves, see Joseph, Spicer, and Chesky, *The Desert People*, 73–77; Nabhan, *The Desert Smells Like Rain*, 25–38; Underhill, "The Autobiography of Chona, a Papago Woman," 39–40; McCarthy, *A Papago Traveler*, 109–111.

31. Booth, "Creation of a Nation," 242; Erickson, *Sharing the Desert*, 128. For a 1940s description of the dances, see Joseph, Spicer, and Chesky, *The Desert People*, 84–85.

32. J. Woodruff, Quarterly Report on the Outing Girls, September 30, 1924, Field Matron Weekly Reports Janette Woodruff 1925–26, SRFM, Box 191, RG 75 NAR.

33. J. Woodruff, Quarterly Report on the Outing Girls, September 30, 1924, Field Matron Weekly Reports Janette Woodruff 1925–26, SRFM, Box 191, RG 75 NAR. J. Woodruff, Annual Report on the Working Girls Ending June 30, 1927, Field Matron Weekly Reports Janette Woodruff 1927–1929, SRFM, Box 191, RG 75 NAR.

34. Manuel and Neff, *Desert Indian Woman*, 19. On division between the traditionalist "conservatives" and the "progressives" among the O'odham on the issue of the *naiwat* ceremonies, see Booth, "Creation of a Nation," 264.

35. Jensen, *Calling This Place Home*, 231. For the 1920s dance culture generally, see Jensen, "'I'd Rather Be Dancing,'" 10–13. And see, for an instructive call to scholars to take note of Indian cultural resilience and creativity with modernity, Deloria, *Indians in Unexpected Places.*

36. Inspector E. M. Sweet Jnr., Outing System, May 15, 1919; L. McCoy, June 11, 1919; C. Sells, Circular No—, June 12, 1919, Sells 47652-19-824, CCF 1907–1939, RG 75 NAB.

37. Meriam et al., *The Problem of Indian Administration*, 712. L. McCoy, June 11, 1919, Sells 47652-19-824, CCF 1907–1939, RG 75 NAB. Memorandum (unsigned) Commissioner, March 19, 1929, General Services 20561-29-920, CCF 1907–1939, RG 75 NAB.

38. Woodruff, *Indian Oasis*, 244. J. Woodruff, Field Matron's Report, Weeks Ending December 31, 1916, July 31, [1917]; J. Woodruff to Commissioner, June 30, 1917; J. Woodruff to T. McCormick, February 14, 1918, Field Matron Janette Woodruff 1915–1918, SRFM, Box 190, RG 75 NAR. J. Woodruff to H. McCormick, December 17, 1921, Field Matron's Weekly Reports Janette Woodruff 1921–22, SRFM, Box 191, RG 75 NAR. J. Woodruff, Quarterly Report on the Outing Girls, Ending March 31, 1925, J. Woodruff, Field Matron's Weekly Reports, January 3, 1925, November 21, 1925, Field Matron Weekly Reports Janette Woodruff 1925–26, SRFM, Box 191, RG 75 NAR. J. Woodruff, Field Matron's Weekly Report, Week Ending July 23, 1927, Field Matron Weekly Reports Janette Woodruff 1927–1929, SRFM, Box 191, RG 75 NAR.

39. Woodruff, *Indian Oasis*, 246. J. Woodruff, Field Matron's Report, Week Ending July 7, [1917], Field Matron Janette Woodruff 1915–1918, SRFM, Box 190, RG 75 NAR. J. Woodruff to Mr. McCormick, July 1, 1920, Field Matron Correspondence Janette Woodruff 1919–1920, SRFM, Box 191, RG 75 NAR.

40. J. Woodruff, Field Matron Report for the Month of May 1917; J. Woodruff, Field Matron Report for the Month of February 1917, Field Matron Janette Woodruff 1915–1918, SRFM, Box 190, RG 75 NAR.

41. J. Woodruff to Commissioner, January 31, 1916, San Xavier 15834-1916-917.1, CCF 1907–1939, RG 75 NAB.

42. J. Woodruff, Field Matron's Weekly Report, Week Ending November 14, 1925, Field Matron Weekly Reports Janette Woodruff 1925–26, SRFM, Box 191, RG 75 NAR.

43. J. Woodruff to Commissioner, January 31, 1917, Field Matron Janette Woodruff 1915–1918, SRFM, Box 190, RG 75 NAR. See also Field Matron Report, Week Ending January 12, 1918, Field Matron Janette Woodruff 1915–1918, SRFM, Box 190, RG 75 NAR. J. Woodruff, Field Matron's Weekly Report, Week Ending November 14, 1925, Field Matron Weekly Reports Janette Woodruff 1925–26, SRFM, Box 191, RG 75 NAR.

44. J. Woodruff, Annual Report for the Year Ending June 30, 1925, Field Matron Weekly Reports Janette Woodruff 1925–26, SRFM, Box 191, RG 75 NAR. Janette Woodruff, Field Matron's Report, Week Ending July 31 [1918], Field Matron Janette Woodruff 1915–1918, SRFM, Box 190, RG 75 NAR.

45. J. Woodruff to Commissioner, March 31, 1917; J. Woodruff to J. Martin, April 5, 1917, Field Matron Janette Woodruff 1915–1918, SRFM, Box 190, RG 75 NAR.

46. J. Woodruff to Commissioner, April 30, 1917, Field Matron Janette Woodruff 1915–1918, SRFM, Box 190, RG 75 NAR. Janette Woodruff, Field Matron's Report, Week Ending June 14, [1920]; Janette Woodruff, Quarterly Report on the Outing Girls, June 30, 1920, Field Matron Correspondence Janette Woodruff 1919–1920, SRFM, Box 191, RG 75 NAR. J. Woodruff, Report on the Working Girls for the Quarter Ending December 31, 1924; J. Woodruff, Annual Report for the Year Ending June 30, 1925; J. Woodruff, Weekly Report, January 3, 1925, Field Matron Weekly Reports Janette Woodruff 1925–26, SRFM, Box 191, RG 75 NAR. J. Woodruff, Field Matron's Weekly Reports, Week Ending October 22, 1927; J. Woodruff, Field Matron's Weekly Report, Week Ending February 5, 1927, November 5, 1927, Field Matron Weekly Reports Janette Woodruff 1927–1929, SRFM, Box 191, RG 75 NAR.

47. J. Woodruff to J. Martin, April 5, 1917, Field Matron Janette Woodruff 1915–1918, SRFM, Box 190, RG 75 NAR.

48. Woodruff, *Indian Oasis*, 281, 284. J. Woodruff, Annual Report on the Working Girls, Ending June 30, 1926, Field Matron Weekly Reports Janette Woodruff 1925–26, SRFM, Box 191, RG 75 NAR. Woodruff's records and especially her memoirs testify to the devastation tuberculosis wreaked among the Indian girls and women. Tucson had been a refuge for Anglo tubercular sufferers because of its dry climate since the late nineteenth century, and by 1920, it has been estimated that the tubercular population, living in segregated tent cities on the outskirts of Tucson, including a large settlement north of the university, made up possibly one-third of Tucson's population, although the proportion declined after that: Hart, *Tucson*, 94–98.

49. J. Woodruff to Mr. Fuller, September 7, 1917, Field Matron Janette Woodruff 1915–1918, SRFM, Box 190, RG 75 NAR. Janette Woodruff to Supt T. F. McCormick, Annual Report on the Working Girls, July 1, 1919; Janette Woodruff, Quarterly Report on the Outing Girls, March 31, 1920; Janette

Woodruff, Quarterly Report on the Outing Girls, January 10, 1920; Janette Woodruff, Quarterly Report on the Outing Girls, June 30, 1920, Field Matron Correspondence Janette Woodruff 1919–1920, SRFM, Box 191, RG 75 NAR. J. Woodruff to T. McCormick, May 29, 1922, Field Matron's Weekly Reports Janette Woodruff 1921–22, SRFM, Box 191, RG 75 NAR.

50. J. Woodruff, July 16, 1921, Field Matron's Weekly Reports Janette Woodruff 1921–22, SRFM, Box 191, RG 75 NAR. I am using pseudonyms here to protect the privacy of descendants.

51. J. Woodruff to T. McCormick, Annual Report on the Working Girls, July 1, 1919, Field Matron Correspondence Janette Woodruff 1919–1920, SRFM, Box 191, RG 75 NAR. See also J. Woodruff, Report on the Working Girls for the Quarter Ending December 31, 1924, Field Matron Weekly Reports Janette Woodruff 1925–26, SRFM, Box 191, RG 75 NAR.

52. Katzman, *Seven Days a Week*, 270.

53. J. Woodruff, September 19, 1925, Field Matron Weekly Reports Janette Woodruff 1925–26, SRFM, Box 191, RG 75 NAR. Janette Woodruff, Field Matron's Report, Week Ending April 20, [1918], Field Matron Janette Woodruff 1915–1918, SRFM, Box 190, RG 75 NAR.

54. J. Woodruff, Field Matron's Report, Week Ending November 24, [1917], Field Matron Janette Woodruff 1915–1918, SRFM, Box 190, RG 75 NAR. J. Woodruff to T. McCormick, Report of the Working Girls, for the Quarter Ending Dec. 31, 1919, Field Matron Correspondence Janette Woodruff 1919–1920, SRFM, Box 191, RG 75 NAR. J. Woodruff, March 29, 1925, Field Matron Weekly Reports Janette Woodruff 1925–26, SRFM, Box 191, RG 75 NAR. Meeks, *Border Citizens*, 87.

55. J. Woodruff to T. McCormick, Annual Report on the Outing Girls, July 1, 1920, Field Matron Correspondence Janette Woodruff 1919–1920, SRFM, Box 191, RG 75 NAR.

56. J. Woodruff, Annual Report on the Working Girls Ending June 30, 1928, Field Matron Weekly Reports Janette Woodruff 1927–1929, SRFM, Box 191, RG 75 NAR.

57. J. Woodruff to T. McCormick, August 26, 1919; Janette Woodruff, September 30, 1919; J. Woodruff to T. McCormick, October 11, 1919, Field Matron Correspondence Janette Woodruff 1919–1920, SRFM, Box 191, RG 75 NAR.

58. J. Woodruff to T. McCormick, October 11, 1919; J. Woodruff to T. McCormick, January 9, 1920, Field Matron Correspondence Janette Woodruff 1919–1920, SRFM, Box 191, RG 75 NAR. J. Woodruff, Report on the Working Girls, September 30, 1921, Field Matron's Weekly Reports Janette Woodruff 1921–22, SRFM, Box 191, RG 75 NAR. Woodruff, *Indian Oasis*, 245, 299–230. Lynch-Brennan noted that in the case of both nineteenth-century Irish maids in America and Latina live-in workers in late twentieth-century Los Angeles, employers refused to allow them to entertain boyfriends: Lynch-Brennan, "Was Bridget's Experience Unique?" 493, 505. Similar restrictions were in place for domestic servants in nineteenth-century London: see Gillis,

"Servants, Sexual Relations, and the Risks of Illegitimacy," 150–151. An insight into the mix of sexual anxiety and amused disdain that characterized contemporary white attitudes to Indian men in Tucson can be gleaned from the childhood memoir published by Rosemary Taylor (the daughter of Ethel and Mose Drachman), *Chicken Every Sunday*, 6–12.

59. J. Woodruff, Field Matron Report for the Month of May 1917, Field Matron Janette Woodruff 1915–1918, SRFM, Box 190, RG 75 NAR. Janette Woodruff, Quarterly Report on the Outing Girls, June 30, 1920, Field Matron Correspondence Janette Woodruff 1919–1920, SRFM, Box 191, RG 75 NAR. J. Woodruff, Annual Report for the Year Ending June 30, 1925, Field Matron Weekly Reports Janette Woodruff 1925–26, SRFM, Box 191, RG 75 NAR. Woodruff, *Indian Oasis*, 268, 248.

60. J. Woodruff to T. McCormick, April 6, 1918; T. McCormick to Commissioner, April 12, 1918, Field Matron Janette Woodruff 1915–1918, SRFM, Box 190, RG 75 NAR.

61. This final encounter would give Armstrong the impetus she needed to leave the Indian Service and embark on her own campaign to publish her "indictment" of the Indian Service and herself, for her cowardice and acquiescence (not published, however, until 1952): E. Brown, *Stubborn Fool*, 250–258. For Armstrong (Brown) see also Carter, "'Completely Discouraged,'" 66.

62. A. Warren to C. Burke, November 8, 1923, Phoenix 87833-1923-824, CCF 1907–1939, RG 75 NAB. See Trennert, "Victorian Morality," 122–124.

63. Woodruff, *Indian Oasis*, 290–302.

64. Katherine Osburn has offered particularly insightful studies on the impact of the marriage policies on Southern Ute women in Colorado: see Osburn, "To Build Up the Morals of the Tribe"; also, "'Dear Friend and Ex-husband.'"

65. Superintendent [Martin] to J. Woodruff, May 31, 1917, Field Matron Janette Woodruff 1915–1918, SRFM, Box 190, RG 75 NAR. Woodruff, *Indian Oasis*, 271–272, 296–297; Underhill, "The Autobiography of Chona, a Papago Woman," 76–78; Blaine, *Papagos and Politics*, 31–32, 63, 88; Joseph, Spicer, and Chesky, *The Desert People*, 48–49.

66. J. Woodruff to H. McQuigg, January 24, 1916; J. Woodruff to H. McQuigg, April 19, 1916, Field Matron Janette Woodruff 1915–1918, SRFM, Box 190, RG 75 NAR.

67. J. Woodruff to H. McCormick, July 1, 1920, Field Matron Correspondence Janette Woodruff 1919–1920, SRFM, Box 191, RG 75 NAR.

68. Woodruff, *Indian Oasis*, 273–275. Synopsis of cases in the Justice Court, Tucson Precinct, County of Pima, Arizona, reported by Mrs. Minnie M. Estabrook . . . , M. Estabrook, Special Report on [Lilly X] and [X], August 18, 1915, Sells 93873-15-175.2, CCF 1907–1939, RG 75 NAB. I have retained the pseudonym Woodruff employed in her book to protect the privacy of the couple's families.

69. Woodruff, *Indian Oasis*, 275. Lilly actually did pursue him under the illegitimacy law for maintenance and succeeded in getting a ruling, but it would

appear he did not pay as required: J. Woodruff to Mr. McCormick, May 29, 1922; J. Woodruff, June 10, 1922, Field Matron's Weekly Reports Janette Woodruff 1921–22, SRFM, Box 191, RG 75 NAR. Field Matron Correspondence Janette Woodruff 1919–1920, SRFM, Box 191, RG 75 NAR.

70. I have used a pseudonym to protect the privacy of the family and descendants. J. Woodruff, Field Matron Report for the Month of May 1917, Field Matron Janette Woodruff 1915–1918, SRFM, Box 190, RG 75 NAR. J. Woodruff to H. McCormick, June 7, 1920, Field Matron Correspondence Janette Woodruff 1919–1920, SRFM, Box 191, RG 75 NAR. Copy, Superintendent [Martin] to J. Woodruff, May 31, 1917, Field Matron Janette Woodruff 1915–1918, SRFM, Box 190, RG 75 NAR. Tohono O'odham infants were frequently "assigned" to the care of older female children in the 1940s, and presumably this was not unknown in the 1920s. However, the babies in this case were very young indeed, and it is highly unlikely that such tiny nursing babies would have been left by their mother in the normal course of events: see Joseph, Spicer, and Chesky, *The Desert People*, 117–121, 127, 138. The mother's beating of her daughter most enraged the aunt, however. The Tohono O'odham despised even the scolding of children: Underhill, "The Autobiography of Chona, a Papago Woman," 73.

71. J. Woodruff to H. McQuigg, February 14, 1916, February 25, 1916, March 7, 1916, April 19, 1916, Field Matron Janette Woodruff 1915–1918, SRFM, Box 190, RG 75 NAR. J. Woodruff, Quarterly Report on the Outing Girls, Ending March 31, 1925; J. Woodruff, Annual Report on the Working Girls, Ending June 30, 1926; J. Woodruff, Annual Report for the Year Ending June 30, 1925, Field Matron Weekly Reports Janette Woodruff 1925–26, SRFM, Box 191, RG 75 NAR.

72. J. Woodruff, Report on Employment, July 1, 1924, Field Matron Weekly Reports Janette Woodruff 1925–26, SRFM, Box 191, RG 75 NAR.

73. J. Woodruff, Quarterly Report, September 30, 1921, Field Matron's Weekly Reports Janette Woodruff 1921–22, SRFM, Box 191, RG 75 NAR.

74. E. M. Sweet Jr. to Commissioner, Outing System (Papago), June 7, 1916, San Xavier 70352-1916-806, CCF 1907–1939, RG 75 NAB. J. Woodruff, Report on Employment for the Year Ending June 30, 1926; Report of Employment for the Year Ending June 30, 1927; Report on Employment for the Year Ending June 30, 1928, Field Matron Weekly Reports Janet Woodruff 1925–26, SRFM, Box 191, RG 75 NAR. J. Woodruff to E. Stewart, June 30, 1927; J. Woodruff, Report on Employment for the Year Ending June 30, 1928, Field Matron Weekly Reports Janet Woodruff 1927–1929, SRFM, Box 191, RG 75 NAR. Woodruff, *Indian Oasis*, 294–295. According to David Katzman, laundry work was "the mainstay of married working women in service, especially black women," up until World War II: Katzman, *Seven Days a Week*, 85. For the impact of washing machines more widely, see Cowan, *More Work for Mother*, 175.

75. E. Bentley, February 18, 1926, Sells 74585-24-823, CCF 1907–1939, RG 75 NAB. Justification, n.d., c. March 1926, T. McCormick to Commissioner,

March 26, 1926; clipping, *Daily Silver Belt*, December 8, 1925; "Indians Starve on Reserve; Business Men Come to Rescue with 1500 Pounds of Frijoles," Tucson *Daily Star*, July 9, 1925; T. McCormick to Commissioner, August 11, 1925; "Missionaries State Report Indians Are Starving Is Untrue," *Tucson Citizen*, August 10, 1925 (Oblasser letter, July 10, 1925), Sells 91045-24-229, CCF 1907–1939, RG 75 NAB.

76. J. Woodruff, Report on the Outing Girls for the Quarter Ending June 30, 1925; J. Woodruff, Annual Report on the Working Girls, Ending June 30, 1926, Field Matron Weekly Reports Janette Woodruff 1925–26, SRFM, Box 191, RG 75 NAR. J. Woodruff, Field Matron's Weekly Report, Week Ending August 28, 1926, Field Matron Weekly Reports Janette Woodruff 1925–26, SRFM, Box 191, RG 75 NAR. For the Chinese store, see also Manuel and Neff, *Desert Indian Woman*, 16–17, 33.

77. J. Woodruff, Annual Report on the Working Girls for the Year Ending June 30, 1925, Field Matron Weekly Reports Janette Woodruff 1925–26, SRFM, Box 191, RG 75 NAR. J. Woodruff to Commissioner, January 31, 1916, San Xavier 15834-1916-917.1, CCF 1907–1939, RG 75 NAB. J. Woodruff, Report on the Working Girls, Dec. 31, 1921; J. Woodruff, Quarterly Report on the Working Girls, n.d. [Ending March 31, 1922], Field Matron's Weekly Reports Janette Woodruff 1921–22, SRFM, Box 191, RG 75 NAR. The evidence shows that many Indian girls were still living-in in 1925, but that parents did not always like this: for instance, J. Woodruff, March 7, 1925, Field Matron Weekly Reports Janette Woodruff 1925–26, SRFM, Box 191, RG 75 NAR.

78. For a detailed study of this shift, see Clark-Lewis, *Living In, Living Out*.

79. J. Woodruff to T. McCormick, June 30, 1926, Field Matron Weekly Reports Janette Woodruff 1925–26, SRFM, Box 191, RG 75 NAR. The owners of this land were possibly Mexicans: see J. Woodruff, Annual Report on the Working Girls, June 30, 1922, Field Matron's Weekly Reports Janette Woodruff 1921–22, SRFM, Box 191, RG 75 NAR.

80. J. Woodruff to E. Stewart, June 30, 1927, June 30, 1928; J. Woodruff, Annual Report on the Working Girls Ending June 30, 1927, Field Matron Weekly Reports Janette Woodruff 1927–1929, SRFM, Box 191, RG 75 NAR.

81. E. Cunningham to E. Stewart, 23 October 1926, 970 Industries and Employment Field Matron Domestic Employment, SIA, CCF 1925–1951, Box 119, RG 75 NAR. E. Stewart to Commissioner, December 14, 1926, Janette Woodruff Personnel File, RG 146 NPRC. J. Woodruff, Annual Report on the Working Girls Ending June 30, 1927, Field Matron Weekly Reports Janette Woodruff 1927–1929, SRFM, Box 191, RG 75 NAR.

82. J. Woodruff, Annual Report on the Working Girls Ending June 30, 1927, Field Matron Weekly Reports Janette Woodruff 1927–1929, SRFM, Box 191, RG 75 NAR.

83. J. Woodruff, Field Matron's Weekly Reports, Weeks Ending January 3, 1926, June 26, 1926, Field Matron Weekly Reports Janette Woodruff 1925–26, SRFM, Box 191, RG 75 NAR. J. Woodruff, Field Matron's Weekly Reports,

Weeks Ending February 12, 1927, July 2, 1927, October 22, 1927, J. Woodruff, Annual Report on the Working Girls Ending June 30, 1928, Field Matron Weekly Reports Janette Woodruff 1927–1929, SRFM, Box 191, RG 75 NAR.

84. Woodruff, *Indian Oasis*, 249–250.

85. J. Woodruff, Annual Report on the Working Girls Ending June 30, 1927; J. Woodruff, Annual Report on the Working Girls Ending June 30, 1928, Field Matron Weekly Reports Janette Woodruff 1927–1929, SRFM, Box 191, RG 75 NAR. For the Christmas parties, see J. Woodruff, Report on the Working Girls, December 31, 1921, Field Matron's Weekly Reports Janette Woodruff 1921–22, SRFM, Box 191, RG 75 NAR. J. Woodruff, Report on the Working Girls for the Quarter Ending December 31, 1924, Field Matron Weekly Reports Janette Woodruff 1925–26, SRFM, Box 191, RG 75 NAR. An exodus from the village for work picking cotton between October and January during the 1920s meant it was fairly deserted at Christmas: see Meeks, *Border Citizens*, 90.

86. W. Acker to J. Woodruff, Notice of Retirement Status, February 1, 1929, Janette Woodruff Personnel File, RG 146 NPRC. Woodruff, *Indian Oasis*, 318.

87. L. Woods to Commissioner, February 20, 1929; J. Woodruff to Commissioner, February 20, 1929; R. Miller to E. Stewart, March 15, 1929; E. Stewart to Commissioner, March 16, 1929; memorandum by MJV, March 2, 1929; E. Meritt to Stewart, telegram, March 25, 1929; memorandum by C. Burke, March 30, 1929, Secretary, Department of the Interior, April 4, 1929; W. Acker to J. Woodruff, April 5, 1929, Janette Woodruff Personnel File, RG 146 NPRC. E. Meritt to J. Martin, February 26, 1917, Field Matron Janette Woodruff 1915–1918, SRFM, Box 190, RG 75 NAR. J. Woodruff, Field Matron's Weekly Report, Week Ending November 5, 1927, Field Matron Weekly Reports Janette Woodruff 1927–1929, SRFM, Box 191, RG 75 NAR. Woodruff, *Indian Oasis*, 288–289.

88. Woodruff, *Indian Oasis*, 318–319. Gomez, Allen & Otiz to R. Wilbur, telegram, April 18, 1929; H. Ashurst to Commissioner of Indian Affairs, April 19, 1929; H. Corbett to R. Wilbur, telegram, April 18, 1929; R. Wilbur to F. Gomez, April 23, 1929; C. Burke to H. Ashurst, April 23, 1929; R. Wilbur to H. Corbett, April 20, 1929, Janette Woodruff Personnel File, RG 146 NPRC.

89. Woodruff, *Indian Oasis*, 319.

90. On retiring, Woodruff had a brief stint as a "practical nurse" in a Tucson day nursery before leaving: US Bureau of the Census, *United States Federal Census*, 1930. Woodruff, *Indian Oasis*, 319–320.

Chapter 6. "A worthy, industrious people": Libbie Light, 1929–1932

1. E. Meritt to L. Light, March 8, 1929; L. Light to Commissioner, March 13, 1929, Libbie Light Personnel File, RG 146 NPRC.

2. The Gibbs had finally secured a joint appointment at Truxton Canon, where William Light was superintendent, and Lydia's husband retired in 1923:

W. Light, Efficiency Report, Lydia Gibbs, November 1, 1922; C. Burke to W. Light, February 20, 1923; W. Light to Commissioner, March 17, 1923; C. Burke to W. Light, March 27, 1923; L. Gibbs to E. Merritte [*sic*], April 4, 1923; E. Meritt to L. Gibbs, April 11, 1932; W. Light to Commissioner, May 23, 1923; E. Meritt to L. Gibbs, June 7, 1923; L. Gibbs to Commissioner, October 9, 1929; C. Rhoads to L. Gibbs, October 30, 1929, Lydia Gibbs Personnel File, RG 146 NPRC. Temporary employees, as many wives of Indian Service employees like Gibbs and Light were classified when they worked, as well as the majority of Indian employees, were ineligible for retirement pensions: see also Cahill, *Federal Fathers & Mothers*, 250–255.

3. Kelly, "Charles James Rhoads," 264, 270. For the Rhoads-Scattergood administration, see Britten, "Hoover and the Indians"; Rusco, *A Fateful Time*, 94–113.

4. Kelly, "Charles James Rhoads," 263, 266–268.

5. Meriam et al., *The Problem of Indian Administration*, 389–390, 524, 528, 591, 597, 626–628, 645.

6. Emmerich, "'To Respect and Love and Seek the Ways of White Women,'" 282–312.

7. E. Stewart to Commissioner, May 7, 1929, Libbie Light Personnel File, RG 146 NPRC. Woodruff, *Indian Oasis*, 318.

8. L. Light to E. Stewart, May 15, 1929, May 31, 1929, Field Matron Libbie C. Light Correspondence Superintendent E. S. Stewart, SRFM, Box 190, RG 75 NAR.

9. Frankenberg, "Growing Up White," 60–61. Judith Rollins has written extensively on the invisibility of the African American domestic servant: see *Between Women*, 207–232. See also James Clifford's illuminating discussion of the figure "Elsie," an Indian domestic servant depicted in a modernist 1920s poem, in *The Predicament of Culture*, 1–7.

10. W. Light to Commissioner, December 9, 1907, Hayward 97013-07-162, CCF 1907–1939, RG 75 NAB. W. Light to Commissioner, February 1, 1909, Hayward 11136-09-162, CCF 1907–1939, RG 75 NAB. W. Light to Commissioner, May 14, 1923; W. Light to E. Meritt, October 25, 1927, William Light Personnel File, RG 146 NPRC. See also McMillen, "The Birth of an Activist," 40–43, 46–49.

11. W. Light to Commissioner, February 17, 1919; W. Light to A. Hall, Secretary of the Interior, April 14, 1921; see also W. Light to Commissioner, February 11, 1922; C. Burke to W. Light, February 27, 1922; W. Light to Commissioner, March 10, 1922, William Light Personnel File, RG 146 NPRC. W. Light to Commissioner of Indian Affairs, December 17, 1923, April 20, 1925, Libbie Light Personnel File, RG 146 NPRC.

12. H. Drachman to T. McCormick, May 11, 1922, Field Matron Correspondence Janette Woodruff 1919–1920, SRFM, Box 191, RG 75 NAR. For the segregation of Tucson's residential areas in the twentieth century, see Otero, *La Calle*, esp. 52–53, 88–89.

13. L. Light to E. Stewart, June 19, 1929, Field Matron Libbie C. Light Correspondence Superintendent E. S. Stewart, SRFM, Box 190, RG 75 NAR.

14. C. Hauke to E. Stewart, June 13, 1929, Field Matron Libbie C. Light Correspondence Superintendent E. S. Stewart, SRFM, Box 190, RG 75 NAR.

15. L. Light to E. Stewart, June 19, 1929; E. Stewart to Commissioner, July 11, 1929; Stewart to Indian Office, telegram, June 29, 1929; C. Burke to Stewart, telegram, June 29, 1929; memorandum, LWW, Medical Division, July 17, 1929, Libbie Light Personnel File, RG 146 NPRC.

16. L. Light to Commissioner, September 29, 1930, Libbie Light Personnel File, RG 146 NPRC.

17. Field Matron's Weekly Report, Week Ending May 25, 1929, also Weeks Ending June 1, 1929, June 8, 1929, June 29, 1929, September 28, 1929, November 9, 1929, November 16, 1929, January 31, 1931, Field Matron's Weekly Reports, 052.1 G & S Statistical Reports Field Nurses and Matrons Monthly Reports 1928–1931, SRFM, Box 190, RG 75 NAR.

18. Field Matron's Weekly Report, Week Ending June 8, 1929; see also Field Matron's Weekly Reports, Weeks Ending September 28, 1929, October 5, 1929, January 4, 1930, January 18, 1930, February 8, 1930, March 22, 1930, March 29, 1930, May 3, 1930, June 28, 1930, September 13, 1930, November 1, 1930, December 6, 1930, November 22, 1930, January 10, 1931, Field Matron's Weekly Reports, 052.1 G & S Statistical Reports Field Nurses and Matrons Monthly Reports 1928–1931, SRFM, Box 190, RG 75 NAR. E. Stewart to Commissioner, September 30, 1930, Libbie Light Personnel File, RG 146 NPRC.

19. Field Matron's Weekly Report, Week Ending May 18, 1929, Field Matron's Weekly Reports, 052.1 G & S Statistical Reports Field Nurses and Matrons Monthly Reports 1928–1931, SRFM, Box 190, RG 75 NAR.

20. Field Matron's Weekly Report, Weeks Ending May 11, 1929, May 18, 1929, Field Matron's Weekly Reports, 052.1 G & S Statistical Reports Field Nurses and Matrons Monthly Reports 1928–1931, SRFM, Box 190, RG 75 NAR. For telephone etiquette of the day, including that phone calls implied relations of social equality, see Fischer, *America Calling*, 183–188.

21. Field Matron's Weekly Report, Weeks Ending August 17, 1929, August 31, 1929, March 15, 1930, Field Matron's Weekly Reports, 052.1 G & S Statistical Reports Field Nurses and Matrons Monthly Reports 1928–1931, SRFM, Box 190, RG 75 NAR.

22. Field Matron's Weekly Report, Week Ending September 28, 1929; see also Weeks Ending August 31, 1929, November 9, 1929, November 16, 1929, January 25, 1930, Field Matron's Weekly Reports, 052.1 G & S Statistical Reports Field Nurses and Matrons Monthly Reports 1928–1931, SRFM, Box 190, RG 75 NAR.

23. Field Matron's Weekly Report, Week Ending March 22, 1930; see also Weeks Ending October 19, 1929, November 2, 1929, November 9, 1929, December 1, 1929, Field Matron's Weekly Reports, 052.1 G & S Statistical

Reports Field Nurses and Matrons Monthly Reports 1928–1931, SRFM, Box 190, RG 75 NAR.

24. Field Matron's Weekly Report, Weeks Ending June 1, 1929, September 28, 1929, Field Matron's Weekly Reports, 052.1 G & S Statistical Reports Field Nurses and Matrons Monthly Reports 1928–1931, SRFM, Box 190, RG 75 NAR.

25. Field Matron's Weekly Report, Weeks Ending August 24, 1929, September 21, 1929, October 4, 1930, November 15, 1930, Field Matron's Weekly Reports, 052.1 G & S Statistical Reports Field Nurses and Matrons Monthly Reports 1928–1931, SRFM, Box 190, RG 75 NAR. L. Light to J. Elliott, March 16, 1931, Libbie Light Personnel File, RG 146 NPRC.

26. Field Matron's Weekly Report, Weeks Ending September 7, 1929, December 1, 1929, December 28, 1929, January 25, 1930, February 22, 1930, March 1, 1930, March 8, 1930, March 15, 1930, March 29, 1930, April 5, 1930, May 17, 1930, May 31, 1930, July 5, 1930, March 7, 1931, April 18, 1931, Field Matron's Weekly Reports, 052.1 G & S Statistical Reports Field Nurses and Matrons Monthly Reports 1928–1931, SRFM, Box 190, RG 75 NAR.

27. Field Matron's Weekly Report, Weeks Ending December 7, 1929, December 14, 1929, Field Matron's Weekly Reports, 052.1 G & S Statistical Reports Field Nurses and Matrons Monthly Reports 1928–1931, SRFM, Box 190, RG 75 NAR.

28. R. D—— to L. Light, November 25, 1929, Field Matron Libbie C. Light Correspondence 1929–1930, SRFM, Box 190, RG 75 NAR. I use a pseudonym for the young woman and her employer to protect the privacy of their descendants.

29. See De Costa, "'The Contagiousness of Childbed Fever'"; Loudon, *The Tragedy of Childbed Fever*, 151–165; Olasky, *Abortion Rites*.

30. R. D—— to L. Light, November 25, 1929, Field Matron Libbie C. Light Correspondence 1929–1930, SRFM, Box 190, RG 75 NAR.

31. L. Light to A. Kneale, November 19, 1929; L. Light to A. Kneale, December 3, 1929, Field Matron Libbie C. Light Correspondence 1929–1930, SRFM, Box 190, RG 75 NAR. See also Field Matron's Weekly Report, Weeks Ending October 26, 1929, November 2, 1929, Field Matron's Weekly Reports, 052.1 G & S Statistical Reports Field Nurses and Matrons Monthly Reports 1928–1931, SRFM, Box 190, RG 75 NAR.

32. L. Light to E. Stewart, November 1, 1929, Field Matron Libbie C. Light Correspondence Superintendent E. S. Stewart, SRFM, Box 190, RG 75 NAR. Field Matron's Weekly Report, Week Ending December 1, 1929, Field Matron's Weekly Reports, 052.1 G & S Statistical Reports Field Nurses and Matrons Monthly Reports 1928–1931, SRFM, Box 190, RG 75 NAR. The names of this young woman and the Indian Service doctor are pseudonyms to protect the privacy of their descendants.

33. Field Matron's Weekly Report, Week Ending December 28, 1929, Field Matron's Weekly Reports, 052.1 G & S Statistical Reports Field Nurses and Matrons Monthly Reports 1928–1931, SRFM, Box 190, RG 75 NAR.

34. Field Matron's Weekly Report, Week Ending June 8, 1929, Field Matron's Weekly Reports, 052.1 G & S Statistical Reports Field Nurses and Matrons Monthly Reports 1928–1931, SRFM, Box 190, RG 75 NAR.

35. L. Light to J. Brown, May 21, 1929, J. Brown to I. B——, May 22, 1929, with annotations on back; J. Brown to I. B——, June 7, 1929, Field Matron Libbie C. Light Correspondence 1929–1930, SRFM, Box 190, RG 75 NAR.

36. L. Light to J. Brown, June 15, 1930, May 27, 1930, May 22, 1930; L. Light to J. Brown, April 18, 1930, Field Matron Libbie C. Light Correspondence 1929–1930, SRFM, Box 190, RG 75 NAR.

37. L. Light to W. Thack[er]y, May 12, 1930; L. Light to J. Brown, May 12, 1930; W. Thackery to L. Light, May 17, 1930; W. Thackery to L. Light, June 15, 1929, Field Matron Libbie C. Light Correspondence 1929–1930, SRFM, Box 190, RG 75 NAR.

38. Field Matron's Weekly Report, Weeks Ending September 14, 1929, September 28, 1929, Field Matron's Weekly Reports, 052.1 G & S Statistical Reports Field Nurses and Matrons Monthly Reports 1928–1931, SRFM, Box 190, RG 75 NAR. L. Light to J. Brown, October 12, 1929; L. Light to J. Brown, March 5, 1930; J. Brown to L. Light, March 8, 1930; L. Light to J. Brown, June 16, 1930; J. Brown to L. Light, June 17, 1930; F. Conser to L. Light, June 20, 1930, Field Matron Libbie C. Light Correspondence 1929–1930, SRFM, Box 190, RG 75 NAR.

39. Field Matron's Weekly Report, Week Ending March 1, 1930, Field Matron's Weekly Reports, 052.1 G & S Statistical Reports Field Nurses and Matrons Monthly Reports 1928–1931, SRFM, Box 190, RG 75 NAR. US Bureau of the Census, *US Indian Census Schedules, 1885–1940.*

40. Field Matron's Weekly Report, Week Ending March 15, 1930, Field Matron's Weekly Reports, 052.1 G & S Statistical Reports Field Nurses and Matrons Monthly Reports 1928–1931, SRFM, Box 190, RG 75 NAR.

41. J. J—— to L. Light, May 17, 1930, Field Matron Libbie C. Light Correspondence 1929–1930, SRFM, Box 190, RG 75 NAR. I am using pseudonyms for Juana and her sister to protect their families' and descendants' privacy.

42. See definitions and etymology in Partridge, *A Dictionary of the Underworld British and American*, 256–257; and in Green, *Cassell's Dictionary of Slang*, 524.

43. Dayton, "Taking the Trade," 24–25.

44. Woodruff, *Indian Oasis*, 302. I use Woodruff's pseudonym for the young woman to protect her descendants' privacy.

45. E. Stewart to Commissioner, July 1, 1930, Libbie Light Personnel File, RG 146 NPRC. L. Light to A. Chingren, September 9, 1930, Field Matron Libbie C. Light Correspondence 1929–1930, SRFM, Box 190, RG 75 NAR.

46. Field Matron's Weekly Report, Week Ending September 20, 1930, Field Matron's Weekly Reports, 052.1 G & S Statistical Reports Field Nurses and Matrons Monthly Reports 1928–1931, SRFM, Box 190, RG 75 NAR. I am using pseudonyms to protect the descendants' privacy.

47. F. Mann to L. Light, May 31, 1929, Field Matron Libbie C. Light Correspondence 1929–1930, SRFM, Box 190, RG 75 NAR. Field Matron's Weekly Report, Weeks Ending September 14, 1929, January 1, 1930, June 7, 1930, Field Matron's Weekly Reports, 052.1 G & S Statistical Reports Field Nurses and Matrons Monthly Reports 1928–1931, SRFM, Box 190, RG 75 NAR. The employer's name is a pseudonym to protect the descendants' privacy.

48. Field Matron's Weekly Report, Week Ending September 20, 1930, Field Matron's Weekly Reports, 052.1 G & S Statistical Reports Field Nurses and Matrons Monthly Reports 1928–1931, SRFM, Box 190, RG 75 NAR.

49. L. Light to J. Brown, September 22, 1930, Field Matron Libbie C. Light Correspondence 1929–1930, SRFM, Box 190, RG 75 NAR.

50. J. N—— to L. Light, September 19, 1930, Field Matron Libbie C. Light Correspondence 1929–1930, SRFM, Box 190, RG 75 NAR.

51. Field Matron's Weekly Report, Week Ending May 25, 1929, Field Matron's Weekly Reports, 052.1 G & S Statistical Reports Field Nurses and Matrons Monthly Reports 1928–1931, SRFM, Box 190, RG 75 NAR. I am using a pseudonym to respect the privacy of descendants.

52. Field Matron's Weekly Report, Week Ending July 5, 1930, Field Matron's Weekly Reports, 052.1 G & S Statistical Reports Field Nurses and Matrons Monthly Reports 1928–1931, SRFM, Box 190, RG 75 NAR.

53. See McLaren, "Illegal Operations," 806–808.

54. Jones, *A Century of Servitude*, 55.

55. Pfefferbaum, Strickland, Rhoades, and Pfefferbaum, "Learning How to Heal," 377.

56. According to a not very reliable history, the doctor did retire in mid-1930, and as it had to be after Lena's examination in July, it may be that he retired at the time Lena was first arrested, or that he retired around the time that Light got involved: Doris Weston, Brief History of Tucson Indian Employment Bureau, n.d., c. Jan 1935, Employment Reports and Statistics ERA 1934–1935, SIEFCW, Box 144, RG 75 NAR. He did not appear as a resident of Tucson in the 1930 census.

57. L. Light to J. N——, October 6, 1930, Field Matron Libbie C. Light Correspondence 1929–1930, SRFM, Box 190, RG 75 NAR.

58. Field Matron's Weekly Report, Week Ending October 11, 1930, Field Matron's Weekly Reports, 052.1 G & S Statistical Reports Field Nurses and Matrons Monthly Reports 1928–1931, SRFM, Box 190, RG 75 NAR. I am using a pseudonym to protect the privacy of descendants.

59. J. Elliott to L. Light, October 4, 1930; L. Light to J. Elliott, October 9, 1930, Field Matron Libbie C. Light Correspondence 1929–1930, SRFM, Box 190, RG 75 NAR.

60. Field Matron's Weekly Report, Weeks Ending October 18, 1930, October 25, 1930, November 1, 1930, Field Matron's Weekly Reports, 052.1 G & S Statistical Reports Field Nurses and Matrons Monthly Reports 1928–1931, SRFM, Box 190, RG 75 NAR.

61. Field Matron's Weekly Report, Week Ending November 8, 1930, Field Matron's Weekly Reports, 052.1 G & S Statistical Reports Field Nurses and Matrons Monthly Reports 1928–1931, SRFM, Box 190, RG 75 NAR.

62. Field Matron's Weekly Report, Weeks Ending May 23, 1931, June 6, 1931, June 20, 1931, Field Matron's Weekly Reports, 052.1 G & S Statistical Reports Field Nurses and Matrons Monthly Reports 1928 1931, SRFM, Box 190, RG 75 NAR.

63. J. Elliott to "Gentlemen," December 16, 1931; L. Light to M. Stewart, April 18, 1932; Field Matron's Weekly Report, Weeks Ending January 21, 1930, January 31, 1931, February 21, 1931, March 14, 1931, Field Matron's Weekly Reports, 052.1 G & S Statistical Reports Field Nurses and Matrons Monthly Reports 1928–1931, SRFM, Box 190, RG 75 NAR. For 1929 wages, see L. Light to A. Kneale, December 3, 1929, Field Matron Libbie C. Light Correspondence 1929–1930, SRFM, Box 190, RG 75 NAR.

64. Erickson, *Sharing the Desert*, 132–133.

65. M. Romero to L. Light, January 31, 1932; Mrs. Jesus [illeg.] to Mrs. Light, undated, c. June 1932; L. Light to M. Starr, April 18, 1932, Field Matron's Weekly Reports, 052.1 G & S Statistical Reports Field Nurses and Matrons Monthly Reports 1928–1931, SRFM, Box 190, RG 75 NAR.

66. L. Light to M. Stewart, April 14, 1932, Field Matron Libbie C. Light Correspondence 1931–1932, SRFM, Box 190, RG 75 NAR.

67. Meriam et al., *The Problem of Indian Administration*, 28. L. Light to A. Chingren, September 9, 1930, Field Matron Libbie C. Light Correspondence 1929–1930, SRFM, Box 190, RG 75 NAR. Various correspondences, 1930, Amanda Chingren Personnel File, RG 146 NPRC.

68. Various correspondences, 1930–1931, Libbie Light Personnel File, RG 146 NPRC.

69. L. Light to J. Elliott, March 16, 1931, Libbie Light Personnel File, RG 146 NPRC.

70. J. Elliott to Commissioner, April 9, 1931; memorandum "Re Libbie C. Light," initials illegible, April 27, 1931; J. Elliott, Efficiency Report Libbie Light, April 1, 1932; J. Elliott to Commissioner of Indian Affairs, April 5, 1932; Elliott and Tisinger to Ryan, telegram, April 15, 1932, and undated annotations, Libbie Light Personnel File, RG 146 NPRC. For Tisinger, see *Cornell Alumni News*, 34, no. 2 (October 1, 1931), 22. M. Stewart to R. Tisinger, 13 May 1932, Box 3 (T–Z), RSSE, PIS, Boxes 1–3, RG 75 NAR. C. Rhoads, Report of the Commissioner of Indian Affairs, June 30, 1931, *ARCIA* 1931, 7.

71. R. Tisinger to Commissioner, May 19, 1932, Box 3 (T–Z), RSSE, PIS, Boxes 1–3, RG 75 NAR. Doris Weston, Brief History of Tucson Indian Employment Bureau, n.d., c. Jan 1935, Employment Reports and Statistics ERA 1934–1935, SIEFCW, Box 144, RG 75 NAR.

72. L. Light to Commissioner, September 29, 1930; L. Light to J. Elliott, March 19, 1931, Libbie Light Personnel File, RG 146 NPRC. Although she had been in the Indian Service since 1895, there had been long periods when

she was only temporarily employed—by her husband William—which did not count towards her service credit.

73. Notice of Retirement Status, June 1, 1932, L. Light to Commissioner, June 15, 1932, Libbie Light Personnel File, RG 146 NPRC.

74. L. Light to Commissioner, June 15, 1932; C. Rhoads to J. Elliott, April 5, 1932, June 14, 1932; J. Elliott to Commissioner, June 23, 1932, Libbie Light Personnel File, RG 146 NPRC.

75. G. Taylor to J. Scattergood, June 8, 1932, Gracie Taylor Personnel File, RG 146 NPRC. B. Garber (Acting Commissioner of Indian Affairs) to C. Hayden, July 7, 1932; copy, B. Garber to L. Light, July 28, 1932; C. Rhoads to L. Light, September 24, 1932, Libbie Light Personnel File, RG 146 NPRC. Light, predictably, wrangled over this final computation of her record, but the Office remained steadfast. C. Rhoads to L. Light, March 16, 1933, Libbie Light Personnel File, RG 146 NPRC.

Chapter 7. "Mrs. Taylor calls it 'messenger work'": Gracie Taylor, 1932–1934

1. Hamm, "The American Friend Obituary Index"; US Bureau of the Census, *United States Federal Census*, 1880, 1900, 1910, and 1930. Various correspondences, 1916–1930, Gracie Taylor Personnel File, RG 146 NPRC.

2. D. & F. Yarnall to J. Scattergood, August 9, 1930; Rhoads to Kitch, telegram, August 19, 1930; notes, Senior Placement Matron, n.d., c. August 20, 1930; G. Taylor to J. Scattergood, June 8, 1932, Gracie Taylor Personnel File, RG 146 NPRC.

3. Memorandum for the Secretary, March 19, 1929, A bill to authorize the establishment of an employment agency for the Indian Service, H. R. 4567, 72nd Congress, 1st sess., Introduced December 8, 1931, General Services 20561-29-920, CCF 1907–1939, RG 75 NAB. Copy, M. Stewart to Mr. Beatty, January 23, 1939, General Services 170534-34-920, CCF 1907–1939, RG 75 NAB. *ARCIA* 1932, 15.

4. G. Taylor to M. Stewart, April 12, 1932, Gracie Taylor Personnel File, RG 146 NPRC.

5. Burton raised this possibility in June but said that it was Stewart's suggestion. E. Burton to R. Lansdale, June 9, 1932, Gracie Taylor Personnel File, RG 146 NPRC.

6. G. Taylor to J. Scattergood, June 8, 1932; G. Taylor to J. Scattergood, June 8, 1932; E. Burton to R. Lansdale, June 9, 1932; E. Gillespie, quoting from Stewart, airmail letter dated June 10,[1932], June 14, 1932, Gracie Taylor Personnel File, RG 146 NPRC.

7. C. Skinner to Commissioner, June 9, 1932; C. Rhoads to C. Skinner, June 20, 1932, Gracie Taylor Personnel File, RG 146 NPRC.

8. J. Scattergood to Mrs. D. Yarnall, June 16, 1932; J. Scattergood to G. Taylor, June 16, 1932; F. Yarnall to J. Scattergood, June 17, 1932, Gracie Taylor Personnel File, RG 146 NPRC.

9. M. A. Jones to R. M. Tisinger, November 28, 1931; M. Jones to W. Ryan, April 1, 1932, Box 3 (T–Z), RSSE, PIS, Boxes 1–3, RG 75 NAR.

10. Helen Bannan identified 27 field matrons who identified as Indian in her study of 187 field matrons: Bannan, *"True Womanhood" on the Reservation*, 9. Lisa Emmerich highlights that the numbers of Indian women in this position declined markedly from the turn of the century, and that there was in fact only *one* Indian field matron remaining in 1927, out of a total of 29 field matrons: Emmerich, "'Right in the Midst of My Own People,'" 203, 212. As Joan Jensen notes, a reversal of a nineteenth-century policy of recruiting American Indian matrons and teachers occurred under the regime of Estelle Reel: Jensen, *Calling This Place Home*, 391–392.

11. See Emmerich, "'Right in the Midst of My Own People,'" 204.

12. Harvey, "Cherokee and American," 64–65, 79–80, 84, 87, 98. Horne and McBeth, *Essie's Story*, 48–49. J. Holst to Commissioner of Indian Affairs, March 7, 1930; R. Bronson to H. Peairs, March 8, 1929; R. Bronson to H. Peairs, May 2, 1930; R. Bronson to Commissioner of Indian Affairs, July 12, 1930; R. Bronson to Commissioner of Indian Affairs, July 31, 1930; R. Bronson to Commissioner of Indian Affairs, September 5, 1930, General Services 13372-30-920, CCF 1907–1939, RG 75 NAB. M. Bronson to R. Tisinger, September 13, 1932, Box 3 (T–Z), RSSE, PIS, Boxes 1–3, RG 75 NAR.

13. Bronson was a graduate of Mount Holyoke College, Massachusetts, in English, economics, and sociology: Harvey, "Cherokee and American," 47, 55.

14. Memorandum by J. Elliott, July 19, 1932; J. Elliott to Commissioner, October 18, 1933; J. Collier to J. Elliott, November 24, 1933, Gracie Taylor Personnel File, RG 146 NPRC. Copy, G. Taylor to I. Sharp, October 6, 1932, Correspondence of Senior Placement Matron Gracie S. Taylor 1929–1934, SIEFCW, Box 147, RG 75 NAR.

15. G. Taylor to I. Sharp, October 6, 1932; G. Taylor to N. Brown, September 28, 1932; G. Taylor to E. Crockett, October 6, 1932; see also G. Taylor to K. Johnson, September 28, 1932, Correspondence of Senior Placement Matron Gracie S. Taylor 1929–1934, SIEFCW, Box 147, RG 75 NAR.

16. G. Taylor to G. Miller, n.d., c. October 1932, Correspondence of Senior Placement Matron Gracie S. Taylor 1929–1934, SIEFCW, Box 147, RG 75 NAR.

17. G. Taylor to Mrs. M. Easchief, October 6, 1932; see also G. Taylor to E. Enas, September 27, 1932; J. Roberts to G. Taylor, n.d., c. June 1932; G. Taylor to K. Johnson, September 8, 1932, Correspondence of Senior Placement Matron Gracie S. Taylor 1929–1934, SIEFCW, Box 147, RG 75 NAR. Note that in the 1920 census the Easchief family was recorded as Indian, and in 1930 as Mexican (and Mrs. Easchief as born in California): US Bureau of the Census, *United States Federal Census*, 1920 and 1930.

18. T. Shipley, Weekly Report, Week Ending July 16, 1932, 057 Reports to Mr. Burton, PISEO, CCF 1935–42, Box 3, RG 75 NAR. I. Coonan to M. Stewart, May 24, 1933, 052 Reports Mrs. Coonan, PISEO, CCF 1935–42, Box 3, RG 75 NAR.

19. I. Coonan to Mary Stewart, November 23, 1932; US Dept of the Interior authorization notice for Irene D. Coonan, 28 March 1933; copy, I. Coonan to M. Stewart, December 12, 1932, 056 Reports to Miss Stewart, PISEO, CCF 1935–42, Box 3, RG 75 NAR. Copy, Guidance and Placement Officer to W. Juan, November 28, 1932, 162 Applications for Positions (Women), PISEO, CCF 1935–42, Box 9, RG 75 NAR.

20. C. Rhoads to O. Gray, J. Balmer, G. Peters, C. Ziebach, H. Morrison, L. Baumgarten, March 19, 1931; C. Rhoads to O. Gray, May 18, 1931; Outline for Guidance and Placement Center, n.d., enclosed with M. Welsh to H. Shipe, July 24, 1930; M. Welsh to W. Ryan, March 3, 1931, enclosing I. Coonan, Case Studies of Indian Girls, February 1931; M. Welsh to Dr. Ryan, and annotations, March 2, 1931; M. Welsh to Commissioner, May 29, 1931; C. Rhoads to C. Lund, May 29, 1931, General Services 26646-30-920, CCF 1907–1939, RG 75, NAB. F. Adams to I. Coonan, December 5, 1932; I. Coonan to F. Adams, April 21, 1932; F. Adams to I. Coonan, March 20, 1933, 058 Reports from Kansas City, PISEO, CCF 1935–42, Box 3, RG 75 NAR. I. Coonan to R. Bronson, April 29, 1933, 056 Reports to Miss Stewart, PISEO, CCF 1935–42, Box 3, RG 75 NAR.

21. I. Coonan to M. Stewart, February 13, 1933; see also I. Coonan to M. Stewart, November 20, 1932, November 30, 1932, December 5, 1932, December 17, 1932, January 21, 1933, 056 Reports to Miss Stewart, PISEO, CCF 1935–42, Box 3, RG 75 NAR. T. Shipley, Weekly Report, Week Ending November 19, 1932, 057 Reports to Mr. Burton, PISEO, CCF 1935–42, Box 3, RG 75 NAR. 056 Reports to Miss Stewart, PISEO, CCF 1935–42, Box 3, RG 75 NAR. I. Coonan to M. Stewart, February 13, 1933, February 25, 1933, February 25, 1933, 056 Reports to Miss Stewart, PISEO, CCF 1935–42, Box 3, RG 75 NAR. J. Roberts to G. Taylor, January 9, [1933], Correspondence of Senior Placement Matron Gracie S. Taylor 1929–1934, SIEFCW, Box 147, RG 75 NAR.

22. G. Hardgrave to G. Taylor, 21 October 1932; see also G. Taylor to L Champie, October 4, 1932; G. Taylor to Lylah Harvey, October 4, 1932; copy, G. Taylor to G. Hardgreave [*sic*], 11 October 1932, Correspondence of Senior Placement Matron Gracie S. Taylor 1929–1934, SIEFCW, Box 147, RG 75 NAR.

23. G. Taylor to M. Stewart, May 18, 1933; R. Tisinger to Commissioner (marked attn. Mary Stewart), June 15, 1933, Box 3 (T–Z), RSSE, PIS, Boxes 1–3, RG 75 NAR.

24. G. Taylor to I. Coonan, March 8, 1933; I. Coonan to G. Taylor, March 17, 1933, Correspondence of Senior Placement Matron Gracie S. Taylor 1929–1934, SIEFCW, Box 147, RG 75 NAR.

25. G. Taylor to W. Harding, November 17, 1920, General Services 34850-21-131, CCF 1907–1939, RG 75 NAB. See also G. Taylor to Commissioner, January 23, 1917; E. Meritt to J. Buntin, February 13, 1917, Tongue River 13166-17-734, CCF 1907–1939, RG 75 NAB; various reports and correspondences, Gracie Taylor Personnel File, RG 146 NPRC.

26. J. Buntin, Efficiency Report, Gracie S. Taylor, November 1, 1918, Gracie Taylor Personnel File, RG 146 NPRC.

27. I. Coonan to M. Stewart, April 4, 1933; I. Coonan to M. Stewart, April 12, 1933, 056 Reports to Miss Stewart, PISEO, CCF 1935–42, Box 3, RG 75 NAR. I. Coonan to Commissioner of Indian Affairs, April 29, 1933, 052 Reports Mrs. Coonan, PISEO, CCF 1935–42, Box 3, RG 75 NAR. Copy also in Sells 00-33-920, CCF 1907–1939, RG 75 NAB.

28. G. Taylor to M. Stewart, May 18, 1933, Box 3 (T–Z), RSSE, PIS, Boxes 1–3, RG 75 NAR.

29. M. Stewart to I. Coonan, March 21, 1933, 052 Reports Mrs. Coonan, PISEO, CCF 1935–42, Box 3, RG 75 NAR. Copy, I. Coonan to M. Stewart, March 26, 1933; I. Coonan to M. Stewart, April 12, 1933, 056 Reports to Miss Stewart, PISEO, CCF 1935–42, Box 3, RG 75 NAR.

30. Philp, "John Collier," 273–276; Kelly, "Charles James Rhoads," 264–265.

31. J. Collier to I. Coonan, April 25, 1933, 052 Reports Mrs. Coonan, PISEO, CCF 1935–42, Box 3, RG 75 NAR. Copy also in Sells 00-33-920, CCF 1907–1939, RG 75 NAB.

32. J. Collier to G. Taylor, April 26, 1933; I. Coonan to Commissioner, April 29, 1933, Sells 00-33-920, CCF 1907–1939, RG 75 NAB. J. Collier to I. Coonan, May 9, 1933, 052 Reports Mrs. Coonan, PISEO, CCF 1935–42, Box 3, RG 75 NAR. I. Coonan to M. Stewart, May 8, 1933, May 17, 1933, 056 Reports to Miss Stewart, PISEO, CCF 1935–42, Box 3, RG 75 NAR.

33. Report, I. Coonan to M. Stewart, May 24, 1933, 052 Reports Mrs. Coonan, PISEO, CCF 1935–42, Box 3, RG 75 NAR.

34. Stefon, "Willard Beatty and Progressive Indian Education," 98; Reyner and Eder, *American Indian Education*, 217–219.

35. Meriam et al., *The Problem of Indian Administration*, 524.

36. Lavender, *Scientists and Storytellers*, 132–134.

37. See Bernstein, "A Mixed Record"; Greenman, "More than a Mother," 49–49, 54. Scholars have also looked at the "introduction" of Indian women to the wage sector through New Deal programs that organized arts and crafts production for wages from the mid-1930s: Berman, *Circle of Goods*, 74; Berman, "'All We Needed Was Our Gardens'"; O'Neill, *Working the Navajo Way*, 55–108.

38. Report, I. Coonan to M. Stewart, May 24, 1933, 052 Reports Mrs. Coonan, PISEO, CCF 1935–42, Box 3, RG 75 NAR.

39. I. Coonan to M. Stewart, May 24, 1933, 052 Reports Mrs. Coonan, PISEO, CCF 1935–42, Box 3, RG 75 NAR.

40. G. Taylor to M. Stewart, May 18, 1933, Box 3 (T–Z), RSSE, PIS, Boxes 1–3, RG 75 NAR.

41. J. Collier to G. Taylor, June 1, 1933; J. Collier to J. Elliott, June 1, 1933, Box 3 (T–Z), RSSE, PIS, Boxes 1–3, RG 75 NAR.

42. R. Tisinger to Commissioner (marked attn. Mary Stewart), June 15, 1933, Box 3 (T–Z), RSSE, PIS, Boxes 1–3, RG 75 NAR.

43. J. Elliott to Commissioner, June 20, 1933, Box 3 (T–Z), RSSE, PIS, Boxes 1–3, RG 75 NAR.

44. F. Hall to J. Collier, July 11, 1933; I. Coonan to M. Stewart, August 4, 1933; I. Coonan, Phoenix Indian School Girls Placed, June 1, 1933; E. Long to J. Collier, July 1, 1933; G. Taylor to J. Collier, July 3, 1933, General Services 00-1933-920, CCF 1907–1939, RG 75 NAB.

45. J. Collier to R. Tisinger, June 23, 1933, Box 3 (T–Z), RSSE, PIS, Boxes 1–3, RG 75 NAR.

46. R. Tisinger to Commissioner, July 3, 1933, Box 3 (T–Z), RSSE, PIS, Boxes 1–3, RG 75 NAR.

47. W. Zimmerman to G. Taylor, July 6, 1933; W. Zimmerman to J. Elliott, July 6, 1933, Box 3 (T–Z), RSSE, PIS, Boxes 1–3, RG 75 NAR.

48. Memorandum, June 21, 1933, General Services 27328-33-920, CCF 1907–1939, RG 75 NAB.

49. J. Collier to R. Tisinger, August 16, 1933, Box 3 (T–Z), RSSE, PIS, Boxes 1–3, RG 75 NAR.

50. J. Collier to R. Tisinger, August 16, 1933; R. Tisinger to Commissioner, September 2, 1933; J. Collier to R. Tisinger, September 15, 1933, Box 3 (T–Z), RSSE, PIS, Boxes 1–3, RG 75 NAR.

51. W. Zimmerman to G. Taylor, July 6, 1933, Box 3 (T–Z), RSSE, PIS, Boxes 1–3, RG 75 NAR.

52. G. Taylor to I. Coonan, September 3, 1933; G. Taylor to I. Coonan, September 16, 1933; I. Coonan to G. Taylor, October 25, 1933, Correspondence of Senior Placement Matron Gracie S. Taylor 1929–1934, SIEFCW, Box 147, RG 75 NAR. I am using pseudonyms to protect the privacy of descendants.

53. J. Collier to J. Elliott, April 24, 1934, Box 3 (T–Z), RSSE, PIS, Boxes 1–3, RG 75 NAR.

54. R. Tisinger to Commissioner, May 10, 1934, Box 3 (T–Z), RSSE, PIS, Boxes 1–3, RG 75 NAR.

55. Personal History Doris Weston, October 6, 1928, Doris Weston Personnel File, RG 146 NPRC. J. Elliott to Commissioner (attn. W. Ryan), January 15, 1934, Sells 00-34-806, CCF 1907–1939, RG 75 NAB. R. Tisinger to Commissioner, June 5, 1933; J. Collier to J. Elliott, March 13, 1934, Box 3 (T–Z), RSSE, PIS, Boxes 1–3, RG 75 NAR.

56. J. Collier to J. Elliott, August 28, 1934; conversation between Mr. Moyer and Miss Groves, Fort Wingate, New Mexico, August 30, 1934; W. Morgan to T. Hall, September 3, 1934; D. Weston to T. Hall, September 8, 1934; T. Hall

to Commissioner, September 19, 1934; Education Division Memorandum, n.d., c. September 1934, Doris Weston Personnel File, RG 146 NPRC.

57. R. Tisinger to J. Elliott, May 10, 1934; J. Elliott to Commissioner, May 19, 1934, Box 3 (T–Z), RSSE, PIS, Boxes 1–3, RG 75 NAR.

58. Memorandum to employees by M. Stewart, May 31, 1934, Gracie Taylor Personnel File, RG 146 NPRC. W. Zimmerman to J. Elliott, June 11, 1934; W. Zimmerman to G. Taylor, June 11, 1934, Box 3 (T–Z), RSSE, PIS, Boxes 1–3, RG 75 NAR.

59. W. Zimmerman to G. Taylor, June 11, 1934, Box 3 (T–Z), RSSE, PIS, Boxes 1–3, RG 75 NAR. She was entitled to a pension of $343 per annum.

60. H. Ashurst to J. Collier, June 27, 1934; W. Zimmerman to H. Ashurst, July 19, 1934, Gracie Taylor Personnel File, RG 146 NPRC.

61. E. Meritt to H. Ashurst, October 21, 1914; H. Ashurst to E. Merritt, October 19, 1914; J. Light to H. Ashurst, October 13, 1914, San Xavier 89961-1914-154, CCF 1907–1939, RG 75 NAB. H. Ashurst to Commissioner, April 19, 1929; H. Corbett to R. Wilbur, telegram, April 18, 1929, Janette Woodruff Personnel File, RG 146 NPRC. M. H. Lanman (secretary to H. Ashurst) to J. Collier, August 7, 1934; J. Collier to H. Ashurst, August 28, 1934, Gracie Taylor Personnel File, RG 146 NPRC.

62. J. Collier to H. Ashurst, August 28, 1934, Gracie Taylor Personnel File, RG 146 NPRC.

63. I. Greenway to J. Collier, September 25, 1934; W. Zimmerman to I. Greenway, October 16, 1934, Gracie Taylor Personnel File, RG 146 NPRC. According to Weston, Taylor was managing a travel agency in town in January 1935. One wonders if she might have had some help from Greenway, a leader in the revival of Tucson's tourism business in the 1930s. Doris Weston, Brief History of Tucson Indian Employment Bureau, n.d., c. Jan 1935, Employment Reports and Statistics ERA 1934–1935, SIEFCW, Box 144, RG 75 NAR.

Chapter 8. "—For a time, at least": History and the Outing Matrons

1. R. Tisinger to J. Elliott, June 29, 1934, Box 3 (T–Z), RSSE, PIS, Boxes 1–3, RG 75 NAR. Woodruff, *Indian Oasis*, 278. Doris Weston, Present Situation of the Indian Employment Work, n.d., c. December 1935, Employment Reports and Statistics ERA 1934–1935, SIEFCW, Box 144, RG 75 NAR.

2. Doris Weston, Tucson Era Project RK3-I, August 11, 1935, Employment Reports and Statistics ERA 1934–1935, SIEFCW, Box 144, RG 75 NAR.

3. Doris Weston, Employment, n.d., c. August 1935, Employment Reports and Statistics ERA 1934–1935, SIEFCW, Box 144, RG 75 NAR.

4. E. G——, Employment Card, September 5, 1934, Employment Qualification Cards A–L, SIEFCW, Box 146, RG 75 NAR.

5. E. Compton to E. Burton, August 1, 1935; E. Burton to E. Compton, August 10, 1935, Doris Weston Personnel File, RG 146 NPRC. Doris Weston,

Present Situation of the Indian Employment Work, n.d., c. December 1935, Employment Reports and Statistics ERA 1934–1935, SIEFCW, Box 144, RG 75 NAR.

6. R. Tisinger to D. Weston, 16 January 1936; T. Hall to W. Beatty, June 26, 1936, Box 3 (T–Z), RSSE, PIS, Boxes 1–3, RG 75 NAR.

7. For Phoenix, see I. Coonan to Miss Stewart, August 24, 1934, General Services 37016-34-920, CCF 1907–1939, RG 75 NAB. B. Coats to E. Roberts, September 20, 1935; V. Easchief to E. White, June 11, 1937, 162.9 Applications for Positions (Women), PISEO, CCF 1935-42, Box 9, RG 75 NAR. F. Nelson to B. Coats, June 6, 1934, 162 Applications for Positions (Women), PISEO, CCF 1935–42, Box 9, RG 75 NAR. Coonan returned to Phoenix for some months before resigning to get married. Coats was transferred from Phoenix at the end of June 1936 to take up an employment agent position in Oklahoma City, a position she held until the end of February 1942 (when it was possibly abolished): S. Ayers to Officer in Charge, Washington, DC, June 24, 1942, Belva Coats Personnel File, RG 146 NPRC. For Kansas City, see V. Woods to M. Stewart, July 12, 1935, General Services 36566-35-920, CCF 1907–1939, RG 75 NAB. M. Stewart to Mr. Armstrong, October 13, 1934; V. Woods to Dear Madam, June 27, 1936, General Services 37016-34-920, CCF 1907–1939, RG 75 NAB.

8. M. Stewart, An Evaluation of the Indian Placement Work, Oakland, California, May 20, 1937, General Services 170534-34-920, CCF 1907–1939, RG 75 NAB. For Oakland, see also Markwyn, "'It Was a Place for the Girls to Meet,'" 62–63. From 1940, the shared office arrangement with the YWCA at Oakland came to an end, although it is not clear whether the Oakland Indian employment service did also: Copy, E. Armstrong to M. Stewart, January 4, 1940; copy, M. Stewart to A. Landman, September 30, 1939; M. Van Every to A. Landman, September 21, 1939, General Services 170534-34-920, CCF 1907–1939, RG 75 NAB.

9. P. Fickinger to T. B. Hall, July 20, 1936, Box 3 (T–Z), RSSE, PIS, Boxes 1–3, RG 75 NAR. Fickinger replaced Mary Stewart, now the superintendent of Indian education in Californa: M. Stewart to A. Landman, September 30, 1939, General Services 170534-34-920, CCF 1907–1939, RG 75 NAB. Weston had been officially promoted the previous month to "community worker," with a special provision for her experience to be accepted in lieu of qualifications. G. Numbers to Civil Service Commission, April 15, 1936; G. Numbers to D. Weston, April 30, 1936; W. Hogard, Efficiency Report Doris Weston, May 6, 1936; T. Hall to Commissioner of Indian Affairs, May 18, 1936, Doris Weston Personnel File, RG 146 NPRC.

10. T. Hall to J. McCaskill, February 24, 1938; P. Fickinger to T. Hall, March 14, 1938, Doris Weston Personnel File, RG 146 NPRC. D. Weston to J. F. McKale, January 19, 1939, Employment General Correspondence 1935–1942, SIEFCW, Box 144, RG 75 NAR. Various correspondences, April 1939–August 2, 1948, Doris Weston Personnel File, RG 146 NPRC. Weston retired in August 1948.

11. Doris Weston, Brief History of Tucson Indian Employment Bureau, n.d., c. Jan 1935, Employment Reports and Statistics ERA 1934–1935, SIEFCW, Box 144, RG 75 NAR.

12. In fact, Tucson would continue to be remarkable for its high levels of Indian women's employment, particularly for single women, albeit in low-paying jobs. Eric Meeks notes that in the late 1960s "hundreds" of Tohono O'odham women worked, mostly in domestic labor, comparing the 50.7% female employment rate with the 18.7% elsewhere in Arizona: Meeks, *Border Citizens*, 220. A 1969 anthropological study of Tohono O'odham employment, however, barely registered that Tohono O'odham women worked, an example of the curious and persistent blindness to their economic contribution: Waddell, *Papago Indians at Work*.

13. A point made with regard to white women generally by indigenous scholars: see Huggins et al., "Letter to the Editors," 506; Jaimes, "American Indian Woman," 332; Moreton-Robinson, *Talkin' Up to the White Woman*, 94. Jackie Huggins has specifically highlighted the complicity of white women who implemented oppressive government policies in Australia: Huggins, *Sister Girl*, 30.

14. As observed in the Australian context: Curthoys, "Identity Crisis," 174.

15. Clonts, "Graham County, Arizona–Safford Union Cemetery Burial Index."

Bibliography

Theses and Dissertations

Almeida, Deirde Ann. "The Role of Western Massachusetts in the Development of American Indian Education Reform through the Hampton Institute's Summer Outing Program." PhD diss., University of Massachusetts, 1992.

Bell, Genevieve. "Telling Stories out of School: Remembering the Carlisle Indian Industrial School, 1879–1918." PhD diss., Stanford University, 1998.

Booth, Peter MacMillan. "Creation of a Nation: The Development of the Tohono O'odham Political Culture, 1900–1937." PhD diss., Purdue University, 2000.

Cahill, Cathleen D. "'Only the Home Can Found a State: Gender, Labor, and the United States Indian Service, 1869–1928." PhD diss., The University of Chicago, 2004.

Emmerich, Lisa. "'To Respect and Love and Seek the Ways of White Women': Field Matrons, the Office of Indian Affairs, and Civilization Policy, 1890–1938." PhD diss., University of Maryland–College Park, 1987.

Gamber, Wendy E. "The Female Economy: The Millinery and Dressmaking Trades, 1860–1930." PhD diss., Brandeis University, 1991.

Gilcreast, Everett Arthur. "Richard Henry Pratt and American Indian Policy, 1877–1906: A Study of the Assimilation Movement." PhD diss., Yale University, 1967.

Harvey, Gretchen G. "Cherokee and American: Ruth Muskrat Bronson, 1897–1982." PhD diss., Arizona State University, 1996.

Markwyn, Abigail. "'It Was a Place for the Girls to Meet': Community, Native Americans, and the Berkeley Outing Center, 1927–1933." Master's thesis, University of Wisconsin–Madison, 2000.

Osburn, Katherine M. B. "'And As the Squaws Are a Secondary Consideration': Southern Ute Women under Directed Culture Change, 1887–1934." PhD diss., The University of Denver, 1993.

Ricks, Nathaniel R. "A Peculiar Place for the Peculiar Institution: Slavery and Sovereignty in Early Territorial Utah." Master's thesis, Brigham Young University, 2007.

Walker-McNeil, Pearl Lee. "The Carlisle Indian School: A Study of Acculturation." PhD diss., The American University, Washington, DC, 1979.

Books, Book Chapters, and Journal Articles

Adams, David Wallace. *Education for Extinction: American Indians and the Boarding School Experience, 1875–1928.* Lawrence: University Press of Kansas, 1995.

———. "Beyond Bleakness: The Brighter Side of Indian Boarding Schools, 1870–1940." In *Boarding School Blues: Revisiting American Indian Educational Experiences*, edited by Clifford E. Trafzer, Jean A. Keller, and Lorene Sidquoc, 35–64. Lincoln: University of Nebraska Press, 2006.

Ahern, Wilbert H. "An Experiment Aborted: Returned Indian Students in the Indian School Service, 1881–1908." *Ethnohistory* 44, no. 2 (Spring 1997): 263–304.

Archuleta, Margaret L., Brenda J. Child, and K. Tsianina Lomawaima, eds. *Away from Home: American Indian Boarding School Experiences.* Phoenix: Heard Museum, 2000.

Bancroft, Hubert Howe. *History of Arizona and New Mexico, 1530–1888.* 1889. Albuquerque: Horn & Wallace, 1962.

Banerjee, Swapna M. *Men, Women and Domestics: Articulating Middle-Class Identity in Colonial Bengal.* New Delhi: Oxford, 2004.

Bannan, Helen M. *"True Womanhood" on the Reservation: Field Matrons in the United States Indian Service.* Tucson: Southwest Institute for Research on Women, 1984.

Bataille, Gretchen M., and Kathleen Mullen Sands. *American Indian Women: Telling Their Lives.* Lincoln: University of Nebraska Press, 1984.

Belich, James. *Replenishing the Earth: The Settler Revolution and the Rise of the Anglo-World, 1783–1939.* New York: Oxford University Press, 2009.

Berman, Tressa. *Circle of Goods: Women, Work, and Welfare in a Reservation Community.* Albany: State University of New York, 2003.

———. "'All We Needed Was Our Gardens': Women's Work and Welfare Reform in the Reservation Economy." In *Native Pathways: American Indian Culture and Economic Development in the Twentieth Century*, edited by Brian Hosmer and Colleen O'Neill, 133–155. Boulder: University Press of Colorado, 2004.

Bernstein, Alison. "A Mixed Record: The Political Enfranchisement of American Indian Women during the Indian New Deal." *Journal of the West: Indian Leadership* 23, no. 3 (July 1984): 13–20.

Blaine, Peter, Sr., as told to Michael S. Adams. *Papagos and Politics.* Tucson: Arizona Historical Society, 1981.

Bringhurst, Newell G. "The Mormons and Slavery—A Closer Look." *Pacific Historical Review* 50, no. 3 (August 1981): 329–338.

Britten, Thomas A. "Hoover and the Indians: The Case for Continuity in Federal Indian Policy, 1900–1933." *The Historian* 61, no. 3 (1999): 518–538.

Brooks, James F. *Captives and Cousins: Slavery, Kinship and Community in the Southwest Borderlands.* Chapel Hill: University of North Carolina Press, 2002.

Brown, Estelle Aubrey. *Stubborn Fool: A Narrative*. Caldwell, ID: Caxton Printers, 1952.

Brown, Haddington. *Historical Circular of Indian Training School, Tucson, Arizona*. Tucson: The Citizen Printing and Publishing Co., 1905.

Browne, John Ross. *Adventures in Apache Country: A Tour through Arizona and Sonora, with Notes on the Silver Regions of Nevada*. 1871. New York: Promontory Press, 1974.

Burton, Antoinette. *Burdens of History: British Feminists, Indian Women, and Imperial Culture, 1865–1915*. Chapel Hill: University of North Carolina Press, 1994.

Cahill, Cathleen. *Federal Fathers & Mothers: A Social History of the United States Indian Service, 1869–1933*. Chapel Hill: University of North Carolina Press, 2011.

———. "'You Think It Strange That I Can Love an Indian': Native Men, White Women, and Marriage in the Indian Service." *Frontiers: A Journal of Women Studies* 29, nos. 2 & 3 (2008): 106–145.

Carter, Patricia A. "'Completely Discouraged': Women Teachers' Resistance in the Bureau of Indian Affairs Schools, 1900–1910." *Frontiers: A Journal of Women Studies* 15, no. 3 (1995): 53–86.

Castro, Robert Francis. "After the Slavers: Law, Liberation and Captive-Taking in the New Mexican Borderlands." *Slavery and Abolition* 28, no. 3 (2007): 369–386.

Chaudhuri, Nupur. "Memsahibs and Their Servants in Nineteenth-Century India." *Women's History Review* 3, no. 4 (1994): 549–562.

Chaudhuri, Nupur, and Margaret Strobel, eds. *Western Women and Imperialism: Complicity and Resistance*. Bloomington: Indiana University Press, 1992.

Child, Brenda. *Boarding School Seasons: American Indian Families, 1900–1940*. Lincoln: University of Nebraska Press, 1998.

Churchill, Ward. *Kill the Indian, Save the Man: The Genocidal Impact of American Indian Residential Schools*. San Francisco: City Lights, 2004.

Clark-Lewis, Elizabeth. *Living In, Living Out: African American Domestics in Washington, D.C., 1910–1940*. Washington, DC: Smithsonian Institution Press, 1994.

Clifford, James. *The Predicament of Culture: Twentieth-Century Ethnography, Literature and Art*. Cambridge, MA: Harvard University Press, 1988.

Cock, Jacklyn. *Maids and Madams: A Study in the Politics of Exploitation*. Johannesburg: Ravan Press, 1980.

Cole, Anna, Victoria Haskins, and Fiona Paisley, eds. *Uncommon Ground: White Women in Aboriginal History*. Canberra: Aboriginal Studies Press, 2005.

Collins, Cary C. "The Broken Crucible of Assimilation: Forest Grove Indian School and the Origins of Off-Reservation Boarding School Education in the West." *Oregon History Quarterly* 101, no. 4 (Fall 2000): 466–507.

———. "A Future with a Past: Hazel Pete, Cultural Identity, and the Federal Indian Education System." *Pacific Northwest Quarterly* 92, no. 1 (Winter 2000/2001): 15–28.

Comaroff, John L. "Images of Empire, Contests of Conscience: Models of Colonial Domination in South Africa." In *Tensions of Empire: Colonial Cultures in a Bourgeois World*, edited by Frederick Cooper and Ann Laura Stoler, 163–197. Berkeley: University of California Press, 2007.

Connelly, Mark T. *The Response to Prostitution in the Progressive Era*. Chapel Hill: University of North Carolina Press, 1980.

Cowan, Ruth Schwartz. *More Work for Mother: The Ironies of Household Technology from the Open Hearth to the Microwave*. New York: Basic Books, 1983.

Curthoys, Ann. "Identity Crisis: Colonialism, Nation and Gender in Australian History." *Gender & History* 5, no. 2 (1993): 165–176.

Davis, Allen F. *Spearheads for Reform: The Social Settlements and the Progressive Movement, 1890–1914*. New York: Rutgers Press, 1984.

Dayton, Cornelia Hugh. "Taking the Trade: Abortion and Gender Relations in an Eighteenth-Century New England Village." *The William and Mary Quarterly* 48, no. 1 (January 1991): 19–49.

Dean, Mitchell. *Critical and Effective Histories: Foucault's Methods and Historical Sociology*. London: Routledge, 1994.

De Costa, Caroline M. "'The Contagiousness of Childbed Fever': A Short History of Puerperal Sepsis and Its Treatment." *The Medical Journal of Australia* 177, nos. 11–12 (2002): 668–671.

Deloria, Philip J. *Indians in Unexpected Places*. Lawrence: University Press of Kansas, 2004.

Deutsch, Sarah. *No Separate Refuge: Culture, Class, and Gender on an Anglo-Hispanic Frontier in the American Southwest, 1880–1940*. New York: Oxford University Press, 1987.

Drachman, Roy P. *This Is Not a Book: Just Memories*. Tucson, AZ: R. P. Drachman, 1979.

Ellinghaus, Katherine. *Taking Assimilation to Heart: Marriages of White Women and Indigenous Men in the United States and Australia, 1887–1937*. Lincoln: University of Nebraska Press, 2006.

Emmerich, Lisa. "'Civilization' and Transculturation: The Field Matron Program and Cross-Cultural Contact." *American Indian Culture and Research Journal* 15, no. 4 (1991): 33–48.

———. "'Right in the Midst of My Own People': Native American Women and the Field Matron Program." *American Indian Quarterly* 15, no. 2 (Spring 1991): 201–216.

Eppinga, Jane. *Tucson, Arizona*. Images of America. Charleston, SC: Arcadia Publishing, 2000.

Erickson, Winston P. *Sharing the Desert: The Tohono O'odham in History*. Tucson: University of Arizona Press, 2003.

Fahmi, Magda. "'Ruffled' Mistresses and 'Discontented' Maids: Respectability and the Case of Domestic Service, 1880–1914." *Labour/Le Travail* 39 (Spring 1997): 69–97.

Fischer, Claude S. *America Calling: A Social History of the Telephone to 1940.* Berkeley: University of California Press, 1992.

Fontana, Bernard L. *Of Earth and Little Rain: The Papago Indians.* Tucson: University of Arizona Press, 1989.

Franco, Jeré. "Unlawful Love: A History of Arizona's Miscegenation Law." *Journal of Arizona History* 27 (Winter 1986): 377–390.

Frankenberg, Ruth. "Growing Up White: Feminism, Racism and the Social Geography of Childhood." *Feminist Review* 45 (Autumn 1993): 51–84.

Fronc, Jennifer. *New York Undercover: Private Surveillance in the Progressive Era.* Chicago: University of Chicago Press, 2009.

Garza, Sonya C. "Common Law Marriage: A Proposal for a Revival of a Dying Doctrine." *New England Law Review* 40 (2005–2006): 541–553.

Gere, Anne Ruggles. "Indian Heart/White Man's Head: Native-American Teachers in Indian Schools, 1880–1930." *History of Education Quarterly* 45, no. 1 (Spring 2005): 38–65.

Gilbert, Matthew Sakiestwa. *Education beyond the Mesas: Hopi students at the Sherman Institute, 1902–1929.* Lincoln: University of Nebraska Press, 2010.

Gillis, John R. "Servants, Sexual Relations, and the Risks of Illegitimacy in London, 1801–1900." *Feminist Studies* 5, no. 1 (Spring 1979): 142–173.

Goff, John S. "William T. Howell and the Howell Code of Arizona." *The American Journal of Legal History* 11, no. 3 (July 1967): 221–233.

Green, Jonathon. *Cassell's Dictionary of Slang.* London: Weidenfeld & Nicholson, 2005.

Greenman, Nancy. "More than a Mother: Some Tewa Women Reflect on Gia." In *Unrelated Kin: Race and Gender in Women's Personal Narratives*, edited by Gwendolyn Etter-Lewis and Michéle Foster, 49–67. New York: Routledge, 1996.

Guiterrez, Ramon A. *When Jesus Came, the Corn Mothers Went Away: Marriage, Sexuality and Power in New Mexico, 1500–1846.* Stanford, CA: Stanford University Press, 1991.

Hackenberg, Robert A. "Pima and Papago Ecological Adaptations." In *Southwest*, Vol. 10 of *Handbook of North American Indians*, edited by Alfonso Ortiz, 161–177. Washington, DC: Smithsonian Institution, 1983.

Hailman, William N. "Education of the Indian." In Vol. 2, *Monographs on Education in the United States*, edited by Nicholas Murray Butler, 3–36. Albany: J. B. Lyon Co., 1900.

Hansen, Karen Tranberg. *Distant Companions: Servants and Employers in Zambia, 1900–1985.* Ithaca, NY: Cornell University Press, 1989.

Hart, John Bret. *Tucson: Portrait of a Desert Pueblo.* Woodland Hills, CA: Windsor, 1980.

Haskins, Victoria. *One Bright Spot.* Basingstoke, Hampshire, UK: Palgrave, 2005.

Herring, Rebecca J. "The Creation of Indian Farm Women: Field Matrons and Acculturation on the Kiowa-Comanche Reservation, 1895–1906." In *At Home on the Range: Essays on the History of Western Social and Domestic Life*, edited by John Wunder, 39–56. Westport, CT: Greenwood Press, 1985.

Horn, Pamela. *The Rise and Fall of the Victorian Servant.* Stroud: Alan Sutton Publishing Ltd., 1995.

Horne, Esther Burnett, and Sally McBeth. *Essie's Story: The Life and Legacy of a Shoshone Teacher.* Lincoln: University of Nebraska Press, 1998.

Hoxie, Frederick E. *A Final Promise: The Campaign to Assimilate the Indians, 1880–1920.* 1984. Lincoln: University of Nebraska Press, 2001.

Hoyt, John P. *The Compiled Laws of the Territory of Arizona, 1864–1877.* Detroit, MI: Richmond, Backus & Co., 1877.

Huggins, Jackie. *Sister Girl: The Writings of Aboriginal Activist and Historian Jackie Huggins.* St. Lucia, Queensland, Australia: University of Queensland Press, 1998.

Huggins, Jackie, Jo Willmot, Isabel Tarrago, Kathy Willetts, Liz Bond, Lillian Holt, Eleanor Bourke, Maryann Bin-Salik, Pat Fowell, Joann Schmider, Valerie Craigie, and Linda McBride-Levi. "Letter to the Editors." *Women's Studies International Forum* 1, no. 5 (1991): 505–513.

Hurtado, Albert L. "'Hardly a Farm House—A Kitchen without Them': Indian and White Households on the California Borderland Frontier in 1860." *Western Historical Quarterly* 13, no. 3 (July 1982): 245–270.

———. *Indian Survival on the California Frontier.* New Haven, CT: Yale University Press, 1988.

Jacobs, Margaret D. "Clara True and Female Moral Authority." In *The Human Tradition in the American West*, edited by Benson Tong and Regan A. Lutz, 99–115. Wilmington, DE: SR Books, 2002.

———. "The Eastmans and the Luhans: Interracial Marriage between White Women and Native American Men, 1875–1935." *Frontiers: A Journal of Women Studies* 23, no. 3 (2002): 29–54.

———. "Maternal Colonialism: White Women and Indigenous Child Removal in the American West and Australia, 1880–1940." *Western Historical Quarterly* 36, no. 4 (Winter 2005): 453–476.

———. "Working on the Domestic Frontier: American Indian Domestic Servants in White Women's Households in the San Francisco Bay Area, 1920–1940." *Frontiers* 28, nos. 1–2 (2007): 165–199.

———. *White Mother to a Dark Race: Settler Colonialism, Maternalism, and the Removal of Indigenous Children in the American West and Australia, 1880–1940.* Lincoln: University of Nebraska Press, 2009.

Jaimes, M. Annette, with Theresa Halsey. "American Indian Woman: At the Center of Indigenous Resistance in North America." In *The State of Native*

America: Genocide, Colonization, and Resistance, edited by M. Annette Jaimes, 311–344. Boston: South End Press, 1992.

Jensen, Joan M. "'I'd Rather Be Dancing': Wisconsin Women Moving On." *Frontiers: A Journal of Women Studies* 22, no. 1 (2001): 1–20.

———. *Calling This Place Home: Women on the Wisconsin Frontier, 1850–1925.* St. Paul: Minnesota Historical Society Press, 2006.

Johnson, S. L. "Sharing Bed and Board: Cohabitation and Cultural Difference in Central Arizona Mining Towns." *Frontiers: A Journal of Women Studies* 7, no. 3 (1984): 36–42.

Jones, Dorothy Knee. *A Century of Servitude: Pribilof Aleuts under U.S. Rule.* Lanham, MD: University Press of America, 1980.

Joseph, Alice, Rosamund B. Spicer, and Jane Chesky. *The Desert People: A Study of the Papago Indian.* Chicago: The University of Chicago Press, 1949.

Katzman, David. *Seven Days a Week: Women and Domestic Service in Industrializing America.* Urbana: University of Illinois Press, 1981.

Kelly, Lawrence C. "Charles Henry Burke, 1921–29." In *The Commissioners of Indian Affairs, 1824–1977*, edited by Robert M. Kvasnicka and Herman J. Viola, 251–261. Lincoln: University of Nebraska Press, 1979.

———. "Charles James Rhoads, 1929–33." In *The Commissioners of Indian Affairs, 1824–1977*, edited by Robert M. Kvasnicka and Herman J. Viola, 263–271. Lincoln: University of Nebraska Press, 1979.

Knack, Martha C. "Newspaper Accounts of Indian Women in Southern Nevada Mining Towns." *Journal of California and Great Basin Anthropology* 8, no. 1 (1986): 83–98.

———. "Nineteenth-Century Great Basin Indian Wage Labor." In *Native Americans and Wage Labor: Ethnohistorical Perspectives*, edited by Martha C. Knack and Alice Littlefield, 144–176. Norman: University of Oklahoma Press, 1996.

———. *Boundaries Between: The Southern Paiutes, 1775–1995.* Lincoln: University of Nebraska Press, 2001.

Knack, Martha C., and Alice Littlefield. "Native American Labor: Retrieving History, Rethinking Theory." In *Native Americans and Wage Labor: Ethnohistorical Perspectives*, edited by Martha C. Knack and Alice Littlefield, 3–44. Norman: University of Oklahoma Press, 1996.

Lack, Paul D. "Slavery and the Texas Revolution." *The Southwestern Historical Quarterly* 89, no. 2 (October 1985): 181–202.

Lamar, Howard Roberts. *The Far Southwest, 1846–1912: A Territorial History.* New Haven, CT: Yale University Press, 1966.

Lavender, Catherine J. *Scientists and Storytellers: Feminist Anthropologists and the Construction of the American Southwest.* Albuquerque: University of New Mexico Press, 2006.

Leupp, Francis Ellington. *The Indian and His Problem.* New York: C. Scribner's Sons, 1910.

Lindsey, Donal F. *Indians at Hampton Institute, 1877–1923.* Urbana: University of Illinois Press, 1995.

Locher-Scholten, Elsbeth. "So Close and Yet So Far: The Ambivalence of Dutch Colonial Rhetoric on Javanese Servants in Indonesia, 1900–1942." In *Domesticating the Empire: Race, Gender, and Family Life in French and Dutch Colonialism*, edited by Julia Clancy-Smith and Frances Gouda, 131–153. Charlottesville: University Press of Virginia, 1998.

Lomawaima, K. Tsaianina. "Domesticity in the Federal Indian Schools: The Power of Authority over Mind and Body." *American Ethnologist* 20, no. 2 (1993): 227–249.

———. *They Called It Prairie Light: The Story of the Chilocco Indian School.* Lincoln: University of Nebraska Press, 1994.

———. "Estelle Reel, Superintendent of Indian Schools, 1898–1910: Politics, Curriculum, and Land." *Journal of American Indian Education* 35, no. 3 (Spring 1996): 5–31.

Lomawaima, K. Tsianina, and Teresa L. McCarty. *To Remain an Indian: Lessons in Democracy from a Century of Native American Education.* New York: Teachers College Press, 2006.

Loudon, Irvine. *The Tragedy of Childbed Fever.* New York: Oxford University Press, 2000.

Luckingham, Bradford. *The Urban Southwest: A Profile History of Albuquerque, El Paso, Phoenix, Tucson.* El Paso: Texas Western Press, 1982.

Ludlow, Helen Wilhelmina. *Ten Years' Work for Indians at the Hampton Normal and Agricultural Institute, at Hampton, Virginia.* Hampton, VA: The Hampton Institute, 1888.

Lynch-Brennan, Margaret. "Was Bridget's Experience Unique? A Comparative View of American Domestic Service over Time and Space." In *Domestic Service and the Formation of European Identity: Understanding the Globalization of Domestic Work, 16th–21st Centuries*, edited by Antoinette Fauve-Chamoux, 489–515. Bern: Peter Lang, 2004.

Malouf, Carling, and A. Arline Malouf. "The Effects of Spanish Slavery on the Indians of the Intermountain West." *Southwestern Journal of Anthropology* 1, no. 3 (Autumn 1945): 378–391.

Manuel, Frances, and Deborah Neff, with Danny Lopez. *Desert Indian Woman: Stories and Dreams.* Tucson: University of Arizona Press, 2001.

Mathes, Valerie Shere. "Nineteenth-Century Women: The Women's National Indian Association." *American Indian Quarterly* 14, no. 1 (Winter 1990): 1–18.

McBride, Theresa M. *The Domestic Revolution: The Modernisation of Household Service in England and France, 1820–1920.* London: Croom Helm, 1976.

McCarthy, James. *A Papago Traveler: The Memories of James McCarthy.* Edited by John G. Westover. Tucson: Sun Tracks and University of Arizona Press, 1986.

McClintock, Anne. *Imperial Leather: Race, Gender and Sexuality in the Colonial Contest*. London: Routledge, 1995.

McLaren, Angus. "Illegal Operations: Women, Doctors, and Abortion, 1886–1939." *Journal of Social History* 26, no. 4 (Summer 1993): 797–816.

McMillen, Christian. "The Birth of an Activist: Fred Mahone and the Politicization of the Hualapai, 1918 to 1923." *American Indian Culture and Research Journal* 27, no. 1 (2003): 33–60.

Meeks, Eric V. "The Tohono O'odham, Wage Labor, and Resistant Adaptation, 1900–1930." *Western Historical Quarterly* 34, no. 4 (Winter 2003): 468–489.

———. *Border Citizens: The Making of Indians, Mexicans and Anglos in Arizona*. Austin: University of Texas Press, 2007.

Meriam, Lewis, et al. *The Problem of Indian Administration: Report of a Survey Made at the Request of Honorable Hubert Work, Secretary of the Interior, and Submitted to Him, February 21, 1928*. Baltimore: John Hopkins Press, 1928.

Midgley, Claire. *Feminism and Empire: Women Activists in Imperial Britain, 1790–1865*. New York: Routledge, 2007.

Moore, Nicole. "'That Critical Juncture': Maternalism in Australian Feminist Anti-Colonial History." *The Vision Splendid: Journal of Australian Studies* 66 (2000): 95–102.

Moreton-Robinson, Aileen. *Talkin' Up to the White Woman: Aboriginal Women and Feminism*. St. Lucia, Queensland, Australia: University of Queensland Press, 2000.

Murphy, Jacqueline Shea. *The People Have Never Stopped Dancing: Native American Modern Dance Histories*. Minneapolis: University of Minnesota Press, 2007.

Nabhan, Gary Paul. *The Desert Smells Like Rain: A Naturalist in O'odham Country*. Tucson: University of Arizona Press, 1982.

Najmi, Samina, and Rajini Srikanth, eds. *White Women in Racialized Spaces: Imaginative Transformation and Ethical Action in Literature*. Albany: State University of New York Press, 2002.

Newman, Louise. *White Women's Rights: The Racial Origins of Feminism in the United States*. New York: Oxford University Press, 1999.

Olasky, Marvin. *Abortion Rites: A Social History of Abortion in America*. Wheaton, IL: Crossways Books, 1992.

O'Neill, Colleen. "Rethinking Modernity and the Discourse of Development in American Indian History, an Introduction." In *Native Pathways: American Indian Culture and Economic Development in the Twentieth Century*, edited by Brian Cosmer and Colleen O'Neill, 1–24. Boulder: University Press of Colorado, 2004.

———. *Working the Navajo Way: Labor and Culture in the Twentieth Century*. Lawrence: University Press of Kansas, 2005.

Osburn, Katherine M. B. "'Dear Friend and Ex-husband': Marriage, Divorce, and Women's Property Rights on the Southern Ute Reservation, 1887–1930." In *Negotiators of Change: Historical Perspectives on Native American Women*, edited by Nancy Shoemaker, 157–175. New York: Routledge, 1995.

———. "To Build Up the Morals of the Tribe: Southern Ute Women's Sexual Behavior and the Office of Indian Affairs, 1895–1932." *Journal of Women's History* 9, no. 3 (Autumn 1997): 10–27.

Otero, Lydia R. *La Calle: Spatial Conflicts and Urban Renewal in a Southwest City*. Tucson: The University of Arizona Press, 2010.

Paisley, Fiona. *Loving Protection? Australian Feminism and Aboriginal Women's Rights, 1919–1939*. Melbourne: Melbourne University Press, 2000.

Palmer, Phyllis. *Domesticity and Dirt: Housewives and Domestic Servants in the United States, 1920–1945*. Philadelphia: Temple University Press, 1989.

Parman, Donald L. "Francis Ellington Leupp, 1905–1909." In *The Commissioners of Indian Affairs, 1824–1977*, edited by Robert M. Kvasnicka and Herman J. Viola, 221–232. Lincoln: University of Nebraska Press, 1979.

Partridge, Eric. *A Dictionary of the Underworld British and American, Being the Vocabularies of Crooks, Criminals, Racketeers, Beggars and Tramps, Convicts, the Commercial Underworld, the Drug Traffic, the White Slave Traffic, Spivs*. 1949. London: Routledge & Kegan Paul, 1961.

Pascoe, Peggy. *Relations of Rescue: The Search for Female Moral Authority in the American West, 1874–1939*. New York: Oxford University Press, 1990.

———. "Miscegenation Law, Court Cases, and Ideologies of 'Race' in Twentieth-Century America." In *Sex, Love, Race: Crossing Boundaries in North American History*, edited by Martha Hodes, 464–490. New York: New York University Press, 1999.

———. *What Comes Naturally: Miscegenation Law and the Making of Race in America*. Oxford: Oxford University Press, 2009.

Paxton, Katrina A. "Learning Gender: Female Students at the Sherman Institute." In *Boarding School Blues: Revisiting American Indian Educational Experiences*, edited by Clifford E. Trafzer, Jean A. Keller, and Lorene Sidquoc, 174–186. Lincoln: University of Nebraska Press, 2006.

Pfefferbaum, Betty, Rennard Strickland, Everett R. Rhoades, and Rose L. Pfefferbaum. "Learning How to Heal: An Analysis of the History, Policy, and Framework of Indian Health Care." *American Indian Law Review* 20, no. 2 (1995/1996): 365–397.

Philp, Kenneth R. "John Collier, 1933–45." In *The Commissioners of Indian Affairs, 1824–1977*, edited by Robert M. Kvasnicka and Herman J. Viola, 273–282. Lincoln: University of Nebraska Press, 1979.

Pickles, Katie, and Myra Rutherdale, eds. *Contact Zones: Aboriginal and Settler Women in Canada's Colonial Past*. Vancouver: UBC Press, 2005.

Pratt, R. H. "The Way Out." In 52nd Cong., 1st sess., 1892, House Executive Document 1, pt. 5, vol. 2 (1892): 1177–1180.

Pratt, Richard Henry. *Battlefield and Classroom: Four Decades with the American Indian, 1867–1904.* Edited by Robert M. Utley. Norman: University of Oklahoma Press, 2003.

Prucha, Francis Paul. "Thomas Jefferson Morgan, 1889–93." In *The Commissioners of Indian Affairs, 1824–1977*, edited by Robert M. Kvasnicka and Herman J. Viola, 193–203. Lincoln: University of Nebraska Press, 1979.

Rawls, James J. *Indians of California: The Changing Image.* Norman: University of Oklahoma Press, 1984.

Reddick, SuAnn M. "The Evolution of Chemawa Indian School: From Red River to Salem, 1825–1885." *Oregon Historical Quarterly* 101, no. 4 (Fall 2000): 444–465.

Reyner, John Allen, and Jeanne M. Oyawin Eder. *American Indian Education: A History.* Norman: University of Oklahoma Press, 2006.

Riley, Glenda. *Confronting Race: Women and Indians on the Frontier, 1815–1915.* Albuquerque: University of New Mexico Press, 2004.

Rochlin, Harriet, and Fred Rochlin. *Pioneer Jews: A New Life in the Far West.* New York: Mariner Books, 2000.

Rollins, Judith. *Between Women: Domestics and Their Employers.* Philadelphia: Temple University Press, 1985.

Romero, Mary. *Maid in the U.S.A.* New York: Routledge, 1992.

Rose, LaVera. "Susan Bordeaux Bettelyoun: Dakota Images." *South Dakota History* 24, nos. 3 & 4 (Fall/Winter 1994): 248–249.

Rusco, Elmer R. *A Fateful Time: The Background and Legislative History of the Indian Reorganization Act.* Reno: University of Nevada Press, 2000.

Salmon, Lucy Maynard. *Domestic Service.* Facsimile ed. 1897. New York: Arno Press, 1972.

Sheridan, Thomas. *Los Tucsonenses: The Mexican Community in Tucson, 1854–1941.* Tucson: University of Arizona Press, 1992.

Silliman, Stephen W. *Lost Laborers in Colonial California: Native Americans and the Archaeology of Rancho Petaluma.* Tucson: University of Arizona Press, 2004.

Simonsen, Jane E. *Making Home Work: Domesticity and Native American Assimilation in the American West, 1860–1919.* Chapel Hill: University of North Carolina Press, 2006.

Smith, Sherry L. *The View from Officers' Row: Army Perceptions of Western Indians.* Tucson: University of Arizona Press, 1990.

Sonnichsen, C. L. *Tucson: The Life and Times of an American City.* Norman: University of Oklahoma Press, 1987.

Stefon, Frederick J. "Willard Beatty and Progressive Indian Education." *American Indian Culture and Research Journal* 33, no. 4 (2009): 91–112.

Stoler, Ann, and Karen Strassler. "Memory-Work in Java: A Cautionary Tale." In *Carnal Knowledge and Imperial Power: Race and the Intimate in Colonial Rule*, edited by Ann Laura Stoler, 162–203. Berkeley: University of California Press, 2002.

Stoler, Ann Laura, ed. *Haunted by Empire: Geographies of Intimacy in North American History*. Durham, NC: Duke University Press, 2006.

———. "Tense and Tender Ties: The Politics of Comparison in North American History and (Post) Colonial Studies." In *Haunted By Empire: Geographies of Intimacy in North American History*, edited by Ann Laura Stoler, 24–67. Durham, NC: Duke University Press, 2006.

———. *Along the Archival Grain: Epistemic Anxieties and Colonial Common Sense*. Princeton, NJ: Princeton University Press, 2009.

Sutherland, Daniel E. *Americans and Their Servants: Domestic Service in the United States from 1800 to 1920*. Baton Rouge: Louisiana State University Press, 1981.

Szasz, Margaret Connell. *Indian Education in the American Colonies, 1607–1783*. Albuquerque: University of New Mexico Press, 1988.

———, ed. *Between Indian and White Worlds: The Cultural Broker*. Norman: University of Oklahoma Press, 1994.

Taylor, Rosemary. *Chicken Every Sunday: My Life with Mother's Boarders*. New York: Whittlesey House, 1943.

Tetzloff, Lisa. "Elizabeth Bender Cloud: 'Working for and with Our Indian People.'" *Frontiers: A Journal of Women Studies* 30, no. 3 (2009): 77–115.

Thoburn, Joseph Bradfield. *A Standard History of Oklahoma: An Authentic Narrative of Its Developments from the Date of the First European Exploration down to the Present Time, Including Accounts of the Indian Tribes, Both Civilized and Wild, of the Cattle Range, of the Land Openings and the Achievements of the Most Recent Period*, Vol. 4. Chicago: The American Historical Society, 1916.

Thompson, Gregory C. "John D. C. Atkins, 1885–88." In *The Commissioners of Indian Affairs, 1824–1977*, edited by Robert M. Kvasnicka and Herman J. Viola, 181–188. Lincoln: University of Nebraska Press, 1979.

Tonkinson, Myrna. "Sisterhood or Aboriginal Servitude? Black Women and White Women on the Australian Frontier." *Aboriginal History* 12, no. 1 (1988): 27–39.

Trennert, Robert A. "From Carlisle to Phoenix: The Rise and Fall of the Indian Outing System, 1878–1930." *Pacific Historical Review* 52, no. 3 (1983): 267–291.

———. *The Phoenix Indian School: Forced Assimilation in Arizona, 1891–1935*. Norman: University of Oklahoma Press, 1988.

———. "Victorian Morality and the Supervision of Indian Women Working in Phoenix, 1906–1930." *Journal of Social History* 22 (1988): 113–128.

Trolander, Judith A. *Professionalism and Social Change: From the Settlement House Movement to Neighborhood Centers, 1886 to the Present*. New York: Columbia University Press, 1987.

Underhill, Ruth M. "Acculturation at the Papago Village of Santa Rosa." In Vol. I, *Papago Indians*, co-authored by Robert Hackenberg, Ruth M. Underhill, and Gwyneth H. Xavier, 309–348. New York: Garland, 1974.

———. "The Autobiography of Chona, a Papago Woman" [1936]. In *Papago Woman*, Ruth Underhill, 29–86. Long Grove: Waveland Press, 1979.

———. *Papago Woman*. Long Grove: Waveland Press, 1979.

Urban, Andrew. "Irish Domestic Servants, 'Biddy' and Rebellion in the American Home, 1850–1900." *Gender & History* 21, no. 2 (August 2009): 263–286.

Vuckovic, Myriam. *Voices from Haskell: Indian Students between Two Worlds, 1884–1889*. Lawrence: University Press of Kansas, 2008.

Waddell, Jack O. *Papago Indians at Work*. Anthropological Papers of the University of Arizona, no. 12. Tucson: University of Arizona Press, 1969.

Wall, Wendy. "Gender and the 'Citizen Indian.'" In *Writing the Range: Race, Class, and Culture in the Women's West*, edited by Elizabeth Jameson and Susan Armitage, 202–229. Norman: University of Oklahoma Press, 1997.

Ward, Geoffrey C. *Unforgivable Blackness: The Rise and Fall of Jack Johnson*. New York: Alfred A. Knopf, 2004.

Ware, Vron. *Beyond the Pale: White Women, Racism and History*. London: Verso, 1992.

Welter, Barbara. "The Cult of True Womanhood: 1820–1860." *American Quarterly* 18, no. 2, pt. 1 (Summer 1966): 151–174.

Willard, William. "Indian Newspapers, or, 'Say, Aren't You Some Kind of Indians?'" *Wicazo Ca Review* 10, no. 2 (Autumn 1994): 91–97.

———. "Outing, Relocation and Employment Assistance: The Impact of Federal Indian Population Dispersal Programs in the Bay Area." *Wicazo Ca Review* 12, no. 1 (Spring 1997): 29–46.

Witmer, Linda F. *The Indian Industrial School, Carlisle, Pennsylvania, 1879–1918*. Carlisle, PA: Cumberland County History Society, 2000.

Woodruff, Janette, as told to Cecil Dryden. *Indian Oasis*. Caldwell, ID: Caxton Printers, 1939.

Woodworth-Ney, Laura. "The Diaries of a Day-School Teacher: Daily Realities on the Pine Ridge Indian Reservation, 1932–1942." *South Dakota History* 24, nos. 3 & 4 (Fall/Winter 1994): 194–211.

Government Documents

US Bureau of the Census. *United States Federal Census*. Digitized copies available at http://www.ancestry.com.au, "The U.S. Federal Collection," http://search.ancestry.com.au/search/group/usfedcen (accessed August 2010–January 2011).

US Bureau of the Census. *United States Indian Census Schedules, 1885–1940*. Digitized copies available at http://www.ancestry.com.au.

US Bureau of Indian Affairs. *Annual Report, 1920, Narrative Section, Sells Indian School. Superintendents' Annual Narrative and Statistical Reports from Field Jurisdictions of the Bureau of Indian Affairs*. National Archives Microfilm Publications, roll 130, Sells, 1919–1935.

US Bureau of Indian Affairs. *Superintendents' Annual Narrative and Statistical Reports from Field Jurisdictions of the Bureau of Indian Affairs.* National Archives Microfilm Publications, roll 129, San Xavier School, 1910–1918.

US Office of Indian Affairs. *Annual Reports of the Commissioner of Indian Affairs (ARCIA)*, 1826–1932. Digitized copies available at the University of Wisconsin Digital Collections website, "The History Collection: Documents Relating to Indian Affairs," http://digital.library.wisc.edu/1711.dl/History.IndianTreatiesMicro (accessed various dates 2010–2011).

Online Sources

Clonts, Glenna (comp.), "Graham County, Arizona–Safford Union Cemetery Burial Index," Dec. 19, 1999, http://files.usgwarchives.org/az/graham/cemeteries/safford.txt, Arizona USGenWeb Archives, http://usgwarchives.net/az/azfiles.htm (accessed Dec. 18, 2010).

Farish, Thomas Edwin. *History of Arizona*. Vol. III. Phoenix: 1916. Transcript in Arizona Board of Regents (n.d.), "Books of the Southwest, The University of Arizona Library," http://southwest.library.arizona.edu/hav3/body.1_div.5.html (accessed October 5, 2010).

Hamm, Thomas D., comp., "American Friend Obituary Index," 1996–1999, October 31, 1895, p. 1060, available online from Earlham College Libraries, Richmond, Indiana, http://www.earlham.edu/~libr/content/friends/obituaries/n.html (accessed December 20, 2010).

Johnston-Dodds, Kimberly. *Early California Laws and Policies Related to California Indians, Prepared at the Request of Senator John L. Burton, President Pro Tempore.* Sacramento: California Research Bureau, 2002, http://www.library.ca.gov (accessed October 20, 2010).

"Wisconsin Marriages, pre-1907." Provo, UT: The Generations Network, Inc., 2000, http://www.ancestry.com.

Index

About the Author

Associate Professor Victoria K. Haskins is an Australian Research Council Future Fellow in History at the University of Newcastle, New South Wales, Australia. Her publications include *Uncommon Ground: White Women in Aboriginal History*, co-edited with Anna Cole and Fiona Paisley, and *One Bright Spot*.